Good BEER Guide
PRAGUE
& THE CZECH REPUBLIC

EVAN RAIL

CAMRA

BOOKS

Published by Campaign for Real Ale
230 Hatfield Road
St Albans
Hertfordshire AL1 4LW

www.camra.org.uk/books

ISBN: 978-1-85249-233-5

A CIP catalogue record for this book is available from the British Library

Printed and bound by www.print-with-ipp.com

Head of Publications: Joanna Copestick
Managing Editor: Simon Hall
Project Editor: Sylvia Goulding
Project Coordinator: Debbie Williams
Editorial Assistance: Emma Lloyd
Design/Typography: Dale Tomlinson
Typefaces: Comenia and Etelka (Stormtype.com)
Maps: John Macklin
Picture Research: Sarah Airey and Nadine Bazar
Marketing Manager: Georgina Rudman

Contents

Acknowledgements

The first edition of this guide in over a decade was started on a clear, white page. Though the Czech Republic is a small country by many standards, in beer terms it is a miniature mammoth, and the fast wave of changes rushing through here since 1989 has made keeping up with information of any kind a task of Sisyphean proportions. The book you are holding now could not have been completed without the assistance of many.

First of all, a heartfelt thank you to Nina Valvodová, who travelled with me to almost every brewery in these pages, who researched many listings, double-checked facts and spellings, who translated, interpreted and, above all, drove the car. Nina's other roles have included mushroom scout, tent architect, breakfast chef, beer judge and moose photographer. You stay classy, San Diego.

For inspiration, information and countless evenings at Pivovarský dům, thanks to Dr Justin Quinn of Charles University, who introduced me to many of the pubs in this guide and who explained various elements of Czech language and history over the past eight years. This is, of course, to say nothing of the Christmas pudding.

For after-work beer therapy and astute cross-cultural insight, Matěj Novák of Grackle. Díky moc, vole.

For anecdotes, aphorisms, gossip, news and stories: Theo Schwinke, Kateřina Pavlitová, Adam Novák, David Cunningham, Peter Dyer, Matthew Smith, Karen Feldman and Bryn Perkins. Thanks one and all.

For morální podpora, thanks to Sofia Aziz.

For on-the-fly prosodic reference, Evan Mellander.

For inspirational beers from Texas, thanks to Scott Ray.

For even more inspirational beers from Texas, thanks to Sarah Rail and Tom Browne, with much love and raised glasses also going out to Jordan Rail, Cori Rail and Bob Quickel. Thanks and love to my parents, DeWayne and Tori Rail, for unflagging encouragement. Thanks are also due to my uncle, John O'Mara, for an early introduction to good beer (Liberty Ale, autumn 1990, sailing a gaff-rigged schooner on San Francisco Bay). For the sessions way back when that ultimately sent me on this voyage, a tip of the hat to Chris Hess, Mike Kloster and Dave Brewington.

Many thanks are due to Iain Loe and all the kind souls at CAMRA. I'd especially like to thank Joanna Copestick for working with me, Debbie Williams for bringing it all together and Sylvia Goulding for asking the right questions. Special thanks to Roger Protz.

For photographic assistance, thanks to Finbar Quinn.

For warm welcomes and kind assistance, Tomáš Erlich, Tomáš Maier and everyone at Sdružení přátel piva, who continue to fight the good fight. Godspeed, gentlemen.

For his encyclopaedic knowledge of the world of beer, Honza Kočka of Svět piva.

Much of the information contained herein came from articles originally written for The New York Times, The Prague Monitor and The Prague Post. Many thanks are due their editors.

A final salute goes out to Sporťák, the Škoda 120L, that drove us around the country for most of a year on only three cylinders. Sometimes just two.

Introduction

Welcome to the Good Beer Guide to Prague and the Czech Republic, the most complete and up-to-date guide to the breweries and beers of the world's greatest beer-drinking nation.

ALTHOUGH it is a small country, the Czech Republic has earned an oversize reputation for its fantastic lagers and its unsurpassed brewing history. It is widely recognised as the home of the first Pilsner and the first Budweiser, as well as the home of the world's greatest hops, those from Žatec (better known abroad by the German name of Saaz), and the legendary malt from Haná. The Czech lands are home to some of the oldest breweries in Europe, as well as some of the world's first hop farms, the first brewing textbooks and the first brewers' journal. It perhaps says most to note that the Czech Republic is a place where beer is consumed in greater volumes than water. Each year, Czech citizens celebratedly drink well over 160 litres (35.2 gallons) for every man, woman and child – the most beer consumed per capita in the world.

If you want to explore a land where beer is an integral part of the history and culture, look no further.

Way back when

A depiction of the current beer situation in the Czech lands might best begin with a bit on how things used to be. When I returned from my first visit to Prague in 1998, I brought with me labels from beers I particularly admired: Nektar, Opat, Regent and Svitavy, among others. Before I went, I was pretty sure I knew something about beer. Among my convictions: Pilsner, as a style, was crap.

These beers, however, had kicked my expectations in the head. In the place of the boring pale lagers I had known back home I found these heavy malt bodies – sturdier than many ales – topped up with plenty of bitter and aromatic hops. In the place of cloying fizz was often a pleasant, steady flatness. These were decadent, dynamically bittersweet brews, the likes of which I had never tasted before. If these were the real Pilsners, I didn't know what Pilsners were at all.

In 2000, straight from a year of study in Paris, I moved to Prague permanently. The beers I had admired just two years earlier were already becoming rarities. Regent was losing its distribution, Opat and Nektar were rarely seen, and Svitavy was out of business completely. In 1998 you could have bought bottles from a number of small brewers in any neighbourhood market. By 2000, it wasn't just the beers that were disappearing. Facing competition from the likes of Tesco, Delvita (Delhaize/Food Lion), Albert (Ahold) and Julius Meinl, the neighbourhood shops were also going belly-up. Suddenly, you could walk into a supermarket the size of an airplane hangar and find beers from just three or four breweries, two of which were owned by mammoth international conglomerates. Instead of 20,000 or 2,000 or 200 breweries in this beer-loving land – the land that had invented the Pilsner style – there were only about 60, and the smaller marques were not looking particularly quick.

Back from the dead

That was then, this is now: fast-forward to 2007 and the Czech Republic is home to more than 100 breweries. For the first time ever, brewpubs and restaurant-breweries – the so-called *mikropivovary* – outnumber big bottlers, at least in absolute numbers, if not production volume. Svitavy is still out of business, but Regent, Opat, Nektar and a number of other smaller breweries are growing, some by as much as 20 per cent annually. And this year, at least ten new independents are scheduled to open, most of which will be brewpubs, but at least one of which is to be an independent bottler.

Even better, the past few years have seen a profusion of beer styles beyond the ubiquitous golden lager. (In this Guide, the term 'Pilsner' is reserved for Pilsner Urquell, as it is throughout the Czech Republic.) Instead, the country is rapidly re-embracing wheat beer, called *pšeničné pivo* in Czech, and a sortie of good ales has launched the first major assault on the hegemony of lagers here.

In addition, a number of smaller breweries are advertising that their beers are unpasteurised, which often means much more dynamic and flavourful brews, and quite different from the homogenized (and pasteurised) beers from the factories. The public seems to be able to tell the difference, and *nepasterované pivo* is becoming something of a trend.

How we roll

This Guide is an independent take on all of the Czech beers and brewers we know of. Our judgement is entirely based on how each beer tastes: not its marketing, not its history, not its label. We're happiest when we can point out that a beer tastes disgusting.

More than once we have completely changed our preconceptions about a given brewery, a certain beer or even an entire beer style. Many times we were surprised to discover that beers we assumed to be of low quality were, when tasted objectively, actually at the top of the league. Many more times we've been disappointed by slacking standards from big names. In every case, we've said so as clearly as possible.

While we remain madly in love with Czech beer, this Guide is not a love fest. It is not intended to make us friends, and it will probably make us more than a few enemies.

To all the people we've offended by our evaluations: We're sorry. Honestly, we are. It's not about you. It's not about us either. It's just about the beer.

The local scene

In beer terms, the situation here has been helped in no small part by the Sdružení přátel piva, or Union of Friends of Beer, a consumer group which started life as a pro-beer political party right after the Velvet Revolution. (Really. We couldn't make up a story like that.)

Today, the SPP is CAMRA's equivalent in the Czech lands, fighting for consumers' rights and better beer, and the SPP has recently become a fellow member of the European Beer Consumers' Union. To kick things off, we've asked SPP Chairman Tomáš Erlich to contribute a few words about the current state of Czech beer culture as he sees it.

As much as we love Czech beer, it remains just part of the story: from Aš to Opava and Varnsdorf to Vimperk, the Czech Republic is a fantastic country in all senses of the word, one which deserves numerous visits and revisits. It is our great wish that this Guide play some small role in introducing more of the storied kingdoms of Bohemia and Moravia to a new generation of deserving, curious travellers.

Na zdraví!

EVAN RAIL
Prague, February 2007

A note from the front lines

In beer terms, the Czech Republic is the centre of the universe, at least according to the people here, who base their opinion on the very scientific fact of having the greatest per capita consumption of the beverage in the world (160 litres annually, or about 281 UK pints). Only neighbouring Bavaria could possibly endanger the Czechs' primacy, assuming Bavaria might secede from the rest of Germany, and would carry on with its Oktoberfest. However, to the surprise and astonishment of the local majority, the reality here is somewhat different.

Unfortunately, the amount of beer consumed isn't directly related to the state of a country's beer culture, although in this respect, much has improved in recent years. Beer culture is no longer an abstract term with no meaning, and the Czechs are slowly starting to discover the world of top-fermented and spontaneously fermented beers, an entire world that has so far been unknown to them, one with beers other than lagers. Nonetheless, nearly 97 per cent of Czech beer production consists of light, bottom-fermented beer in the Pilsner style. That indicates the sealed-off nature of the Czech market, where imports account for just 1 per cent of consumption, and which means, generally speaking, that Czechs drink Czech beer only. (This is true, in part, for economic reasons as well as for those of taste.)

Unfortunately, in so doing, they do themselves harm. Czechs scorn foreign beers, especially different types of beers, but on the other hand they allow the 'tastes' of the uniform Euro-beers and licensed beers to be pushed down their throats in the name of globalisation. Then the important aspects for many Czechs remain the price and the place of brewing (in the Czech Republic). How it is brewed and what ingredients are used for brewing 'their' beer does not interest them.

The basic question today is: who still brews Czech beer? The production processes of breweries owned by international concerns completely destroy the traditional production techniques of Czech brewing – double or triple decoction mash, long maturation, no pasteurisation, brewing to original gravity, etc. Instead, international brewers are replacing quality Czech ingredients with low-grade malt and Chinese hop extract, creating a beer served with a huge portion of advertising and intrusive marketing, one which is brewed in the same way anywhere in the world (using cylindro-conical tanks, high-gravity brewing, and so forth). So, real Czech beer is only going to be in every second or third bottle, depending on how strictly we're judging it according to our traditions.

A note of hope: in the last two years, the Union of Czech Breweries and Malt Houses has been trying to register a geographical trademark for 'Czech beer', which would have clear and strict rules about where, how and from what it must be brewed. This is a commendable move, but apparently unfeasible in legal terms. Moreover, much will depend on the particular terms of the trademark, so that it doesn't become a burial ground for real Czech beers.

The only possible way to defend Czech traditional beer against the unified Euro-beers is clear – we need to drink them. It is nice to realise that things start to break here, in the soul of the Czech consumer. The community of people who seek the authentic taste and quality – and not just quantity – is growing. We are glad that the SPP is trying to take a small part in this enlightenment, even outside its membership. Essentially, the policy of predominantly large breweries to spit out the same beer over and over again means a chance for traditional Czech brewers. They just have to stick to their traditions and restrain from seeking the third way or trying to copy the competition that could lead them to an easy destruction.

Another bright and positive prospect, not just for 'Czech' beer, but any other good and honest beer (ale, *Weißbier, Bock*, etc.) is the constant growth of microbreweries, which have experienced a massive boom, especially in recent years. This year won't be any different, with another ten new and interesting microbreweries opening simultaneously, in a number of cases right on the site of an original brewery which was bankrupt or closed by the previous regime.

Only one microbrewery, U Fleků, made it through the Communist era. It is of course very familiar to most tourists in Prague, and remains the oldest Czech brewery in continuous production, dating back to 1499. Today there are 62 small breweries in total, excluding contract breweries and educational facilities, a number which clearly overwhelms the industrial brewers in absolute terms, both in the number of beers they offer, and their quality.

However, the ruthless hand of the market, globalisation and international owners who value their own economic interests above the needs of their customers are just some of the 'enemies' of honest Czech beer. European bureaucrats who justify their positions by making up new rules often offer laws which, in their essence, complicate life for everyone. And so it is impossible to contemplate Czech beer without considering the proposal to setting energy limits on beer production, because it is obvious that the traditional and honest methods of brewing will have problems meeting these new limits. The question of who is going to profit from this is also quite timely. The European inspectors approach the increase of a consumer tax on beer just as deviously (and entirely against the principle of flat taxation), suggesting automatic annual increases, while wine is paradoxically free from such a tax. Who is behind this is obvious.

Everybody understands that beer is part of the Czech national culture and remains the national drink. This is visible even in the country's attitude to the EU, when the Czech government was the only one to refuse this unjust tax proposal. With a bit of stretch we could even cite the old Czech saying, 'A government that increases the price of beer will fall!', as being behind this move. (Surely no Czech government is going to risk that.)

I'd like to close on a positive note. Regardless of the bad news above, Czech *pivo* remains a unique high point in the world's brewing culture. Many beers around the world pride themselves on using a Czech recipe or Czech hops. Beer was being brewed here even before the first Slavic settlements, but with their arrival came the important introduction of hops in beer. That was also the reason for Czechs to bring hop cultivation to perfection, and the *poloraný červeňák* (semi-early red) from Žatec (Saaz) is still widely considered the plant's apex. Czechs, of course, also gave Pilsner-style beer to the world, and it was the Czech brewer František Ondřej Poupě who revolutionarily introduced the thermometer to brewing. The tradition of excellent brewers in the Czech Republic continues, descending from father to son and grandson and beyond.

That alone is a good reason for learning more about Czech beer. And what better place than in a picturesque Czech pub? For it is in the pub where Czechs have always solved their problems, groused, lamented, but also laughed and rejoiced together, from time immemorial, and where they always will.

TOMÁŠ ERLICH
Chairman, Sdružení přátel piva
(Union of Friends of Beer)

How to use this Guide

Order! Order!

The order of this Guide is geographic. The Czech Republic is composed of two ancient kingdoms, Bohemia in the west and Moravia in the east, where a small bit of the old region of Silesia remains just along the upper border with Poland. Bohemia and Moravia are together divided into 14 administrative units comprising 13 regions, or *kraje* (singular *kraj*) and one capital city, Prague, in the very centre of Bohemia.

This Guide arranges breweries by chapters, one for each *kraj*, starting with the capital and continuing out through the 14 administrative regions. The order is as follows: after Prague comes Central Bohemia, which surrounds the city like a doughnut.

Primarily out of deference to Budvar, this Guide continues next to South Bohemia and then traces a clockwise trail through the remaining *kraje* in Bohemia: Pilsen and Karlovy Vary to the west, Ústí nad Labem, Liberec and Hradec Králové to the north and Pardubice out to the east. Next, roughly along the border between Bohemia and Moravia, lies the Vysočina, home to the lovely Czech-Moravian highlands.

In Moravia, our chapters start in South Moravia and move north through Zlín and Olomouc to finish in Moravian Silesia, the home of a dynamic new brewpub scene.

We tried to make it more complicated, but this is the best we could come up with.

Where are all the pubs?

This Guide has chapters for interesting pubs in the two largest cities, Brno and Prague, which are also the only Czech cities with direct flight connections to the UK. When we have found them, we have listed other noteworthy pubs in the breweries chapters. These chapters also include listings for dozens of brewery taprooms and brewery restaurants, as well as fantastic brewpubs in every corner of the country. Approximately 50 of the country's total of 102-and-growing breweries are brewpubs. All are worth seeking out.

Easy as A, B, Č

This Guide uses Czech names and spellings throughout. However, all listings are alphabetised in the English manner. This means that we treat C and Č as the same letter (and S and Š, and so on), while they are considered different letters in the Czech language.

This distinction is perhaps most important for words which begin with Ch. In Czech, Ch is a letter of its own which, confusingly for outsiders, comes after H in the alphabet. However, we have treated it in the English manner, listing words that begin with Ch among those that begin with C.

Maps

This Guide contains many maps detailing all the breweries and brewpubs in the various regions of the Czech Republic, as well as several maps showing the locations of recommendable pubs in Prague and Brno. However, considering this historic country's highly... *idiosyncratic* system of streets, roads and highways, it is also recommended that visitors keep an additional, large-scale map with them at all times, and that drivers always travel with an auto atlas, perhaps supplemented by a compass, a GPS unit, a two-way radio, a machete, emergency flares and enough provisions to survive several weeks in the wilderness.

The Trúba watchtower above Štramberk, Moravian Silesia

A Brief History of the Czech lands

If there were balm in Gilead, I would go
To Gilead for your wounds, unhappy land,
Gather you balsam there...

EDNA ST VINCENT MILLAY, 'Czecho-Slovakia'

IT'S NOT A QUICK and easy story by any means: the history of Bohemia and Moravia goes back a long way, includes some of the greatest tragedies in Europe, and follows a plot line that remains intractably convoluted (at least seven major players are named Václav, or Wenceslas). If, after five or six half-litres, someone in a pub starts to recount a beery history of the Czech lands, it might sound something like this.

Beautiful beginnings

An early start takes us very far back indeed: in South Moravia, the Venus of Dolní Věstonice (Věstonická Venuše) is created sometime around 28,000 BC. The earliest ceramic human figurine yet discovered, the Venus is a female terracotta form with ample hips and large breasts, displaying a shapeliness for which locals in this area will become quite famous in about 30,000 years. Settlements from the area indicate that humans here are making ceramics and extremely fine textiles woven from nettles.

Skip forward to around 400 BC. Around the Mediterranean, Hellenic culture is in full florescence. Bohemia, however, is rife with Celts, whose Boii tribe ultimately give the area its name. The Boii live here in relative prosperity, trading with Greeks and other faraway nations, until they are forced out by Germanic tribes, the Marcomanni and the Quadi, sometime around the birth of Christ. (The later subjugation and enslavement of the Boii by the Romans is a possibility for the origin of the English word 'boy', just as it is the subjugation of the Slavs that gives us 'slavery'.) The Germanic tribes are replaced by waves of Slavs, who migrate here around the 6th century AD and begin to farm hops.

According to legend, the first Slav to arrive here is Čech, also known as Praotec Čech, or 'forefather Czech'. Lore says that Čech comes to this land from the south, stopping upon the pinnacle mountain Říp, a 460-m (1,509-ft) lone hilltop in North Bohemia. Various forms of the story exist, but most agree that mythical Čech has two equally mythical brothers, Lech and Rus. Lech travels north to found the Polish nation, Rus heads east. Čech stays here, where the people and the land will take his name.

Regardless of fact or lore, there still isn't anything like an organised state. There is, however, the ever-increasing likelihood of attack from roving bands of Avars, a nomadic people from the Asian steppes who dominate much of Central Europe. Against them comes King Samo, a Frankish merchant in the area who creates a mini-state with an expressed anti-Avar foreign policy which lasts until his death in 658.

Things rock on without much organisation until the foundation of Great Moravia, a powerful Central European state which rivals that of the Franks. Not mere military rivals, the Franks are also converting the people of Moravia to their Christian faith. In order to subvert the power of the foreigners, Great Moravia's leader Rastislav asks Byzantine Emperor Michael III to send some priests who can talk to the people in a Slavic tongue. In 863, Cyril and Methodius – two Greeks who learned the Slavic vernacular during their childhood in Thessaloniki – show up. They invent a Slavic alphabet and convert the local people to the Eastern faith, neither of which really sticks (though they will have more success with both of these in points further east). Great Moravia breaks apart in the 10th century under pressure from the Magyars.

Just about this time, a Slav dynasty is being formed in Bohemia: the Přemyslids. The first ruler is Duke Bořivoj I, who is baptised by Methodius in 874. The Přemyslids largely remain Christians, though Vratislav I (915–19) marries a pagan, Drahomíra. Their son is the first important Václav in the Czech lands and is said to be devoted to his grandmother, Ludmila, who raises him in the Christian faith. Drahomíra, being evil and jealous, perhaps not in that order, has Ludmila murdered in her castle in Tetín, not far from Beroun. Václav, assuming the throne a few years later, has his mother banished.

True to the faith of his grandmother, Václav I promotes Christianity, angering the pagan nobles. One angry noble is Václav's brother, Boleslav, who has Václav hacked to death against a church door in 935, making him, in short order, Saint Wenceslas.

Boleslav I may be a fratricidal maniac, but historians point out that he turns out to be a good ruler, leading Czech and Bavarian forces to a decisive victory over the Magyars in 955. Under his son, Boleslav II, Prague's diocese is founded in 973, the Polish region of Silesia is captured and the rival Slavníkovec dynasty is wiped out in 995, ensuring Přemyslid rule for centuries.

In 1088, Duke Vratislav II declares that the Bohemian estates must pay a hop tithe for the making of beer. By 1101, Bohemian hops are being exported to the main hop market in Hamburg, where they bring high prices. In order to protect their wealth, the Přemyslids will ban the export of hop rhizomes under the penalty of death.

In 1212, the Přemyslid dynasty receives the Golden Bull of Sicily from Frederick II, Holy Roman Emperor, elevating their title to Kings of Bohemia. Breweries are founded in Svitavy (1256), Žatec (1261), České Budějovice (1265) and Plzeň (1290).

Despite continuing fratricides, patricides, matricides and of course regicides, the Přemyslids continue to rule until the death of King Václav III in Olomouc 1306 (and yes, he was murdered). His sister's husband, John of Luxembourg, assumes the throne.

John, being cosmopolitan, sends his son (also Václav) off to the French court of his uncle, Charles IV of France, for an education. When he returns, Václav has adopted his uncle's name and rules Bohemia and Luxembourg as Charles IV, also becoming King of Germany in 1346. In 1355 Charles IV is crowned King of Italy and Holy Roman Emperor. For the first time, Prague is the centre of the universe.

Empire and conflict

Under Charles IV, Prague blooms. After the coronation, Petrarch writes to ask if Charles will be moving the capital of the empire to Rome. Instead, St Vitus Cathedral and much of Prague Castle is completed, Charles Bridge is erected across the Vltava, Charles University is founded in 1349, Karlovo náměstí is laid out in New Town and Karlštejn and Karlovy Vary are built.

It doesn't go quite so swimmingly under Charles' son, Václav IV, aka 'The Drunkard'. Though Václav inherits both roles of King of Bohemia and Holy Roman Emperor in 1378, he is a weak and ineffective king, suffering from bouts of epilepsy and a proclivity for drink. The princes of the German states turn on him in 1400. In part, they believe he is paying too much attention to his domestic duties, rather than his imperial tasks.

In part, Václav IV is consumed by the conflict between a protestant reformer, Jan Hus, and the religious establishment.

Among other issues, Hus, a rector at Charles University and a preacher at Bethlehem Chapel in Prague, is incensed by the accumulation of wealth among the priesthood and the selling of indulgences. Because of his Czech translation of John Wycliffe's *Trialogus* and his push for the primacy of the Czech department at Charles University, many German members leave to found a new university in Leipzig. Hus continues to rail against the Church and in 1415 is burned at the stake in Konstanz, Germany. You can bet that doesn't go down well.

In 1419, the followers of Hus – known as the Hussites – storm Prague's Novoměstská radnice (New Town Hall) and perform the First Defenestration of Prague, throwing seven members of the town council out of the tower windows and onto a small armoury of Hussite-wielded spears below.

You can bet that doesn't go down well either. The death-by-throwing-and-gravity-stabbing of the aldermen causes the subsequent death-by-epileptic-fit of Václav IV and kicks off the Hussite Wars.

These pan-Bohemian civil wars last until 1434 and maintain a distinction for being one of the first European wars in which gunpowder is used, giving the English language one of its few words of Czech origin: howitzer, from the Hussite cannon known as a *houfnice*. The legendary one-eyed Hussite general Jan Žižka – one of the few military leaders in history never to lose a battle – tears up the countryside, destroying many monasteries and monastery breweries in the process. Noting that she is otherwise busy fighting the English at the moment, Joan of Arc sends the Czechs a threatening letter on 23 March 1430.

A few years later, Bohemia returns to normality of a kind under a Hussite king, George of Poděbrady, and an agreement on religion is reached with the Catholic authorities which is later annulled by Pope Pius II in 1462.

A few more Czech breweries are founded, including Prague's U Fleků in 1499. Around this time, 50 per cent of the income in many Czech towns is said to come from brewing. In cities like Rakovník, the figure is closer to 90 per cent.

After a brief spell of rule under a Polish king, the Czechs come under Austrian Habsburg rule, that of Ferdinand I, in 1556.

That's about when things start heading south. By now, Bohemia has been a powerful country for hundreds of years with dozens of powerful nobles. The Habsburgs are into centralisation. The Bohemian estates elect Ferdinand I as ruler under the condition that he respect their rights and privileges. He forgets. (He does, however, continue the practice of handing out brewing rights to nobles, setting the foundations for many more Czech breweries.)

Religious conflicts break out around 1547. The Catholic Church declares a stated goal of re-Catholicisation of the Czech lands. The Czech Protestants enter an agreement with new Holy Roman Emperor Maximilian II whereby they are guaranteed religious freedom in exchange for support of his son, Rudolph, as King of Bohemia. When Rudolph becomes Rudolph II, Holy Roman Emperor, in 1576, he makes Prague the imperial capital once again. In 1583, he buys the Krušovice brewery.

Rudolph's rule makes Prague even more cosmopolitan than it was under Charles IV. He employs the painter Giuseppe Arcimboldo, the jeweller Ottavio Miseroni and the sculptor Alessandro Abondio; Czech families with Italian last names bear witness to this small invasion to this day. Prague becomes a centre of alchemy and astronomy, the home of Tycho Brahe, Copernicus, Edward Kelley and John Dee. Even though Rudolph himself alternates between bouts of madness and lethargy, Prague experiences its second great rebirth, and Rudolph guarantees religious freedom throughout Bohemia in 1609.

But just a few years after the end of Rudolph's rule in 1611, things get worse again. Feeling repressed under the rule of devoutly Catholic Holy Roman Emperor Ferdinand II, an army of Czech Protestants march into Prague Castle on 23 May 1618 and put the two imperial governors on trial. Somewhat unsurprisingly, the governors are found guilty and thrown out of the windows of Prague Castle. In a cartoon-like twist, the Second Defenestration of Prague ends with the governors landing atop a large pile of manure, from which they emerge unscathed.

By general agreement across Europe, the next three decades will be set aside for the Thirty Years' War. The Czech rebellion largely plays out by 8 November 1620, when Protestant forces are routed at Bílá Hora, or White Mountain, today a part of Prague just to the west of Prague Castle, after which 27 Czech noblemen are executed on Old Town Square.

In 1643, the town of Kutná Hora pays off Lennart Torstensson's pillaging Swedish troops with barrels of beer.

Sprechen Sie Deutsch?

The rebellion of the Bohemian estates is not fundamentally a linguistic issue, and among the murdered rebels are German-speakers as well. But from this point on, it becomes distinctly less likely that someone in power is going to speak Czech, and the language is erased from literature, education, government and the church for about 200 years.

But at the end of the 18th century, in the full glow of the Enlightenment and straining under the rule of far-off Vienna, people here start expressing an interest in 'Bohemian' language and culture. Though German remains the official language, the study of Czech – which has survived primarily among illiterate peasants – begins in earnest, leading to the strange situation whereby the first Czech grammars and histories of the language are actually written in German. Many of the students of Czech language come from families who have kept their Hussite faith a secret for the past several centuries.

The whole of the 19th century sees an explosion of interest in Czech culture and the return of the use of the Czech language. This will later be known as the Czech National Revival or Czech National Awakening. In Prague, the National Museum and National Theatre are founded.

Then there is the beer. Until now, beer has been a local product made on a small scale, usually by burghers or lords with brewing rights. But in 1842 the burghers of Pilsen get together to found a new brewery, due to the remarkably bad beer in their town. They hire a Bavarian, Josef Groll, as their first brewmaster. The beer he invents comes out unusually clear and light in colour.

Coincidentally, this new beer from Pilsen appears at around the same time as industrial glassware starts to become cheap enough for common people to drink from it. The unusual colour and clarity of the beer makes its popularity spread quickly throughout Bohemia, then throughout Europe. In its wake, hundreds of indigenous beer styles disappear as brewers adopt the new Pilsner style of brewing. The Czech lands, once famous for wheat beers and dark ales, convert almost entirely to light lagers. With industrialisation, large factory breweries start to appear.

The Habsburgs begin to lose control throughout the empire. The Czech nationalist movement grows stronger. In opposition to the brewery held by the minority German property owners in České Budějovice, aka Budweis, a Czech brewery is founded in the town in 1895. In an indication of things to come, it is soon the dominant brewery in the region.

The happy 20th century

Czechs and Slovaks remain subjects of the Austro-Hungarian empire until the end of World War I. With a push from a magnetic statesman, Tomáš Garrigue Masaryk, and tireless campaigning abroad, a combined Czech and Slovak free state becomes reality on 28 October 1918. Now known as the First Republic, the 20-year role of independent Czechoslovakia is regarded by many as a golden era, bringing untold prosperity to Bohemia and Moravia and a third rebirth of Prague as an international capital.

Until 1938. Hitler's rise to power is partly due to his claim on the border regions of Bohemia and Moravia – the so-called Sudetenland, most of which is historically German-speaking – as rightfully German. With a lot of sabre-rattling, he convinces Britain, France and Italy to abandon the new state of Czechoslovakia at Munich on 29 September 1938. After signing the treaty with Hitler, Neville Chamberlain dismissively speaks of 'a quarrel in a far-away country between people of whom we know nothing.' Somewhat more presciently, Winston Churchill declares: 'In a period of time which may be measured by years, but may be measured by months, Czechoslovakia will be engulfed in the Nazi regime.'

Though not allowed to attend the Munich talks, Czechoslovakia, under pressure from its so-called allies, reluctantly agrees to surrender the Sudetenland to Germany on 30 September 1938. On 15 March 1939, German troops march into Prague. Bohemia and Moravia become protectorates of the Reich; Slovakia becomes a separate pro-Nazi state.

On 17 November 1939, Charles University is stormed by German troops after a protest over the killing of a medical student, Jan Opletal, at an earlier anti-Nazi rally. Nine student leaders are executed and 1,200 students are sent to concentration camps. The date becomes a significant anniversary for students and anti-totalitarian movements around the world.

Rather charitably overlooking recent history, the Czech government-in-exile takes up residence in England during World War II.

On 27 May 1942, Czech commandos sent from Britain complete Operation Anthropoid, ambushing and killing Reichsprotektor Reinhard Heydrich in Prague's Holešovice district. The ensuing reprisals see random Czech citizens pulled off trains and shot. The villages of Lidice and Ležáky are entirely razed. At least 93 children from the villages end up in a concentration camp, where they are gassed. In total, at least 1,200 Czechs die in the Nazi revenge killings alone. During the war, 70,000 Czech Jews are murdered in concentration camps.

Czech factories of all kinds are taken over to serve the Nazi cause. The brewery in Velké Březno – which has called itself 'Sudetenbräu' since 1938 – supplies beer to Rommel's Afrikakorps.

Liberation in the form of the Soviet Red Army comes on 9 May 1945.

Implausibly, things get worse.

After the war, Czechoslovak President Edvard Beneš issues what are now known as the Beneš Decrees, which result in the expulsion of 90 per cent of Czechoslovakia's German and Hungarian populations. People of German and Hungarian background are viewed collectively as traitors (even, confusingly, many who are Jewish). Approximately 2.6 million Germans are expelled to Germany and Austria, often on forced marches. Many die along the way.

Backed by the Soviets, in February of 1948 Klement Gottwald and the Communist Party take control of Czechoslovakia. President Edvard Beneš resigns.

The early Communist era is notable for its show trials. In particular, military leaders who served in Britain during the war and most of the country's few remaining Jewish intellectuals are persecuted. Collectivisation means that many factories, farms and breweries are grouped together in large co-operatives. Inefficient breweries, such as Dalešice, are closed by the central planners.

After 20 dark years, Czechoslovakia experiences a brief period of sunlight during the Prague Spring of 1968. This period of reforms, openness, press freedom and 'Socialism with a human face' lasts just eight months until 21 August, when Soviet tanks invade.

Things get worse. Apparently not without a sense of irony, the Communist hardliners under Gustáv Husák refer to the resulting crackdown as 'normalisation'.

In 1974, the playwright and dissident Václav Havel is put to work in the brewery in Trutnov for nine months.

In 1977, Havel and others write Charter 77, a human rights manifesto, largely in response to the arrest of members of the rock band Plastic People of the Universe. Havel is imprisoned from 1979–83, when he is released for reasons of ill health.

In 1984, the Communist government raises the price of a half litre of beer from 1.70 to 2.5 crowns.

In January 1989, Václav Havel is arrested again and serves four months in prison. On 17 November 1989, the Socialist Youth Union in Prague organises a march to commemorate the Nazi attack on Charles University students in 1939. The march is blocked at Národní třída by riot police, who attack and beat the students. A rumour of a student being killed leads to immediate strikes, boycotts and mass protests. From here on out, things move very quickly.

On 29 November, parliament removes from the constitution a platform declaring Marxism the official state ideology.

On 30 November, the teaching of Marxism-Leninism is cancelled at all universities.

By 4 December, Czechoslovak citizens are free to travel to Austria without special documents.

On 11 December, the border to West Germany is opened.

On 29 December 1989, the still-Communist parliament elects Václav Havel president of Czechoslovakia.

That's all it takes.

Full speed ahead

Unbelievably, after the Velvet Revolution, things go even faster. The newly democratic Czechoslovakia begins restitution of seized property. Public property is privatised, often under less-than-transparent conditions. Millions of dollars of what was once public property ends up in the hands of a limited number of individuals. Stories abound of Western investors losing everything in the country's anything-goes era of cowboy capitalism.

In 1992, brewpubs open at Chýně, just outside of Prague, and in Brno.

In 1993, increasing pressure from nationalist elements leads to the break-up of Czechoslovakia, also known as the Velvet Divorce. Václav Havel is elected president of the newly independent Czech Republic, which, like a clumsy teenager, will try on various other names over the years, including Czechia and Česko.

Throughout the 1990s, breweries trade hands repeatedly. Bass sells Radegast to Nomura, the Japanese investment bank, and sells Staropramen and Braník to Interbrew. Nomura also buys Pilsner Urquell, selling both breweries later to South African Breweries, which will merge with Miller. Dozens of breweries close down entirely. A few brewpubs open.

In 1999, the Czech Republic joins NATO.

In the new millennium, capitalism goes crazy. Hypermarkets are opened around the country. Tourism begins to grow by 10 per cent and more yearly. Prague adds hundreds of hotel beds annually and still cannot keep up with demand.

After 13 years, Václav Havel leaves office in February of 2003, replaced by President Václav Klaus. Before Havel leaves, a neon heart is installed above Prague Castle. It is promptly taken down when Klaus arrives.

In 2004 the Czech Republic joins the EU.

In 2006 the Czech Republic heroically battles a suggested 31 per cent EU tax increase on beer.

Despite a barely functioning government – there is no government at all for much of 2006 – the country enjoys a robust economy. (There might be a lesson in this.) In the first half of the year, Czech beer exports grow by 17 per cent. Many small bottlers export 50 per cent or more of their production.

In 2007 small breweries open in every corner of the country. Perhaps for the first time since the advent of industrialisation, micro-breweries and brewpubs outnumber mega-brewers.

Getting There

Given its location at the heart of Europe – halfway from Stockholm to Rome – the Czech Republic is quickly turning into one of the Continent's central transport hubs. Renovated airports in both Prague and Brno and a profusion of quality, low-cost airlines make it easier than ever to reach the land of great Pilsners.

AIR ROUTES

FLYING TO PRAGUE

Prague Ruzyně Airport   www.prg.aero

Oh, Lordy. With the proliferation of low-cost flights like so many mushrooms on a damp summer morn, keeping up with incoming flights to Prague's Ruzyně airport is a mug's game. This is to say nothing of the growth of the airport itself, which expanded from one to two terminals in 2006 and added almost a million passengers (to 11.6 million) from the year before. Considering the city's prime tourist attractions – by which we mean great beer, of course – the 10 per cent annual growth rate is expected to continue well into the foreseeable future.

So here's our stab in the dark: at the time of writing (early 2007), the following airports in the United Kingdom and the Republic of Ireland have direct flights to Prague:

From the UK

Belfast
Jet2 (Channel Express)   www.jet2.com

Birmingham
British Midland   www.bmibaby.com

Blackpool
Jet2 (Channel Express)   www.jet2.com

Bournemouth
Thomsonfly.com   www.thomsonfly.com

Bristol
EasyJet   www.easyjet.com

Doncaster/Robin Hood Airport
Thomsonfly.com   www.thomsonfly.com

East Midlands
British Midland   www.bmibaby.com
EasyJet   www.easyjet.com

Glasgow
Flyglobespan   www.flyglobespan.com

Leeds/Bradford
Jet2 (Channel Express)   www.jet2.com

London Gatwick
EasyJet   www.easyjet.com
British Airways   www.britishairways.com

London Heathrow
Czech Airlines   www.csa.cz
Korean Air   www.koreanair.com
British Airways   www.britishairways.com
American Airlines
    www.americanairlines.co.uk
Cathay Pacific Airways
    www.cathaypacific.com

London Luton
Thomsonfly.com   www.thomsonfly.com

London Stansted
EasyJet   www.easyjet.com
Czech Airlines   www.csa.cz
Korean Air   www.koreanair.com

Manchester
Aeroflot   www.aeroflot.ru/eng
British Midland   www.bmibaby.com

Czech Airlines **www.csa.cz**
Korean Air **www.koreanair.com**

Newcastle
EasyJet **www.easyjet.com**

From Ireland

Cork
Aer Lingus **www.flyaerlingus.com**

Dublin
Aeroflot **www.aeroflot.ru/eng**
Aer Lingus **www.flyaerlingus.com**
Czech Airlines **www.csa.cz**

Transport from Ruzyně airport into Prague

Just outside the arrival gate of Terminal Sever 1 (Terminal North 1, used by flights from non-Schengen countries, including all flights from Britain and Ireland) is a taxi stand.

Forget the crooked cabbies: they are by and large disappearing, especially at Ruzyně Airport. Our favourite cars are the super-clean Škoda Superbs from the AAA company. The airport is about a 30-minute drive from downtown, and a taxi connection should cost around 700 Kč, or about £17 at the time of writing. The Visa-brand taxis – a fleet of grey VW Passats – look attractive, but they have a reputation for bad driving. After AAA, other preferred cab services are Profi and Rony.

Prague Airport Shuttle
www.prague-airport-shuttle.com
Larger groups may wish to book a minivan or bus from Prague Airport Shuttle, which carries up to 20 people, charging a flat fee per vehicle and offering a door-to-door service.

Almost as fast and far cheaper is public transport. The easiest is the No. 119 bus, with a bus stop just on the other side of the taxi queue. A 20-Kč ticket is good for one person all the way to the line's terminus at Dejvická metro station, and is also valid for a onward metro or tram ride.

Depending on your ultimate destination, you may wish to take the No. 100 express bus from the same stop, though it's worth noting that it arrives at Zličín, in the far southwest of the city, and is probably useful only if you are staying in that area or somewhere directly on the metro B line.

If your final destination is not in Prague but somewhere else in the country via a train connection, you might need the new AE Airport Express bus. It leaves the airport every 30 minutes from 5:00 to 22:00, heading directly to Prague's Holešovice train station, the main launch pad for the high-speed Pendolino. It costs 40 Kč.

If you're taking the bus into town and think you might use the metro or trams more than a few times, consider buying a three-day (220 Kč) or week-long (280 Kč) travel pass. You can start right at Prague airport, where two Travel Information Centres sell passes and mini-maps every day until 22:00. Passes are valid for both of the regular buses from the airport, though not the AE line.

Remember to stamp your ticket when you first use it, either at the entrance to the metro or on a tram. It's not valid otherwise, and if you get caught by one of the plainclothes inspectors, it's the same as riding without a ticket, subject to an annoying fine and an even more annoying lecture.

FLYING TO BRNO

Brno Tuřany Airport   www.airport-brno.cz
Currently, the Czech Republic's second city only offers direct connections with Britain on Ryanair, which flies to Brno's Tuřany airport from London Stansted.

Ryanair   www.ryanair.com
Of course, schedules may change and flights may be added (or dropped) at any time, so take the following with a not-so-healthy dose of sodium chloride:

From London, the current schedule for departures is Su–Fr at 13:40, Sa at 17:05.
From Brno, current departures take place Su–Fr at 17:05, Sa at 20:30.

Flying time from London is approximately 2 hours 10 minutes.

Transport from Tuřany airport into Brno

The cheapest and easiest method is to take bus No. 76 from the airport to Hlavní nádraží, the main train station. From 04:30 until 23:00, buses run every 30 minutes. The trip takes 20 minutes and tickets cost 13 Kč for adults, or 6 Kč for children.

A taxi will take almost the same length of time and should cost about 300 Kč. Confirm the price before boarding.

You can buy tickets for Brno public transport from the Information Centre at the Airport, or from coin-operated vending machines, newsstands and some shops. Tickets cost 13 Kč for a 40-minute ride, including transfers, or 8 Kč for a simple 10-minute trip without a transfer. A one-day pass for the entire public transport system is just 50 Kč, valid for 24 hours, or 100 Kč for three full days.

Do not forget to stamp your ticket once you step inside the first bus or tram. Plainclothes ticket inspectors may ask to see your ticket at any time, and travel without a valid ticket is subject to a fine of 1,000 Kč, payable on the spot.

SURFACE ROUTES

BY TRAIN AND BUS

To Prague

National and international timetables: **www.idos.cz**

Most international trains arrive in Prague at either Holešovice or Hlavní nádraží (Main Station), both of which lie on Prague's C metro line. The new Pendolino line has shortened connections from Vienna and Bratislava by half an hour or more, down to less than 4 hours.

Bus travel is one of the fastest ways to get to the Czech capital from neighbouring destinations like Dresden. Most buses arrive at the Florenc bus station, just steps from the Florenc metro, a connecting station for the C and B lines.

To Brno

National and international timetables: **www.idos.cz**

In late 2006, the Czech Republic's high-speed Pendolino line was extended from Brno out to Vienna and Bratislava, speeding up trips from the Austrian and Slovak capitals. Pendolino trains connect Brno's Hlavní nádraží to Prague's Holešovice, Vienna's Südbahnhof and Bratislava's Hlavná stanica. Via Pendolino, a trip from Vienna is just under 90 minutes. From Bratislava, it can be as fast as 1 hour 24 minutes. From Prague, a Pendolino connection is about 2 hours 25 minutes.

Other lines are less speedy, though with many more connections throughout the day.

Being There

CZECH REPUBLIC

POPULATION (2006 est.): **10,235,455**
AREA: **78,866** sq km (30,442 sq miles)
BREWERIES (7.2.07): approx. **102** (and climbing)

The Czech Republic is composed of two halves, Bohemia in the west and Moravia in the east, with a little strip of the old region of Silesia remaining on Moravia's northern border with Poland. Though many people here will refer to regions like Eastern Bohemia and Vallachia (the one in Moravia, not Romania), often these are unofficial terms, usually with ambiguous borders and non-existent end-points. Currently, the Czech Republic has 13 official administrative regions, or *kraje* (singular *kraj*), and one capital city, or *hlavní město*, Prague. For the sake of our own sanity, we have organised this Guide's chapters on breweries and beers according to those 14 delineable administrative zones.

BASICS

Telephones

Czech country code: 420
Since 2002, all Czech telephone numbers have been composed of nine digits, e.g. 222 333 444. Mobile numbers are now more common than land lines, even for businesses. In the Czech Republic, mobile numbers start with a 6 or a 7 and, like land lines, they are always nine digits long.

To phone a Czech number from the UK, you will need to dial the international dialling code (00), followed by the country code (420), followed by the nine-digit number, for example: 00 420 222 333 444.

To phone a Czech number from within the Czech Republic, whether landline or mobile, you will need to wait for a dial tone, then punch in the nine digits, without any dialling codes.

To phone a UK number from the Czech Republic, dial the international dialling code (00), followed by the UK country code (44), followed by the UK dialling code omitting the 0, followed by your respondent's number, e.g. 00 44 20 1234 5678.

The weather

The Czech Republic has a continental climate, meaning hot summers and cold, cloudy, wet winters, with snowfall possible anytime between early October and late April, though most commonly from Christmas through March. In winter, daytime temperatures well below freezing are common. Spring and early summer are the wettest seasons of the year, while in June, July and August temperatures are often above 30°C (86°F), sometimes up to 38°C (100°F) and higher.

Month	Av min. °C (°F)	Av max. °C (°F)
Jan	−5 (23)	0 (32)
Feb	−4 (25)	1 (34)
March	−1 (30)	7 (45)
April	3 (37)	12 (54)
May	8 (46)	18 (64)
June	11 (52)	21 (70)
July	13 (55)	23 (73)
Aug	13 (55)	22 (72)
Sept	9 (48)	18 (64)
Oct	5 (41)	12 (54)
Nov	1 (34)	5 (41)
Dec	−3 (27)	1 (34)

Czech Republic

GERMANY

LIBEREC REGION

ÚSTÍ NAD LABEM
REGION

KARLOVY VARY
REGION

● Prague

CENTRAL BOHEMIA

PILSEN REGION

SOUTH BOHEMIA

GERMANY

0 KM   50

The language

You'll never learn it.

However contradictory or oxymoronic this might sound, that's meant to encourage you to learn a few words. Think of it this way: no, you'll never speak it perfectly, so you might as well go ahead and speak it as best you can. And by all means learn the following:

Czech	Pronunciation	English
prosím	(pro-seem)	please
děkuji	(dyeh-koo-yee)	thank you
díky	(dyee-kee)	thanks
dobrý den	(dough-bree-den)	hello
nashledanou	(na-skled-a-now)	good-bye

Much like Latin or German, Czech is pronounced as it is spelled and has what linguists refer to as a 'standard five-vowel system', meaning the A, E, I, O and U are going to sound much as they do in Spanish, for example. Stress is usually on the first syllable of the word, resulting in a trochaic feel, as opposed to the iambic of Shakespearean English. With sharp consonants (rolled Rs, crisp Ts and Ks), it sometimes sounds like English spoken backwards, or perhaps a Latinised Slavic tongue.

For foreigners, the hardest sounds are letters marked by the accent known as háček (ˇ): ě (y+e, as in 'yes'), č (ch, as in 'chocolate'), ň (n+y, like the Spanish 'niño'), ž (zh) and ř (r+... well...)

Yes, ř: supposedly the most difficult sound in the world to make, a voiced, trilled, palatal fricative. For non-native speakers it is already difficult, and it gets no easier next to a consonant, as in tři, three. 'I usually describe it by telling people to roll an r while saying zh', one linguist told us. So try that.

Other sounds are the t with háček, written ť and pronounced as a 'soft' t, and the similar d with háček, written ď and pronounced like a d with a small y behind it. Vowels such as á and é are pronounced as standard vowels though almost twice as long, and ů is pronounced as a fairly lengthy 'oooh'. The ou in a phrase such as dobrou noc ('good night') sounds like a long 'oh', and the letter c is always pronounced as ts: dobrou noc becomes 'dough-brohh nots'.

And that's it: you're fluent.

Perhaps more important than the language itself is learning about Czech customs: it is considered rude to enter a room (or pub) without a greeting, and even one in English would likely go down better than none at all. When you meet someone, you should say dobrý den, and when you give someone something you should say prosím. However, you probably won't be penalized for not speaking perfect Czech: people here are rarely nationalistic, at least in terms of linguistic nationalism, and even the most dim-witted of bar owners will realise his business will be helped, not hindered, by his welcoming of foreign tourists. (This is less likely to be the case in small suburban bars, pubs in remote regions, or those few local places in areas that are completely overrun by throngs of backpackers.) Most waiters, waitresses, hotel staff and publicans will speak enough English to get you a beer and something to eat, though they'll almost always appreciate even the slightest effort made to learn the Czech language.

Money matters

The Czech Republic uses the koruna, or crown, denoted as Kč domestically and CZK internationally. Koruny come in coins of 1, 2, 5, 10, 20 and 50, as well as banknotes of 50, 100, 200, 500, 1,000, 2,000 and 5,000. (Each koruna is worth 100 haléřů, or hellers, which are virtually worthless themselves. The 50-heller coin is the smallest unit of value for cash transactions.) For a long time the Czech Republic was expected to join the Eurozone in 2010, but that is now viewed as extremely unlikely, with an adoption of the euro currently postponed until 2011 or later. Euros, however, are often accepted here, especially in hotels and tourist-friendly restaurants in the centre. Generally, Czech businesses which accept payment in foreign cash – euros, dollars or sterling – do not offer the best rates. (In our experience, the best rates come when you pay by credit or bank card, depending on the fees charged back home for a transaction in a foreign currency.) In terms of withdrawing cash, Czech cash machines work perfectly fine with most foreign bank cards. Our particular experience is that an in-the-bank teller withdrawal using your credit card will result in the lowest charges overall.

Above all, do not trade money with shady characters on the street: the practice is illegal and almost certainly a scam.

Accommodation

Bohemia and Moravia have a long tradition of hostelry. Many places of lodging date back to Prague's rule over the Holy Roman Empire in the 14th and 16th centuries, and some go back even earlier, when crusaders had bivouacs here on their way out to the Holy Land.

At the bottom, things have remained at about the same level of luxury as they were in the 12th century. This is the *ubytovna*, and it is extremely cheap: at the time of writing this Guide, two people could often find a room in an *ubytovna* for less than 600 Kč, at least in remote villages that saw few tourists. At this kind of price, you won't often get breakfast, and you'll probably need to bring your own towels, shampoo and soap. But at less than £15 for two, you can afford plenty of towels, and with enough left over to splurge on lunch and dinner. Private rooms for rent are usually marked with a German *Zimmer frei* sign, and the **www.ubytovani.cz** website is very good for affordable lodging. It also works in English.

The next step up is the *penzion*, a modest family hotel. (The name does not necessarily mean that you can get your meals here, though you might.) Above that is the hotel, a name which usually implies something grander and more formal, though not necessarily, and which probably has its own restaurant. In fact, many *Zimmer frei* places and *penziony* are better than a lot of hotels, which may well be run down.

However, if you think it's all cheap sleep, think again. Prague is home to a Four Seasons and a Mandarin Oriental, among other high-end addresses, and more fancy places arrive each year. It's very easy to sleep well, at least in Prague, but it can be hard to do so for less than 100 euros per night, especially in high season. Some helpful websites are **www.ubytovani.cz**, **www.czecot.com**

(the tourist server of the Czech Republic), and Mary's Travel Services, which books short-term apartments and rooms to rent at **www.marys.cz**.

GETTING AROUND

GETTING AROUND IN PRAGUE

Bring sturdy shoes: Prague is made for walking, though the cobblestones and hills can be tiring. You'll probably need a good pocket-size map like the Prague Pocket Atlas, available at most newsstands, though getting lost in the mirror-maze of the Old Town and Malá Strana is part of the fun.

For trips outside of the centre, trams and the metro are extremely efficient ways to cover long distances. Consider buying a three-day (220 Kč) or week-long (280 Kč) travel pass, either at the airport or from a main metro station (Muzeum, Můstek, Nádraží Holešovice and Anděl). For tram, bus and metro schedules, maps and complete information in English, check **www.dpp.cz**.

Although the taxis in Prague have largely been cleaned up, the unassociated cars lurking outside the city's Irish pubs and other tourist haunts are more likely to be among the few remaining crooks. But who on earth would come all the way to Prague only to go to an Irish pub?

Trains

Do you remember when Britain had a good rail system? Neither does this Guide, but we imagine it might have resembled České dráhy (Czech Rail): a single nationwide network of inexpensive trains which almost always arrive on time. There is virtually nowhere in the country that cannot be reached from Prague by early afternoon, depending on how early your day begins, making quick trips possible to all but the most remote locations. Tickets are cheap and further reductions are given for groups, return journeys and weekend travel.

Schedules are very easy to find online at the Czech transport ministry's nationwide timetable, **www.idos.cz**, which also has information for buses and municipal transport systems around the country. Many of the older trains may be low-frills, if not a bit run-down, but České dráhy remains extremely punctual, and the high-speed Pendolino trains from Prague to Pardubice, Olomouc, Ostrava, Brno, Vienna and Bratislava are among the most modern in Europe, reaching speeds of 160 km/h (100 mph), and (point of pride) playing the role of the bullet train to Montenegro in *Casino Royale*.

For more information on the Czech Pendolino, see **www.scpendolino.cz**. České dráhy's own website, **www.cd.cz**, also has information in English on reduced fares, schedules and special offers, such as the bike hire service: from 1 April to 31 October of each year, ČD rents bikes at many of the most popular tourist destinations, including South Bohemia and Český ráj.

Driving

In recent years there have been conflicting reports that Czech drivers are (a) the third deadliest in Europe after the Greeks and the Portuguese, and (b) among the safest drivers on the Continent, with far fewer road accidents than the European average. They cannot both be true; this Guide is inclined to believe the former. Based on personal experience, it takes only five minutes on a Czech road before some maniac passes you on the shoulder at 140 km/h (87 mph).

That said, driving on the back roads of Bohemia and Moravia is a beautiful experience, and rolling over a plum-tree-lined country lane, undulating over hilltops and through valleys of wheat and barley, often feels like a trip to an earlier time rather than one to a different place. The roads are lovely, but be prepared for bad drivers, especially on the motorways. Generally the need for speed is explained thus: 'We had crappy cars for so long. Now that we can afford nice cars, we want to go fast.'

But this is not the Autobahn: speed limits are relatively low. Unless marked, the limit is generally 50 km/h (31 mph) in towns, 90 km/h (56 mph) outside of towns and 130 km/h (81 mph) on expressways. All motor vehicles must have their lights on at all times, day and night. All passengers must wear seat belts, it is illegal to hold or otherwise use a mobile phone without a hands-free kit, and pedestrians must be given the right of way at crossings.

Most importantly for readers of this Guide, THERE IS A ZERO-BLOOD-ALCOHOL LIMIT FOR DRIVERS. Choose a designated driver or plan your drinking around your driving, perhaps with a stay at a brewery hotel (see 'Brewery Hotels'). Or, for Pete's sake, just use the excellent and affordable public transport system.

Cycling

Cycling in Bohemia is both paradise and a roll of the dice, as drivers here are often less courteous to cyclists than in other countries. That's the roll of the dice. The heavenly aspect is the view of verdant hills and forgotten villages with tumbledown Baroque churches and ruined castles.

GUIDEBOOKS

General guides

Being something of a tourist draw means there's no shortage of guidebooks for Prague. For many years, the overall best has been *TimeOut Prague*, although DK's *Top 10: Prague* and Fodor's *Prague* are also good. (Full disclosure: this Guide's writer contributed to the food and drink section of a recent Fodor's.) For boutique hotels and swish night spots, *Avant Guide: Prague* is probably the leader.

Whatever you buy, check carefully for the original date of publication: many guides seem to keep printing the same information without updates. If you consider most of the hotels, bars and restaurants in Prague to be of post-1989 vintage, this thousand-year-old city is far too 'new' and dynamic for old information. At least a dozen hotels, a score of restaurants and another of bars are added every year.

We can only hope that the Guide you are holding will be similarly outdated within a few years by the arrival of dozens and dozens of new pubs, brewpubs and independent breweries, as that would mean so much for the country's beer culture. If so, you can bet that we will enjoy updating a new edition just as much as we've enjoyed researching this one.

Maps

When the armies of the Warsaw Pact invaded Prague just before midnight on 20 August 1968, thus ending Alexander Dubček's Prague Spring and the dream of 'Socialism with a Human Face', the good people of Prague removed many of the street signs from the Old Town, confusing Soviet troop movements for several days. Streets in Prague tend to bend and jump and dip and split, only to reconnect again in some alternate universe. Until you understand the theoretical physics of the Old Town, you should probably carry a map with you at all times.

Do not be alarmed if, while puzzling over a map on a street corner for half an hour, no one comes to offer you assistance. If you want assistance, here's one way of doing it: pick someone young (who probably speaks English); smile and walk up to them, say *Dobrý den*, point to the map and ask *Prosím, kde to je?* (Please, where is this?). No matter how nice they look, keep an eye on your wallet and camera and smile again. Rinse. Repeat. Wipe hands on pants.

It would not be fun to travel around the country without an atlas, as many of the Czech roadways date to the medieval era and, when seen from above, resemble the bloodshot eyes of an insane man, perhaps as drawn by an insane child. An *autoatlas* ('road map') can be had at any bookstore for around 400 Kč (£10) and most include information on tourist attractions, as well as the sites of frequent accidents.

The online service **www.mapy.cz** works miraculously, even without typing the correct Czech diacritical markings, and the Guide rarely sets out for an unknown pub, restaurant or brewery without consulting it first.

FOOD AND DRINK

No one is going to come here for the food. Instead, it's a question of sights, atmosphere and of course beer. But Czech cooking?

In all honesty, Czech cuisine can be delicious, equal to or better than the similar recipes of its neighbours, Germany and Austria. At the turn of the century, the city with the second-largest population of Czech speakers was Vienna, and many Austrian recipes have their origins in the Czech lands, brought there by the lovely Bohemian and Moravian lasses who went to the capital to work as cooks, maids and au pairs. Czech cooking is still held in some esteem by the Czech Republic's neighbours, as witnessed by the signs for 'Bohemian baked goods' in nearby Saxony.

Here, however, grandmother's recipes had to go through Nazi occupation and Communist collectivisation. Just as many of today's Czech policemen were policemen before the Velvet Revolution, many of today's Czech chefs were trained in Communist-era hotel schools. The younger generation, by and large, have shaken off the vestiges of the former regime, at least when it comes to cooking. But if every pub in Orlické hory seems to serve the same five recipes, and not one of them is any good, now you know why.

Breakfast

Don't be surprised to see people drinking *pivo* at 8 am – labourers are often on their second or third by that time, and many pubs open for breakfast. Most of the population, however, skips the beer until lunch. Instead, a typical breakfast usually consists of a slice of bread and a slice of ham or cheese. Many restaurants have adopted a new recipe, *hemenex*, which, just as it is pronounced, is a slice of ham fried with eggs.

The English influence is visible in another ingredient, *anglická slanina*, English bacon, which resembles streaky bacon. Müsli, porridge and *rohlíky* (rolls) with *džem* (jam) and *máslo* (butter) are common at the breakfast table.

To wash it down, you might ask for *čaj* (tea) or *káva* (coffee). In earlier times, the most

common form of coffee was euphemistically called 'Turkish', though no Turkish *cezva* is used: instead, boiling water is poured into a cup filled with ground coffee and served, unfiltered, to the guest or victim. *Turecká káva*, or *turek*, is still around today, unfortunately, although the Italian espresso has gained ground in even the most rustic of regions. Called *presso*, an espresso can be *malé* (small) or *velké* (large). Most come from common Italian brands like Lavazza and are perfectly palatable.

Lunch

For many, the largest meal of the day, though often one of the simplest: roast pork and potatoes, goulash and dumplings. With your dumplings you might have goulash, a thicker and less oily paprika-based soup than the Hungarian version. *Vepřové maso* (pork) is ubiquitous, and the *koleno* (knuckle) can be a masterpiece of simple cooking, with a crispy skin and tender, juicy chunks of meat coming easily off the bone. Many times *koleno* is cooked in dark beer, adding a sugary note to the skin. Naturally, this pairs very well with a cold one.

Dumplings

The *knedlík* (dumpling) is an aspect of Czech national identity whose importance would be hard to overstate. (If you travel across the country and elect not to eat *knedlíky*, you will probably go hungry.) The two principal kinds are the denser ones made from potatoes (*bramborové knedlíky*) and the lighter (if that is the right term) *houskové knedlíky*, made from rolls. They are the most common side dish for many meals, in particular those with a rich sauce or gravy.

Game

One of the country's great culinary resources – only now getting the attention it deserves – is wild game. Come autumn, venison, boar, wild duck and goose are all frequently served, often with sauces made from wild fruits like rose hips (*šípky*) or blueberries (*borůvky*). Since such dishes are only seasonal delicacies, if one is on the menu, try it.

Fish

Much is made of the country's yuletide obsession with *kapr* (carp), which, come Christmas eve, is ritually slaughtered, cut into steaks, breaded and fried. Christmas carp can be good or less-than-good, though most Westerners seem to prefer fish with lower olfactory profiles. The nation's trout farms supply plenty of fresh *pstruh*, often served simply fried whole in butter or breaded and deep-fried. The native zander or pike-perch (here called *candát*) is a working man's delicacy, and was brought to Western Europe from this region especially for that reason. Catfish (*sumec*), tench (*lín*), pike (*štika*), eel (*úhoř*) and perch (*okoun*) are occasionally listed on menus. The area around Třeboň has been famous for its fish ponds since at least the 16th century, and many good fish restaurants are found there today.

Dinner

You lucky dog: your second chance to eat dumplings. And goulash. And *koleno*.

In fact, lunch and dinner here are virtually indistinguishable. In many pubs and restaurants, dinner may mean more complicated recipes or a longer list of dishes. Schnitzel, called *řízek*, may be made from pork (*vepřový*) or chicken (*kuřecí*). Both are breaded and fried and usually served with a lemon wedge.

In the Czech lands, vegetarianism is a long, narrow path along a sheer cliff face composed of stacks of streaky bacon and pork sausages. Pork is ever-present, occasionally even in dishes labelled *bez masa*, or 'without meat'. However, one pub favourite usually is meatless: *smažený sýr*, or fried cheese, which is breaded and served in the manner of a schnitzel. It is usually accompanied by *hranolky*, fast-food-style French fries, and *tatarská omáčka*, a mayonnaise-like tartar sauce.

In most pubs, you won't find many salads beyond a primitive coleslaw, a bowl of grated carrots and the ever-present *šopský salát*, a would-be Greek-style mix of chopped cucumber, tomato, peppers and a feta-like 'Balkans' cheese, made from cow's milk.

Desserts

Grandma's kitchen has a passel of wonderful dessert recipes that you'll almost certainly never see in any Czech restaurant. However, that doesn't mean there's no sweet finish – only that you'll have to get invited to a Czech home to taste the best ones.

In a restaurant, however, you can almost always get good *palačinky*, the Czech style of crêpes, which are thinner and less crisp than the Breton version, and usually served with jam or compote and topped with whipped cream. You're especially lucky if you find *lívanečky*, thick yeasty pancakes which resemble blinis, and best served with blueberries. Many Czech bakers make *závin*, aka *štrůdl*, or strudel, layers of flaky pastry usually filled with *jablko*, or apple. In recent years, there has been a proliferation of the so-called *medovník*, a crumb-cake made with honey which is excellent with coffee. And of course, there's always room for more dumplings: *ovocné knedlíky*, or fruit dumplings, are a delicious dessert, especially when *jahody* (strawberries) are in season.

Cheese

Forty-one years of collectivisation didn't do much for the country's unusual cheeses, but one or two rarities stand out. The first, *olomoucké tvarůžky* or *olomoucké syrečky*, is an extremely stinky soft cheese from Olomouc. In Austria it is known as *Olmützer Quargel*, and still spoken of with some affection. It has been produced in Olomouc since the 15th century, but today just one firm makes it. It is slightly rubbery, low in fat and, at its best, smells like old socks. It may be fried, served with toast or used for crowd control by riot police.

Pivní sýr, beer cheese, is another soft cheese, though more buttery and much less noisome than *tvarůžky*. It is served with mustard, chopped white onions and paprika, and is meant to be mashed up with a fork and a splash of beer from your glass and spread on a slice of Šumava rye bread. In Prague, U Zlatého tygra boasts that it was one of the first pubs to serve *pivní sýr*, lending it an aura of authenticity.

Other varieties are more or less copies of well-known *fromages* from the West, like *niva*, which resembles a low-fat Roquefort, and the ever-present *eidam*, a version of Edam.

Wine

Well, it's getting better. But for the love of all that is sacred, think about where you are in geographic terms before ordering a Cabernet and expecting it to remind you of those warm summer nights in California. This country has a long and esteemed winemaking tradition that is slowly recovering from years of Communist abuse, but it does not receive enough sunlight to create big, meaty reds.

Instead, look to the whites, and try regional varietals that might be more familiar when you think of neighbouring Austria, Germany or not-so-far-off Hungary: Müller-Thurgau, *veltlínské zelené* (grüner Veltliner) and *tramín* (Traminer) all can make very good white wines, though in many years the colder climate and short amount of sunlight may produce a greater degree of acidity, which could cause difficulty with food pairings. Confusingly, Czech wines are often priced at the same level as the imports, though they're often far off in terms of quality. Two domestic winemakers with very good whites are Dobrá Vinice and Nové Vinařství. In particular, their Rieslings and Riesling blends (often with *rulandské šedé*, or Pinot Gris, or *rulandské bílé*, Pinot Blanc) have been outstanding. Because of the climate, Czech Sauvignon Blanc has the possibility to someday do just as well as its cousins from France, and usually makes an excellent local choice.

Reds are trickier although more interesting, due to the unusual varietals. With game dishes, Czech *modrý portugal* (blauer Portugieser) and Zweigeltrebe can be perfectly functional and very flavourful, as can *svatovavřinecké* (St Laurent) and *rulandské modré* (Pinot Noir). The most common red wine is *frankovka* (Lemberger, or Blaufränkisch) and despite its usual acidity, it is ubiquitous and widely beloved. Occasionally, though rarely, and in the right hands, *frankovka* can make a very nice, medium-bodied red wine. But if you need a big, round red, you're probably better off buying an import. Normally this Guide is all about local products in local places, but then again, you didn't come here for the wine, or why would you have bought this book?

Spirits

After dinner, or very early in the morning, or anytime before, in-between or after, you might be asked if you would like a *panák*, literally a 'little man', but here meaning a shot of the strong stuff. It invariably seems to mean 'several shots', and it is not recommended if you have to get behind the wheel or testify in court or do anything at all, anytime within the next several days. No matter how small your shot is promised to be, they always end up quite a bit larger.

That said, the country's spirits can be very good, especially the *slivovice* (plum brandy, aka slivovitz), especially if it is homemade and from Moravia. The best stuff is not the stuff in the bottles with fancy labels. The tough, throat-cleaning solvents from the Jelínek distillery are just shadows of the ethereal, clean-tasting eau-de-vies made by old men out near the Austrian and Slovak borders. If you have the chance, take it.

In addition to plum distillates, brandies are made from apricots *(meruňkovice)*, pears *(hruškovice)*, sweet cherries *(třešňovice)*, sour cherries *(višňovice)*, apples *(jablkovice)*, and just about anything else that bears fruit or has leaves.

In addition, Czech gastronomy has two traditional bitter liqueurs, usually thought of as digestifs: Fernet Stock, a version of Italy's Fernet Branca, and Karlovy Vary's Becherovka. Both are syrupy drinks, sweet and bitter, laced with loads of herbal flavour. One after a meal is a great idea. Six is a death sentence.

Beer snacks

If you're in a simple place, don't plan on eating much: the most spartan Czech *pivnice* or *výčep* will probably only have crisps, here called *čipsy* or *brambůrky*. The best ones, often, are the cheap, extremely greasy crisps in the clear cellophane bags. Sometimes these are called *České brambůrky* (as opposed to those fancy crisps from abroad). The packaging may look unprofessional: just think of that

as 'home-made', in both the best and the worst possible ways. Alternately, there may be peanuts, called *arašídy* or *buráky*. If this is all there is, you probably won't be very hungry, as a place with such a limited menu will also offer a constant supply of second-hand smoke.

The next step up is the *utopenec*, or 'drowned man', a thick, fat pork sausage which has been pickled in a mix of water, vinegar, salt, sugar and spices, usually with onions and peppers. *Utopenci* are a subject of derision for many outsiders, though this Guide endorses them wholeheartedly. Beer cheese *(pivní sýr)*, mentioned above, is another great way to soak it all up.

If there is a kitchen of some kind, there probably will be *topinky*, fried slices of rye bread. These can come with *pomazánka*, or spread, but the most common way to serve them is *s česnekem*, with garlic, a clove of which you will rub over their crisp surfaces with fury, just as if you were preparing a bruschetta.

This part of Central Europe is traditionally considered the home of one type of potato cake (as north Connacht might be called the home of Ireland's boxty). Here, it is called *bramborák* (or *bramboráčky*, if they are numerous and small). Other names, often specific to certain regions, are *báč* (near Prostějov), *kramflek* (in the foothills of the Orlické hory), *křapáč* and *křapanec* (in Eastern Bohemia), *prskanec* (near Benešov), *smrazek* (in the Central Vysočina), *škrample* (near Pardubice) and *vošouch* (in Plzeň, where it consists of chunks of smoked pork). The ingredients are: grated raw potatoes, flour, eggs, garlic, salt and spices. It is generally very greasy and often quite good. It may be served alone, or with smoked pork or another meat, with cabbage, or even used as the casing for a cutlet.

You might also encounter *sádlo*, or lard, served with sliced rye bread. It is cheap, rich, peasant food and exactly the kind of thing for which the Guide will walk across town, especially *škvarkové sádlo*, lard mixed with crisp lardons, spread over a thick slice of Šumava bread and paired with a *světlý kvasničák*. Across town, and through a rainstorm.

Beer Tourism

ALMOST EVERY Czech brewery – from the tiniest brewpubs up to the 8-million-hectoliter mammoths – offers brewery tours, usually for a nominal fee. While Czech is naturally the main language, tours in English are often available, sometimes only with advance notice and occasionally just for large groups. (At the very least, you'll be allowed to join a Czech-language tour after being handed a slip of paper with the guide's banter written out in something which approximates the Bard's tongue, and which in many cases forms a bizarre kind of poetry on its own.)

When we've learned that Pivovar XYZ does not offer tours, that information is included in the brewery's listing. Otherwise, you should be welcome. You might be welcome only one day each week – possibly only in the summer, probably only with advance reservations – but by and large, you should be able to spend an hour kicking the tyres, so to speak, before taking one out for a test drive.

BREWERY MUSEUMS

Many small and medium-size breweries – Chodovar and Dalešice, for example – incorporate small 'brewery museums' into their premises, often comprising just a few maps, some old glasses and sepia photographs of the brewing family. Here are a few independent beer-themed museums:

Chmelařské muzeum/Hop Museum
Mostecká 2580
438 19 Žatec
T 397 626 125
www.beers.cz/hopmuseum
The hop museum in the capital of the Czech hop industry has information on the crop's history here, which dates back a millennium or more, spread out over several floors of a former hop storage and packaging plant. The museum closed for reconstruction in early 2007, but was scheduled to reopen by summer.

Salesiánské pivní muzeum/ Salesian Beer Museum
Salesiáni Dona Boska
Kobyliské náměstí 1
182 00 Praha 8–Kobylisy
T 283 029 324
www.sdb.cz/pivo/
Call for reservations.
Don't ask us why, this collection of 5,000 beer labels, 4,000 coasters and much, much more is held by the Salesians of Don Bosco, a Roman Catholic religious order. The collection is kept in the brothers' youth centre located directly at Prague's Kobylisy metro station, and visitors are requested to phone in advance.

Plzeňské Pivovarské muzeum/ Pilsner Brewery Museum
Veleslavínova 6
301 14 Plzeň
T 377 235 574
www.prazdroj.cz
This Gothic brewery and malt house in Plzeň tells the story of Pilsner, Urquell and otherwise, with a stunning collection of glassware, coasters, labels and photographs. Life-size dioramas depict every aspect of malting, brewing, cooperage and of course drinking. Located next door to the Na Parkánu pub, currently the only place in the world to serve Pilsner Urquell's version of *kvasnicové pivo*. Apr–Dec: *daily* 10–18; Jan–Mar: *daily* 10–17.

Pivovarnické muzeum Oselce/ Brewery Museum Oselce

Oselce 2
335 01 Oselce
T 371 591 665
www.obecoselce.cz | www.bbkult.net
Not far from Nepomuk, the Oselce Brewery Museum opened at the beginning of 2004 with more than 600 beer bottles, glasses, porcelain coasters and antique bottlers. Located inside the *Obecní úřad* (Municipal Office), with a government office's opening hours.
CLOSED SATURDAY. *Mon & Wed* 8–17, *Tue & Fri* 8–noon, *Thu* 8–15, *Sun* 14–17.

Šumavské Pivovarnické Muzeum/ Šumava Brewing Museum

Vimperská 12
341 92 Kašperské Hory
T 728 124 463
www.volny.cz/pivovarske-muzeum
The Southern Bohemian town of Kašperské Hory lies not far from Strakonice in the direction of the German border. There, the Šumava Brewing Museum uses a restored pub from the 1930s as a showcase for hundreds of historic bottles dating back to 1870, glasses from 1890–1950, as well as old placards, taps, antique bottling equipment and more. *Daily* 9–17.

CZECH BEER CALENDAR

Though relatively under-promoted, dozens of beer festivals – called *pivní slavnosti* – light up weekend nights around the country. The majority are annual Friday to Saturday rock festivals in the grounds of medium-to-large breweries, the so-called 'open door' days that usually come just once a year. (As such, only that particular brewery's beer is usually available.) But other festivals from the capital all the way to the far corners of the countryside invite multiple breweries, often smaller producers, to show off their wares, and include entertainment ranging from mechanical bull rides to puppet shows.

As with almost everything in the Czech Republic, dates and times listed here are mere estimates. By all means, double-check online and call ahead to make sure your event wasn't moved to a different city, in a different region, in a different month... and cancelled at the last minute due to 'technical reasons'.

JANUARY

Last week
Táboře (South Bohemia), Amber Hotel Palcát, Třída 9. května
Slavnosti piva v Taboře
Annual four-day beer festival, tasting and awards ceremony (*Česká pivní pečet*) taking place since 1990.
More details on slavnostipiva.topweb.cz

FEBRUARY
No events.

MARCH

Early March
Prague, Na Perštýně 7, U Medvídků
X-33 Release
Fast becoming a semi-annual event, the arrival of U Medvídků's X-33 strong beer is cause for a small celebration.
More details on www.umedvidku.cz

March (biennial)
Brno (South Moravia), Exhibition Centre
Pivex
Every two years, this international brewing and malting trade fair takes place in the Czech Republic's second city, with the next one scheduled for 2008.
More details on www.bvv.cz

APRIL

Last Saturday
Černá Hora (South Moravia)
Černá Hora 3/5
Vítání jara
The 'welcoming of spring' beer festival takes place at the Černá Hora brewery.
More details on www.pivovarch.cz

Friday nearest April 30
Pardubice (Pardubický kraj), Palackého 250
Čarodějnice
The Pernštejn brewery celebrates *Čarodějnice*, the Czech lands' annual 'burning of the winter witch' bonfire night, akin to the Celtic festival of Beltane.
More details on www.pernstejn.cz

MAY

First Saturday
Žatec (Ústecký kraj), main square
Chmelfest
The opening of the hop-growing season brings about this madcap festival with prizes for 'beer athleticism' and an anti-beauty competition for the 'ideal' beer-drinker's body. Brought to you by the wacky people who do *Chmelovín*, the Halloween hop festival in October.
More details on www.chrampiva.cz

Second weekend
Olomouc (Olomoucký kraj), 17. listopadu, city centre
Olomoucký pivní festival
The largest beer festival in the Czech Republic takes place in Olomouc, with beers from 25 or

more domestic breweries, as well as concerts and a Miss Beerfest ČR beauty contest, all spread out over five very beery days.
More details on **www.pivnifestival.cz**

Mid- to late May
Brno (South Moravia), Stará Radnice (Old Town Hall)
Radniční dny s Pivem
The country's second city hosts a two-day festival of the smaller Czech breweries, right at Brno's Old Town Hall.
More details on **www.kultura-brno.cz**

Mid-May (Saturday)
Pelhřimov (Vysočina)
Pivovar Poutník, Pivovarská 856
Poutník Fest
An annual rock concert taking place in the courtyard of the Poutník brewery.
More details on **www.pivovarpoutnik.cz**

Saturday closest to May 20
Náchod (Královéhradecký kraj)
Pivovar Primátor, Dobrošovská 130
Primátor Beer Festival
The Primátor brewery opens the doors for a one-day beer and music festival.
More details on **www.primator.cz**

Last weekend
Třebíč (Vysočina), Karlovo náměstí
Třebíčské slavnosti piva
This ten-year-old beer festival brings music and brews to a lovely, UNESCO-listed town in the 'largest people's festival of golden brews in Moravia'. The beers from 17 or more breweries include many of the usual suspects as well as a few underdogs.
More details on **www.dan-production.cz/slavnosti**

JUNE

First weekend
Znojmo (South Moravia), Hradní 2
Pivní slavnosti
The beer festival at Heineken's Hostan brewery.
More details on **www.hostan.cz**

First Saturday
Velké Popovice (Central Bohemia), Ringhofferova 1
Den Kozla
The 'Day of the Goat' at the Velkopopovický Kozel brewery includes folk, country and rock groups playing on two stages.
More details on **www.kozel.cz**

Second weekend
České Budějovice (Southern Bohemia), Antonínský Jarmark
Slavnosti piva
A decade of beer festivals in Budweis has regularly brought in more than 40 breweries each year, including some of the country's smallest. Free entry.
More details on **www.vcb.cz**

Saturday nearest June 16
Broumov (Královéhradecký kraj), Osvobození 55
Naše Pivo
Opat Brewery's 'Our Beer' open-door festival brings barrel-rolling competitions, musical groups and games for kids to the brewery grounds all day Saturday.
More details on **www.pivovarbroumov.cz**

Saturday nearest June 16
Krušovice (Central Bohemia)
Pivní slavnosti
The massive Krušovice brewery's open-door beer festival.
More details on **www.krusovice.cz**

Second or third Saturday
Benešov (Central Bohemia), Táborská 306
Slavnosti pivovaru Benešov
The open-door festival at Benešov's Ferdinand brewery entertains with Czech rock groups, contests and tours of the premises.
More details on **www.pivovarferdinand.cz**

Mid-June (Saturday)
Ostrava (Moravskoslezský kraj), Hornopolní 57
Pivní slavnosti
The open-door festival at InBev-owned Ostravar brewery.
More details on **www.staropramen.cz**

Mid-June (Saturday)
Ústí nad Labem, Amfiteátr letního kina
Pivní slavnosti
Zlatopramen, Březňák, Kutná Hora and Louny beers are available at this summer beer festival taking place in Ústí nad Labem's open-air cinema.
More details on **www.drinksunion.cz**

Mid-June (Saturday)
Nymburk (Central Bohemia), Pražská 581
Pivní slavnosti
On one Saturday sometime around June 15–20, the Nymburk brewery opens its doors.
More details on **www.postriziny.cz**

Mid–June (weekend)
Prague, Nádražní 84
Pivní slavnosti
On one weekend in mid-June, Staropramen, Prague's biggest brewer, opens its doors for the city's biggest beer festival: upwards of 20,000 spectators drawn in by pivo in plastic cups, musical concerts and massive crowds.
More details on **www.staropramen.cz**

Weekend nearest June 22
Český Krumlov (South Bohemia), Old Town
Five-Petalled Rose Festival
The UNESCO-listed Gothic town in South Bohemia puts on a three-day medieval-themed festival to celebrate the solstice, including characters in historical dress, night processions, concerts, games and more. Many of the events and performances take place in the grounds of the Eggenberg Brewery.
More details on **www.ckrumlov.info**

Saturday nearest June 22
Malý Rohozec (Liberecký kraj), Malý Rohozec 29, near Turnov
Svatojánské slavnosti
On a Saturday close to the summer solstice, the Malý Rohozec brewery opens its doors for a St. John's Day midsummer festival.
More details on **www.pivorohozec.cz**

Late June
Chodová Planá, Pivovarská 107
European Barrel-Rolling Championships
The Chodovar brewery sponsors this yearly barrel-rolling competition, setting against each other teams from the Czech Republic, Germany, Britain, America and elsewhere, with further competitions in in-line skating (with beers) and a Mini Cooper rally (without).
More details on **www.chodovar.cz**

Last weekend
Vratislavice nad Nisou (Liberecký kraj), Tanvaldská 163   Pivovar Konrad
Pivní slavnosti Konrad/Konrad Fest
The brewery in Vratislavice nad Nisou hosts three days of rock concerts at this bustling, open-air fair.
More details on **www.pivo-konrad.cz**

Last Saturday
Polička (Pardubický kraj), Pivovarská 151
Den otevřených sklepů
The Polička brewery opens its cellars and the brewery grounds to the public for tours, concerts and more.
More details on **www.pivovar-policka.cz**

Last Saturday
Havlíčkův Brod (Vysočina), Dobrovského 2027
Pivní slavnosti
The Rebel brewery hosts an on-site beer festival and rock concert.
More details on **www.hbrebel.cz**

Last Saturday
Klášter Hradiště nad Jizerou (Central Bohemia)
Pivní slavnosti
The beer festival at the brewery next to the eponymous monastery in Klášter Hradiště brings rock music to what was once a calm and introspective place. In recent years there has been a shuttle bus running from the town of Mnichovo Hradiště to the festival's hilltop location.
More details on **www.pivovarklaster.cz**

Last Saturday
Strakonice (South Bohemia), Podskalí
Pivovarská pouť
The Strakonice brewery's all-ages Saturday fair, beer festival and concert.
More details on **www.pivovarnektar.cz**

Sometime in June

Pardubice (Pardubický kraj), Palackého 250
Pardubické léto s Pernštejnem
Apparently, this 'Pardubice Summer with
Pernštejn' festival has no set date, just
'sometime in June'. At Pivovar Pernštejn.
More details on www.pernstejn.cz

JULY

Thursdays (through August)
Plzeň, Pilsner Urquell Brewery
Léto s Prazdrojem
A free summer concert series on the brewery
grounds, every Thursday evening at 19.30,
through to the end of August.

Mid-July (Saturday)
Svijany (Liberecký kraj), Svijany 25
Svijanské pivní slavnosti
Svijany holds its beer festival on the first
Saturday after July's state holidays – Saints
Cyril and Methodius Day on 5th July, and
Jan Hus Day on 6 July. In 2007, the big party
takes place on 14 July.
More details on www.pivovarsvijany.cz

Second Saturday
Žamberk (Pardubický kraj)
Pivní slavnosti
This mountain village hosts a beer festival
on its local soccer field, with a number of
brews from around the region.
More details on www.zamberk.cz

Second-to-last Saturday
Harrachov (Liberecký kraj), Harrachov 95
Harrachovské pivní slavnosti
The mountain brewery-cum-glassworks-
cum-ski-resort hosts an annual party where
Bohemian polka bands and rivers of molten
glass collide. One can only hope.
More details on www.sklarnaharrachov.cz

Last Saturday
Třeboň (South Bohemia), Trocnovské
náměstí 124
Tradiční slavnosti piva
Regent, one of the most beautiful breweries
in all of Bohemia, hosts its big open-door
party on the last weekend of July. Raffles,

fireworks, music, performances and plenty
of fresh fish from the nearby carp ponds.
More details on www.pivovar-regent.cz

Last weekend
Protivín (South Bohemia), Pivovarská 168
Pouťový víkend pod platany
The festival weekend under the plane trees
includes tours of the Platan brewery on the
hour, a market for collectors of Czech
breweriana and open-air rock concerts.
More details on www.pivo-platan.cz

AUGUST

Second weekend
Humpolec (Vysočina)
Pivovar Bernard, Ul. 5. května 1
Pivní slavnosti Bernard
Folk and rock concerts, as well as a rock-
climbing wall, games for kids and plenty of
Bernard beer at the brewery's open-door days.
More details on www.bernard.cz

Second weekend
Vrchlabí (Královéhradecký kraj), main square
Krkonošské pivní slavnosti
The Giant Mountains' beer festival brings
together a handful of small brewers from the
region, including Nová Paka, Opat Broumov,
Primátor, Svijany and others.
More details on www.kpivnislavnosti.cz

Sunday nearest August 15
Vyškov (South Moravia)
Pivovar Vyškov, Čs. armády 116/4
Open Doors
Though open-door day at the Vyškov brewery
is normally scheduled for Sunday only, it
may also be backdated to include Friday and
Saturday. Music, culture and beer.
More details on www.pivovyskov.cz

Mid-August (Saturday)
Pelhřimov (Vysočina)
Pivovar Poutník, Pivovarská 856
Poutník pivní slavnosti
Apparently, Pilgrims know how to rock: yet
another summer beer festival taking place
on the grounds of the Poutník brewery.
More details on www.pivovarpoutnik.cz

Mid-August (Saturday)
Dolní Cetno/Podkováň (Central Bohemia)
Pivovar Podkováň, Podkováň 24
Slavnosti podkováňského piva
Play safe: the open-door beer fest at the
normally closed Podkováň brewery combines
beer and fireworks – plus the added danger
of country music. Czech country music.
Mixed with house. Take heed!
More details on www.podkovan.cz

Third or fourth weekend
Chodová Planá (Plzeňský kraj), Pivovarská 107
Pivní slavnosti Chodovar
The Chodovar brewery's second major
yearly event is this festival in late August,
including a ride on the 'Chodovar Express',
a special steam train running from the town
of Plzeň directly to the brewery.
More details on www.chodovar.cz

Third Saturday
Litovel (Olomoucký kraj)
Pivovar Litovel, Palackého 934
Litovel pivní slavnosti
The Litovel brewery throws its open-door beer
festival on the third weekend of the month.
More details on www.litovel.cz

Last Saturday
Oslavany (South Moravia)
Pivovar Oslavany, Zámek 1
Oslavany pivní slavnosti
The tiny brewery in Oslavany's summer beer
festival takes place in the castle grounds.
More details on zamek.oslavany-cz.eu

Last weekend
Uherský Brod (Zlínský kraj)
Pivovar Janáček, Neradice 369
Janáček Beer Festival
This remote bottling brewery not far from the
Slovak border holds its open-door weekend
party. *More details on* www.pivovar-janacek.cz

Last weekend
Choceň (Pardubický kraj), Park Peliny
Choceňské pivní slavnosti
A small-town beer festival with rock concerts
in the park.
More details on www.pivnislavnosti.unas.cz

**Last weekend before first working day
in September**
Dalešice (Vysočina)   Pivovar Dalešice
Dalešice pivní slavnosti
Pay careful attention to that date, as Dalešice's
beer festival and 'open doors' day is usually
(but not always) in August: in 2007, for example, the big party takes place on 1 September.
More details on www.pivovar-dalesice.cz

SEPTEMBER

First weekend
Žatec (Ústecký kraj), main square
Žatec Hop Festival
The city of hops hosts its annual harvest
festival on the main square.
More details on www.mesto-zatec.cz

Doctor's orders

Hops have been used in folk medicine for
centuries, primarily in the treatment of liver
and skin disorders, and anyone who loves
Czech beer knows that Žatec hops have their
own particularly powerful mojo. In fact, hops
actually have measurable pharmacological
properties, including significant levels of phytoestrogens – naturally occurring substances
that resemble the female hormone oestrogen.

From its offices on Prague's Ječná ('barley')
street, the Czech Research Institute of
Brewing and Malting is currently developing
a beer especially for women, using the
phytoestrogens in hops in an attempt to
alleviate the symptoms of the menopause.
In an initial two-month experiment funded
by the Ministry of Agriculture, the institute's
high-hopped, low-alcohol 'Lady Beer' showed
an ability to reduce such complaints as
fatigue, accelerated heart rate and insomnia.
Far from bitter medicine, the special brew
was reported by participants in the study to
taste quite the same as any good Czech lager.

First weekend
Hanušovice (Olomoucký kraj), Pivovarská 261
Pivní slavnosti
An annual party on the grounds of northern-
most brewery in the Olomouc region.
More details on www.holba.cz

Second weekend
Brno (South Moravia), Hlinky 12
Starobrno pivní slavnosti
Heineken's Starobrno brewery opens the doors for a beer festival, concerts and tours.
More details on **www.starobrno.cz**

Mid-September (Saturday)
Hlinsko v Čechách (Pardubický kraj)
Pivovar Rychtář, Resslova 260
Pivní slavnosti
The open-door festival at Rychtář always takes place on a Saturday in the middle of September – in 2007, that date is 15 September.
More details on **www.rychtar.cz**

Mid-September (Saturday)
Nošovice (Moravskoslezký kraj),
Pivovar Radegast
Pivní slavnosti
SAB-Miller's Radegast subsidiary opens the doors for an on-site party usually taking place on the Saturday closest to 20 September.
More details on **www.radegast.cz**

Mid-September
Prague, Na Perštýně 7
X-33 Release
A party celebrating the second annual release of U Medvídků's X-33 strong beer.
More details on **www.umedvidku.cz**

Second half of September (Saturday)
Pardubice (Pardubický kraj), Palackého 250
Velký den piva
Pivovar Pernštejn's September 'Big Day of Beer' takes place on the expansive brewery grounds. *More details on* **www.pernstejn.cz**

Last Saturday
Černá Hora (South Moravia)
Pivní pouť
The annual beer fest at the wickedly cool Černá Hora brewery. Music, tours, food and bowling. *More details on* **www.pivovarch.cz**

Sometime in September
České Budějovice (South Bohemia)
Budějovický Měšťanský Pivovar, Lidická 51
Pivní slavnosti
The most we could get out of Budějovický

Měšťanský Pivovar, aka Samson, aka Budweiser Bürgerbräu, aka Budweiser 1795, is that they hold an annual beer festival on the brewery grounds 'in September'.
More details on **www.budweiser1795.com**

Sometime in September
České Budějovice (South Bohemia)
Budweiser Budvar, Karolíny Světlé 4
Budweiser Budvar Open Doors
The 'open doors' day at Budvar takes place sometime in September. That much we know. As to which weekend…
More details on **www.budvar.cz**

OCTOBER

First week
Plzeň, Pilsner Urquell brewery
Pilsnerfest
The anniversary celebration of the first brewing of the first Pilsner always takes place in October, usually in the first week. Beer, music and more.
More details on **www.pilsner.cz**

October 31
Žatec (Ústecký kraj), main square
Chmelovín
An unofficial, spontaneous, hop-themed Halloween party taking place in the city of hops. *More details on* **www.chrampiva.cz**

NOVEMBER
No events.

DECEMBER

Weekend before Christmas
Prague
Výstaviště Praha, Průmyslový palác
Christmas Beer Market
The Prague fairgrounds open up for a Christmas market of seasonal beers and paraphernalia from around the Czech Republic and farther afield.
More details on **www.svetpiva.cz**

ANNO 1379

Pivnice

nabízí

15.- 10°

18.- 12°

18.- 13° *řezané*

11°

22.- *krušovický special*

20 12° *krušnicové*

Czech Beer Styles

A QUICK SPIN THROUGH Czech legal edict 357/1997 ('Non-alcoholic drinks and concentrates for the preparation of non-alcoholic drinks; fruit wines; other wines and mead; beer; spirits; liquor and other alcoholic drinks; vinegar') would make it seem as if Czech brewing was mired in a mess of EU gobbledygook resembling one of the funnier passages from Václav Havel's absurdist plays.

In fact, things here are relatively straightforward, with a few Czech twists to keep things interesting. To make it simple, 95 per cent of all beer is largely brewed in the Pilsner style, and would be called 'Pilsner' anywhere else in the world. However, in this country that term is reserved for the original Pilsner, *Plzeňský Prazdroj*, also known as Pilsner Urquell. It may be the appropriate term elsewhere, but this Guide defers to local taste, history and language in the matter, using 'Pilsner-style' or 'golden lager' in the place of 'Pilsner' whenever possible.

Furthermore, as Czech brewing expands, the number of terms is growing as well, and not in ways that make things easier to understand. The first headache is the legal terminology, which, in an effort to simplify things, promptly created more confusion. The second headache comes when people use different terms for the same thing: *světlý ležák*, or 'light-coloured lager', is often translated into English as 'pale ale', which it clearly is not, and one brewer, when asked about the *kvasnicové pivo* on his list, told us that it was not *kvasnicové pivo* at all but that he was serving *nefiltrované pivo*. When asked why he was calling his unfiltered beer a 'yeast beer' – somewhat similar, but clearly not the same – he replied, 'Well, most people don't know the difference.'

And, of course, they never will, as long as this is common practice. With confusing legal terms and an anything-goes attitude from the brewers, it's difficult to define all Czech beer styles in absolute terms. (Is a *tmavé*, or dark, different from a *černé*, or black?)

The most difficult thing to get your head around is that there might be two words for the same beer, or two very different beers with the same name, and the terms can stack up like VWs in an ice storm: Primator's *Hefeweizen* can also be called a *svrchně kvašené světlé pšeničné kvasnicové pivo* (although perhaps not by your average English-speaking beer drinker) or 'upper-fermented, light, wheat yeast beer'. In other words, if you can handle synonyms, homonyms, cognitive dissonance and a constant supply of oxymorons, you'll do just fine.

Basic legal categories

The following terms make up the basic scaffold upon which most current Czech beer styles are built.

Lehké 'Light' beer is brewed anywhere up to 7.99° Balling and must have less than 130 kJ per 100 ml. Very rare.

Výčepní 'Tap', though it can refer to bottles as well. The legal definition for beer brewed between 8° and 10.99° on the Balling scale. The country's most common type.

Ležák Confusingly, the legal definition for a beer brewed between 11° and 12.99° on the Balling scale is 'lager', regardless of brewing technique. Considered the flagship of any brewery.

Speciál 'Special', referring to all beers brewed above 13° on the Balling scale.

THE BEER STYLES

Ale

Not a single style, but rather a whole new family of styles that didn't exist here even just 10 years ago: top fermentation (*svrchní kvašení*). Before the new Pilsner style burned across the country in the mid-19th century, many of the best Czech beers were ales. By the time of the Velvet Revolution, all were long gone, ancient history, forgotten by even the oldest oldsters.

Early reappearances after the year 2000 included the Belgian-style ales from the Želiv monastery brewery, as well as the surprising *Altbier* and *Kölsch* at Richter Brewery in Prague. By 2006, IPAs and other international ale styles had begun to appear at brewpubs in every corner of the Czech lands, finally showing up in the excellent bottled English Pale Ale from Primátor. More like this, please.

BEST ALES
Alt, *Richter*
English Pale Ale, *Primátor*
Gottschalk, *Želiv*

Dia

A beer with lower carbohydrates intended for diabetics (not a low-cal 'diet' beer for slimmers). Produced by several breweries, but invariably a disappointing product for a speciality market. Not regular beers, generally of low quality, and largely ignored by this Guide.

Flavoured beers

Generally speaking, sour cherry beers, eucalyptus beers, stinging-nettle beers and the like are produced from a standard *světlý* or *tmavý ležák* with an adjunct of syrup after lagering. Some can get the balance right, sometimes, but most are cloyingly sweet and annoyingly chemical in taste.

BEST FLAVOURED BEERS
Kaštanomedový ležák (chestnut honey), *Rambousek*

Kávové pivo (coffee), *Pivovarský dům*
Kopřivnové pivo (nettle), *Pivovarský dům*
Višňové (sour cherry), *U Richarda*

Kvasnicové pivo/ kvasnicový ležák

A reason to move here. *Kvasnicové pivo*, or yeast beer (sometimes called *kvasničák*), is a standard Pilsner-style lager with a dose of 'young beer' – fresh yeast and wort – added after lagering, thus reactivating the fermentation process. Although usually cloudy, it can sometimes be perfectly clear (and though most are light in colour, dark or half-dark yeast beers occasionally appear). As a 'living' beer, it is comparable to a *Hefeweizen*, and it is almost exclusively found on tap, not in bottles, either at brewpubs or brewery taprooms. Occasionally found in Germany as *Kräusen*, it is far more common in the Czech lands. Yeast beer has the same basic flavour profile as *světlé výčepní* or *světlý ležák*, with an additional bread-like yeast scent to the nose and a refreshing tartness in the mouth.

Best 10° yeast beer
10°, Oslavany

Best 11° yeast beers
11° kvasnicové, *Dalešice*
11° Lipnický ležák, *Lipník*
Světlý ležák, *Pivovarský dům*
Kvasnicové pivo 11°, *Zlatá labuť*

Best 12° yeast beers
12° Kvasnicové, *U rytíře Lochoty*
12° Kvasnicové hukvaldské pivo, *Hukvaldy*
12° Medlešický ležák světlý, *Medlešice*
12° Záviš světlý kvasnicový, *Polička*
12°, *Oslavany*
Arthur's Old Keltic Beer, *Arthur's*
Forman, *Velichov*
Richter ležák, *Richter*
Světlý ležák, *Novoměstský pivovar*
Světlý ležák kvasnicový, *Pegas*
Světlé pivo Lipan, *Pivovarský dvůr Lipan*

Světlý ležák, *Vendelín*
Vulkán 12°, *Kopřivnice*

Best 13° yeast beer
13° kvasnicová světlá, *Dalešice*

Nealkoholické pivo

Non-alcoholic beer, often called by the nickname *pito*. Very good, high-hopped versions from Bernard and Budvar have appeared recently. Ignored for the purposes of this Guide, but not a bad option for drivers.

Nefiltrované pivo

Unfiltered beer. Similar to, but technically not the same as *kvasnicové pivo*, though the terms are often confused. In this case, merely beer which has not been filtered, rather than beer to which fresh yeast has been added. Can be golden, half-dark or dark, bitter or sweet, low alcohol or high. Thus, not its own style, but often a distinguishing sign of a good, traditional Czech lager.

Best Nefiltrované pivo
Moravské sklepní nefiltrované, *Černá Hora*
Dvorní světlý ležák jedenáctka, *Chýně*

Nepasterované pivo

Any beer which has not been pasteurised. Technically not a style, but something of a nationwide phenomenon, contributing to the popularity of Bernard and Svijany.

Pilsner/Plzeňské pivo

Although the term is used for all sorts of beers around the world, in this country there is just one, Pilsner Urquell, making it something of its own style. Characterised by a deep golden-amber colour and a rich, sugary malt body, Urquell has a strong hoppy bitterness in the finish from a healthy dose of hops from Žatec, known by its German name of Saaz. As the original, Urquell remains the standard for most Czech beers today, though it is losing its edge in this regard. (Many brewers now speak of trying to emulate the Pilsner

invented in the 19th century by Anton Dreher: 4.5–5.5% alcohol, a lightly toasted taste and some serious malt complexity followed by a balanced hop finish. A high-gravity version, *polotmavé speciál*, can be the equivalent of a German *Märzen*.

BEST POLOTMAVÉ LEŽÁK

11° polotmavé pivo, *Bernard*
Granát, *Nová Paka*
Oldgott Barrique, *U Medvídků*

Porter

A dark beer in the Baltic style, usually bottom-fermented and required to be brewed above 18° Balling. For years, the only remaining Baltic-style porter has been Pardubický Porter, brewed at 19° and finishing with a robust 8% alcohol. As a lager, it is very dark brown with a sugary taste of roasted malt, sweet-and-sour and slight pepper notes, light carbonation and a deep, molasses-like finish with little hop bitterness. A style which deserves a comeback.

BEST PORTER

Pardubický Porter, *Pernštejn*

Urquell of 20 years ago.) It has a moderate amount of alcohol, just 4.4% compared to the 5% of most similar European beers. The remaining sugars contribute to the body's richness, differentiating the Czech style from its less robust cousins abroad.

Polotmavý ležák

'Half-dark'. In a strangely heroic move, Staropramen almost single-handedly revived this century-old Czech style in 1999 with a beer called Millennium. It has since caught on at other brewers, usually called *granát* (garnet) or *jantar* (amber). While many people call half-darks *řezané*, they are not, in fact, the same: *řezané* is a mix of separately brewed light and dark lagers, while *polotmavé* is a single beer that is brewed to a reddish, half-dark colour.

Unlike Pilsner-style brews, which usually require extremely soft water, half-darks can be made with a higher carbonate content and can include caramel and dark malt to various degrees, as well as Pilsner malt. Extremely clear and reddish-amber in colour, they are perhaps closest to the Vienna lager

Pšeničné pivo

'Wheat beer', and once called *bílé pivo*, or 'white' beer, equivalent to the Belgian *wit*. Before the invention of the Pilsner style in 1842, the Czech lands were famous for this style. Today only a few bottlers (Herold and Primátor, most significantly) sell *pšeničné pivo*, though the style is clearly gaining in popularity, and is more and more commonly found in brewpubs. Vanilla, clove and banana notes are often present in the aroma. Wheat must make up at least 33% of the grist, creating a light body with very little hop flavour, though a crisp, yeasty tartness is often present in a beer that generally has 4.3–5.6% alcohol. One of the few Czech beers regularly produced with top-fermenting yeast.

BEST WHEAT BEERS
13° Weißbier, *U Krále Ječmínka*
Pšeničné pivo, *Pivovarský dům*
Weizen, *Richter*
Weizenbier, *Primátor*

Řezané/řezaný

Not a style so much as a beer cocktail: a 'cut' mix of *světlé* and *tmavé pivo* from the same category (e.g. *výčepní, ležák*). This can be done at the brewery and bottled and kegged for distribution, though it is most commonly done at the tap by your barman. Not the same as *polotmavé*, but the terms are often confused.

Speciál

According to Czech law, a 'special' is any beer with an original gravity above 13° Balling, though that can mean dark or light, clear or opaque, or any combination thereof. In general, most are strong lagers comparable to a German *Bock* (ram) or *Doppelbock*, and some producers here even use the Czech equivalent words of *beran* (ram), *kozel* (goat) or the diminutive *kozlík* (kid). These commonly range from 5.5–9% alcohol and beyond. Hop aroma is low to non-existent. Hop flavour is similarly reduced, especially in the dark versions.

BEST DARK SPECIALS
13° tmavé pivo, *U Krále Ječmínka*
Double 24°, *Primátor*
Oldřich 18°, Xaver

Speciál tmavý 13⁰, *Zlatá labuť*
Speciální černý ležák 13⁰, *Bernard*
Speciální tmavé pivo XIII, *Sentice*
Tmavý ležák 13⁰, *Příbor*

BEST GOLDEN SPECIALS
1530, *Černá Hora*
Exklusiv 16⁰, *Primátor*
Jihlavský Grand, *Ježek*
Jubiler, *Vyškov*
Opat speciál 13⁰, *Opat*
Prácheňská perla, *Platan*
Speciál 14⁰, *Poutník*
Žamberecký Kanec 13⁰, *Žamberk*

BEST HALF-DARK SPECIALS
16⁰ speciál, *Pegas*
Bohemian Granát Lager, *Herold*
Březňák světlý výčepní 14⁰, *Velké Březno*
Eso, *Konrad*
Polotmavý 13⁰, *Primátor*
Rytířský 21⁰, *Primátor*
X-Beer 33⁰, *U Medvídků*
Žamberecký Kanec 14⁰, *Žamberk*

Světlé výčepní

Generally speaking, 'light tap' beer is a Pilsner-style brew, pale gold in colour, usually produced with relatively low alcohol content due to the lower amount of malt at 8–10.99⁰ Balling. The German equivalent is known as *Schankbier*. Usually 3.5–4% alcohol, often with much less malt and much less hop aroma and bitterness than the premium *světlý ležák*. If such beers go too far in this direction, they are no longer within the parameters of the true Czech style, resembling instead something closer to a German brew.

BEST SVĚTLÉ VÝČEPNÍ
10⁰ Hradební světlé výčepní, *Polička*
Březňák 10⁰, *Velké Březno*
Pepinova desítka, *Nymburk*
Podkováňské výčepní světlé 10⁰, *Podkováň*
Světlé výčepní pivo, *Budvar*
Světlé výčepní, *Louny*
Žamberecký Kanec 10⁰, *Žamberk*

Světlý ležák

'Light lager', a category which includes both Pilsner Urquell and Budvar. A clear deep gold colour and a more or less pronounced malt body with the strong, citrusy scent of Czech hops and a bittersweet finish. Contrary to received wisdom, the best examples here are not very fizzy, even rather flat. Generally 4.4–5.2% alcohol by volume and nowadays often considered the premium or flagship brew at any brewery.

BEST 11° SVĚTLÝ LEŽÁK
11° světlé pivo, *Klášter*
Bednářův truňk 11°, *Podkováň*
Zlatopramen 11°, *Zlatopramen*

BEST 12° SVĚTLÝ LEŽÁK
12° světlý ležák, *Bernard*

B. B. Budweiser Bier, *Budějovický Měšťanský Pivovar*
Baronka, *Žatec*
Budweiser Budvar světlý ležák, *Budvar*
Export, *Žatec*
Opat 12°, *Opat*
Pilsner Urquell
Premium 12°, *Ostravar*
Premium 12°, *Rychtář*
Premium, *Žatec*
Světlá dvanáctka, *Bon*

Tmavé výčepní

'Dark tap' beer is a low-gravity, low-alcohol (roughly 3.5–4%) dark brew, the equivalent of a German *Dunkles Schankbier*. Thinner body, often with much less coffee and cola flavours than the premium *tmavý ležák*. Sugary, malty, with very little bitterness. Often overlooked is its ability to pair well with food.

BEST TMAVÉ VÝČEPNÍ
Granát, *Černá Hora*
10° tmavý, *Ježek*

Tmavý ležák

Approximately 5% of Czech beers – and the fastest-growing export segment – are dark lagers, meaning beers produced with the same yeast and similar techniques as Pilsner-style beers, but with a portion of dark or caramel malts and much less of a hop presence. Related to German *Dunkles* and *Schwarzbier*, and occasionally called *černé/černý*, or black, although this is not an official term. Generally around 5% alcohol, dark amber to black in colour with a tan or sandy head and more sweetness in the mouth, often with rich coffee, cola, chocolate and ginger notes, and with far less bitterness than most golden lagers here.

BEST TMAVÝ LEŽÁK
Bohemian Black Lager, *Herold*
Flekovské pivo, *U Fleků*
Malvaz 12°, *Rychtář*
Tmavé pivo, *Pivovarský dům*
Tmavý ležák, *Velké Meziříčí*
Lučan Premium tmavé, *Žatec*
Troobacz tmavý ležák 12°, *Štramberk*

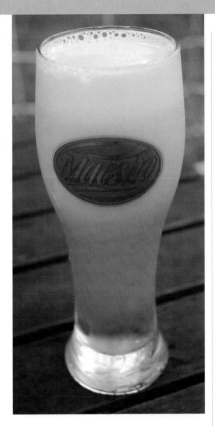

Vánoční

Christmas beer, also known as *sváteční*, or holiday beer. In the past, largely an occasion to print a special 'Christmas' label and put it on the same old golden lager that appears year-round. (Really.) Recently, a few smaller breweries and brewpubs have started making true special beers for Christmas, usually a deep gold or half-dark *speciál* brewed between 14–17° Balling, heavy on the malt and light on the hops, averaging 5.5–6.6% alcohol.

BEST VÁNOČNÍ
12° svateční ležák, *Bernard*
Speciál 14°, *Krakonoš*
Sváteční speciál 17°, *Opat*

Weird beers

A category, if not a style, which includes everything else: Nová Paka's marijuana-tasting Hemp Valley Beer; occasional rye beers; Ferdinand's spiced Sedm kulí; the stinging-nettle beer on draught at Pivovarský dům; Konrad's Jocker (made with a wheat adjunct) and bright-red Červený Král; and so on...

Some like it hot

What's the correct temperature for beer? Many experts believe that Pilsner-style brews taste best at about 10° C (50° F) – relatively warm by most standards. In fact, the owner of one Czech micro-brewery told us that when he serves his beer anywhere above 7° C (45° F), his customers complain that it's not cold enough.

However, not everyone likes frigid lager. If you travel far and wide in the Czech lands – and spend a lot of time in pubs – you may eventually see an *ohříváček*. Roughly the size and shape of a cigar tube with a clip on the end, an *ohříváček* is filled with hot water and hung in a beer glass in order to bring a too-cold brew up to the desired temperature. Still a common sight in Czech pubs of the early 1900s, the *ohříváček* nowadays is a fairly rare bird.

What's in a name

IF YOU SEE '12%' on a Czech beer label, don't expect the drink inside to be as strong as your favourite chardonnay. Also written as '12°', the number refers to the percentage of malt sugar present before fermentation, not the amount of alcohol in the beer afterwards.

In the West, this is usually referred to as the Plato scale. However, its inventor was the Bohemian scientist Carl Josef Napoleon Balling (1805–68), the director of the department of chemistry at Prague's technical college and the creator of the hydrometer in 1843. (The eponymous Fritz Plato improved on Balling's work a few years later.) A similar scale used in the wine industry is called Brix. Out of deference to local history and tradition, this guide refers to Balling numbers.

Unfortunately, such numbers are less and less in use. For many years, a Balling number was a legal term – if a beer was labelled '12°' or '12%', it had to have started life with 12% malt sugar (equivalent to an original gravity of 1.048). In this way, consumers were guaranteed at least a small indication of the value of the drink they were about to purchase.

But on 12 December 1997, Czech law was changed to bring it closer in line with EU norms, and beer labelling was changed to a few broad categories. These were given nonsensical names, the most common of which are *výčepní pivo* (tap beer) for beers brewed from 8–10.99° Balling, *ležák* (lager) for those brewed between 11–12.99° and *speciál* (special) for anything above 13°.

These terms almost appear to have been designed to confuse. In the way it is brewed and the type of yeast it uses, almost every Czech *výčepní pivo* is technically a *ležák*. In the same way, nearly every *speciál* is also a *ležák*, and of course both types are found in a *výčep*, or taproom.

Understandably, most consumers still think of and refer to their beer as a 10° (*desítka*), 11° (*jedenáctka*), 12° (*dvanáctka*), 13° (*třináctka*), 14° (*čtrnáctka*), and so forth.

Not only are the older terms outdated, but they're also inaccurate. Because the new categories are so broad, brewers can cut costs and quality while selling what is legally considered to be the same product. For example, a beer that was formerly brewed at 10° Balling may now be brewed at 9° or less, yet both versions are legally called *výčepní pivo*. In this case, the weaker, cheaper wort can then be fermented longer or otherwise manipulated to ensure the 'right' amount of alcohol. To a consumer just glancing at the label, both old and new beers will appear the same.

But in the mouth, the difference is clear: a true Czech Pilsner-style beer has a solid malt body composed of lots of residual malt sugar. When the amount of initial malt in the wort is reduced, the resulting malt body is also diminished. And with less malt, much less bittering hops are needed to balance the sugars. And in this manner, a Czech beer suddenly starts to taste like something from Germany, or, God forbid, St. Louis.

It is a sign of what this really means to note that the country's big breweries have embraced the new categories wholeheartedly. Small brewers, however, often continue to label their beers with Balling numbers (one of them, Zlatopramen, even made its Balling number the focus of a nationwide ad campaign, thus kicking off the craze for 11° beers). With proper labelling and a guaranteed amount of a principal ingredient, is it any wonder that such brews often taste better?

The Breweries
and Brewpubs
of the
Czech Republic

The brewers of the Czech Republic

FOR A SMALL COUNTRY, the Czech Republic has left a Yeti-size footprint in the vast meadow of global beer culture. There are smaller countries with more breweries, but there are few countries of any size with a comparable brewing history, and even fewer where the people pray at the temple of malt on such a regular basis. The 100-plus Czech breweries and brewpubs included in this Guide date from the relatively antique – like Prague's U Fleků, founded in 1499 – to several which arrived within the past year. Despite a severe contraction in the number of bottlers, more brewpubs are opening every year, with at least ten set to appear in 2007 (see 'Future Breweries', pp 166).

Sadly, most of the large Czech breweries are now owned by foreign conglomerates: Pilsner Urquell, Radegast, Gambrinus and Velké Popovice, all owned by SAB-Miller; Staropramen and Ostravar, owned by InBev; Krušovice, owned by Germany's Radeberger (itself owned by the great frozen-pizza maker, Dr. Oetker); Starobrno and Hostan, owned by Heineken's BBAG.

As such, a number of the foreign-owned domestics now serve as ~~Trojan Horses~~ distributors for their foreign overlords. By and large, the trick has not caught on: most locals still have a fairly good idea of what a real beer is supposed to taste like. Whatever that may be, it is certainly not Stella Artois. The marketing drones do keep trying, however.

The Czech beer market

It is a celebrated fact that the Czech Republic consumes the world's largest amount of beer per capita annually, just under 1 beer per day for every man, woman and child. This figure is aided in part by the wonderful tourists who come to the country to drink lots of great lager. Please do your part while you are here.

For all that volume, don't expect much variety: 95 per cent of the market is Pilsner-style golden lager (and some 40 per cent is produced by the Pilsner Urquell group alone). A further 4 per cent or so is the traditional dark lager. Unless you make an effort, you will probably see the same four or five brands everywhere you go.

For most of us outsiders, it is difficult to get a handle on the true Czech attitude towards beer. While the drink is clearly beloved, it is – surprisingly – cheaper than water and is sometimes treated with even less respect. For many, beer is not anything special, but merely what you drink with a meal – almost every meal, and certainly with nearly every lunch and dinner. But while most locals know what a beer should taste like, few would be able to tell you the difference between a typical Czech brew and an English one, or what the 12% posted on the bottle of their favourite lager actually means. 12% of what?

In recent years, consumption has remained relatively flat while exports are approaching the speed of sound. With the entry of the Czech Republic into the EU on 1 May 2004, import duties to fellow EU countries – most significantly, Germany and Poland – disappeared instantly. Since the domestic market is largely locked up, the main source of growth for many breweries lies abroad, and many smaller brewers survive (and thrive) by increasing their exports 20 per cent or more each year, while at home they might remain almost invisible.

On the domestic front, the biggest news has been the increase in speciality beers and non-alcoholics. Drivers, put aside all evil thoughts of the latter: Budvar's NA is one of the hoppiest, maltiest drinks in the country, real beers included. Bernard makes a similarly good malt soda. Of course, it's still not beer.

Speciality beers, however, are. Not 'specials', meaning 'strong beers', but specialities in the form of reclaimed territory. In the past three or four years, Czech brewers have begun producing more wheat beers and half-darks – traditional favourites which fell out of fashion long ago – and brews such as rye beers, smoked beers and a few entirely acceptable Belgian-, English- and American-style ales. Look for more of these in the future. Or so we pray.

What counts as a beer?

The beers listed in this guide include every regularly produced version that we know of except non-alcoholic beers and the few reduced-sugar brews intended for diabetics. We do not include beers produced outside of the Czech Republic.

We pay little attention to beers produced under licence for supermarket labels unless they are of particularly high quality.

The cheapest swill, sold in oversized plastic bottles, primarily to the destitute, is also ignored. (Měšťan! What happened?)

When we can, we include information on regular seasonal beers such as those produced for Christmas and Easter. However, many so-called 'seasonal' beers in fact turn out to be one-offs, brewed once and then never again. In general, this Guide focuses on beers which are available year-round. Barring that, we list those beers which are brewed with a sense of regularity that does not require an innate understanding of geologic time.

Capricious whimsy

In tasting and rating over 400 Czech beers, we have studied, considered, pondered and reflected. We have consulted with experts and novices alike. But in the end, our views are our views alone.

It should be noted that we have made every effort to rate beers according to the generally accepted profiles of the style. Czech beers are often richer, sweeter and bitterer

than similar beers from other countries. Instead of comparing them to less dynamic beers from abroad, we have judged each beer in this Guide based on the generally accepted local standards as we understand them, together with a dash of our own subjective, capricious whimsy.

After many years of drinking little other than Czech lagers, the idea of spending ten months travelling around the country to taste beers at 100 Czech breweries seemed a daunting, very nearly unpleasant task. (How we have suffered for the greater good!) However, this holiday-like toil provided us with the means to compare these brews almost simultaneously, back-to-back-to-back. Through the course of our evaluations, we returned to many breweries and many pubs more than once. Occasionally, we revised our earlier ratings. Generally, they seemed to stick.

Following the lead of our colleagues at Good Beer Guide Belgium, we adopted the following scale:

★★★★★	*One of the world's great beers*
★★★★/★	*A classic of its kind*
★★★★	*Highly enjoyable and well-designed*
★★★/★	*An above-average performer*
★★★	*Good quality brew that is worth sampling*
★★/★	*May disappoint but should not irritate*
★★	*Unexciting*
★	*Not worth getting out your wallet*

We have rated every beer that we have had the chance to taste recently, though more than a few oddballs escaped us, even at the breweries themselves. We have included information on the amount of alcohol, except in those few cases where it was not available.

It's worth noting once again the transient nature of this wonderful drink and the very dynamic local market: a one-time five-star brew can quickly turn into sewer-water under new ownership. Several breweries listed herein were once internationally known as grand marques, though they have fallen immensely in recent years. Because we are independent, we're free to say that Krušovice sucks.

Furthermore, beer can improve or worsen depending on where and how it is served. A Czech aphorism says that the quality of a beer depends half on the brewer, half on the barman. Due to the long history of beer culture in this country, most people know how to correctly store and serve lager. But differences will always exist, and some may affect the taste. In all cases we have tried to judge beers under optimal conditions: directly inside the brewery, at the brewery's own taproom or at the best pub or restaurant nearest the brewery.

The brewery descriptions

In almost all cases, we try to tell you where the brewery or brewpub is, how to get there and some information about its location, situation, history and renown. If we have been told that tours are definitely not available, we have said so. Otherwise, most breweries should be able to arrange tours of the grounds and cellars, almost certainly for groups. However, most will need advance notice.

In terms of amounts of production, we have queried every brewery directly. Almost all of them have answered, more or less incredulously. Nearly all of the information listed herein comes from their replies, some of which were quite mistrustful indeed. They must have thought we were from the secret EU tax police.

The amounts of production are broken into general categories based on hectolitres (hl) brewed per year:

- < **250 hl** per year implies a part-time, hobby brewer or minor micro-brewery
- < **1,000** hl per year covers most brewpubs and smaller micro-breweries
- > **20,000** hl per year means a significant regional brewer
- > **1,000,000** hl per year is a major, mass-market, factory brewer

Beer names

Due to centuries of oppression, occupation and tyranny, people here tend to be quite comfortable with nomenclatural equivocation: you say Budweis, I say České Budějovice. As such, many beers and breweries seem to thrive on pseudonyms, heteronyms and *noms de guerre*. We attempt to list beers by the most common names in current local use, generally by the name on the label if there is one, or by the name on the beer menu in the case of a brewpub.

It is quite often the case that a beer has a different name in 'real life' than on the brewery's website or English-language PR brochure, in which case we will use the term which is more closely based in reality. Often seemingly translated by a squadron of drunken bonobos armed with manual typewriters, many such pamphlets and menus will erroneously use 'pale ale' in the place of *světlý ležák*, and so on and so forth.

Almost always, this Guide uses Czech names.

In the quest for better marketing, it has become common practice for some breweries to suddenly rename beers, often with monikers that have historically been used for beers in quite different styles. If a beer with a different name is brewed at the same original gravity, in the same style with the same amount of alcohol, it is probably the same beer listed here.

Figures for degrees Balling are included wherever possible. Figures for alcohol content are always for amount of alcohol by volume (ABV). In the case of the living *kvasnicové pivo*, or yeast beer, alcohol content may change over the life of the brew, becoming stronger as it continues to ferment. When such figures are known, we list alcohol content for these beers as an approximate range.

Prague

POPULATION: **1,130,000**
www.pis.cz

AFTER THE VELVET REVOLUTION of late 1989, Prague crept into the world's consciousness as a latter-day Paris, an overlooked medieval burg filled with heart-stopping architecture and a glorious setting on the Vltava river. Largely unspoilt by war and the ravages of 20th-century history, Prague was, is and most likely will remain, one of the most beautiful cities in Europe.

The city's high points, literally, are the hundreds of spires, starting with the peaks of St. Vitus' Cathedral soaring above thousand-year-old Prague Castle. This is Hradčany, the castle district, with Malá Strana – sometimes translated as "Lesser Quarter" – nestled just below it on the west side of the Vltava river. Across the 650-year-old Charles Bridge (Karlův most) is Staré Město, or Old Town, filled with Baroque and Gothic churches, cobblestone lanes, and the ancient astronomical clock on Old Town Square (Staroměstské náměstí). On the north side of Staré Město is Josefov, the old Jewish district, home of the Old-New Synagogue, Europe's oldest active *Shul,* from 1270. To the southwest but still in the centre is Nové Město, or New Town, founded in the mid-14th century but mostly developed over the past 200 years. Its core is Wenceslas Square (Václavské náměstí), a setting for palatial Art-Nouveau and Beaux-Arts cafés and hotels, all of which add to the city's never-ending visual feast. It's no surprise why so many people speak of Prague with wonder – even those who have lived here their entire lives. To the eye, it's almost too much.

And then, of course, there is the beer. As wealth has returned to the Czech lands, more locals are beginning to splurge on Burgundy and Champagne, but the default beverage for even the most serious occasions – opera galas and state dinners – is *pivo,* or beer. It is consumed so widely and so commonly that it is not considered an alcoholic beverage by many, and it is so ubiquitous that many locals don't even realise how good it is. It is simply what you drink.

With only eight functioning breweries, Prague is certainly not the biggest city in the republic in terms of production, but it remains the country's best destination for drinking: there are individual streets here which are home to more than 300 pubs, ranging from dingy dives to chic cafés, and it's not uncommon to see a pub on all four corners of a given intersection. Most often, the taps will pour Pilsner Urquell, Gambrinus, Budvar or local Staropramen, but a number of rare birds from around the country can also be found here. In addition, the list of brewpubs is a growing tourist draw that is starting to rival the architecture.

With the visual beauty, great brews and attendant crowds have come Western-style luxury hotels and prices, despite the relative weakness of the Czech crown. There is no cheap hotel district, and at the time of writing, €110 was a good price for an inexpensive double in the centre in high season, much less in the off season. Since the city is blessed with such a wonderful public transport system, it doesn't much matter where you stay: all of Prague's best bars, breweries and pubs are accessible via tram, metro or bus. The last metros leave the end stations at midnight, but trams and buses run across the city all night long. Have fun.

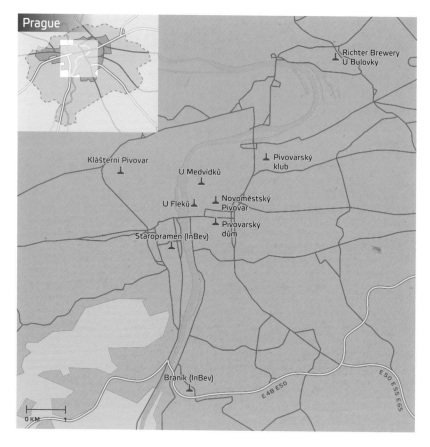

Prague

Richter Brewery
U Bulovky

Klášterní Pivovar

Pivovarský
klub

U Medvidků

U Fleků

Novoměstský
Pivovar

Pivovarský
dům

Staropramen (InBev)

Braník (InBev)

E 48 E 50

E 50 E 55 E 65

0 KM   1

Braník (InBev)

Údolní 1/212
Praha 4–Braník
T 244 018 111
E info@staropramen.cz
www.pivovary-staropramen.cz

Once a dark lager so fine it inspired writers to compose odes and paeans, Braník has turned into a fourth-rate Eurolager under InBev and is slated to close in 2007. The brands might continue to be brewed by InBev, perhaps at Prague's Staropramen brewery, perhaps somewhere in Africa. The dark Braník of legend appears to be available in other countries, but is rarely if ever seen here. A bitter end.

ANNUAL OUTPUT: >1,000,000 hl.

REGULAR BEERS:
Braník světlé výčepní (4.1%: ★★)
  Very pale straw-gold, far too fizzy and flavourless.
Braník světlý ležák (4.9%: ★/★)
  A fourth-rate Eurolager.

Klášterní

Klášterní pivovar Strahov
Strahovské nádvoří 10
Praha 1–Strahov
T 220 516 671
E klasterni-pivovar@iol.cz
www.klasterni-pivovar.cz

Opened in 2001, the 'Cloister' restaurant and microbrewery serves two standard lagers named after Norbert, the patron saint of the Premonstratensian monastic order whose remains are interred nearby: a *jantar*, or 'amber', and a classic dark lager. In addition, seasonal brews have included 18° and 19° Christmas specials, as well as an Easter 14°. In a prime tourist location near Prague Castle, prices here are high and portions small: at the time of this writing, a 0.4-litre glass (just under a pint) ran 49 Kč, almost twice the cost of the average half-litre in town. Unfortunately, service can be indifferent as well, making this place seem like an essential stop only for completists. However, the beers are good, the location can't be beat, and Martin Matuška won the SPP award for Brewer of the Year in 2006.

ANNUAL OUTPUT: <1,000 hl.

REGULAR BEERS:

Svatý Norbert jantar 13° (5.2%: ★★★/★)
Amber in both name and colour with light body and a mild finish.

Svatý Norbert tmavý 14° (5.7%: ★★★/★)
A flat dark lager of reduced sweetness and flavour.

Novoměstský pivovar

Vodičkova 20
Praha 1–New Town
T 222 232 448
www.npivovar.cz

Founded in 1993, the year the Czech Republic and Slovakia finally broke up, this labyrinthine micro-brewery and restaurant serves up decent Bohemian fare – hearty beef goulash and roast suckling pig – in sizeable portions, although the cooking is still several steps down from the crisp, citrus-scented lager. Tourist throngs, inattentive waiters and bad music on the stereo are only here to dissuade the undeserving. Do not be fooled. Enter, take your rightful place and order a round or two.

ANNUAL OUTPUT: <250 hl.

REGULAR BEERS:

Světlý ležák (4%: ★★★★/★)
A yeast beer with a slight orange-grapefruit nose and deliciously bittersweet malt body.

Tmavé pivo (4%: ★★★★)
Molasses-and-coffee tasting dark lager with a long, slightly bitter finish.

Pivovarský dům

Lípová 15
Praha 2–Nové Město
T 296 216 666
www.gastroinfo.cz/pivodum

Established in 1996, this bustling, reservations-recommended brewpub lies downstairs from the Czech Research Institute of Brewing and Malting, a vote of confidence if ever there was one, and the name 'Brewery House' applies to both the institute's domicile (constructed 1937) and the newer arrival. Pivovarský dům gets a lot of talk for its hit-or-miss special beers, flavoured after brewing with fruit and spice extracts (chili, eucalyptus, blackthorn, etc.), but true beer fans come for the standards alone. Seasonal additions to the list make frequent visits a necessity for locals. Only one beer, Šamp, is regularly available in bottles.

ANNUAL OUTPUT: 1,000 hl.

REGULAR BEERS:

Světlý ležák (4%: ★★★★★)
A cloudy, deep gold yeast beer with a bread-like scent and a citrus-like malt body followed by the crisp taste of fresh Saaz hops. Gorgeous.

Tmavé pivo (4%: ★★★★/★)
Classic Czech dark with slight coffee notes and a bittersweet finish.

Pšeničné pivo (4%: ★★★★★)
Wheat beer: one of the first wheats to return to the Czech lands. A pale thirst-quencher with a beautiful clove nose.

Kávové pivo (4%: ★★★/★)
Coffee beer: a deep amber Munich-style dark with plenty of coffee flavouring.

Višňové pivo (4%: ★)
Sour cherry. A light lager flavoured with fruit extract. Medicinal. Unpleasant.

Banánové pivo (4%: ★★)
Banana. Only a slightly better idea than the sour cherry.

Kopřivové pivo (*4%: ★★★/★*)
Nettle. Deep green lager scented with a favourite comestible from the Bohemian forests. Unusual and refreshing.

Šamp (4%: ★★★/★)
Brewed with champagne yeast and only available in bottles, this sweet and bubbly lager has the added aroma of Muscat grapes.

Pivovarský klub

Křižíkova 17 (near metro Florenc)
Praha 8–Karlín
T 222 315 777
www.gastroinfo.cz/pivoklub

A sister bar to the Pivovarský dům micro-brewery, Pivovarský klub ('Brewery Club') opened in late 2005 with only one beer of its own: the killer 17° *sedmnáctka* ('seventeen') lager, named after the street address, brewed off-site by its cross-town sibling. A small 40-litre brewery here allows fans and home-brewers without equipment to make small batches for personal consumption, though waiting four weeks for lagering seems several bridges too far, and it is unclear if this will continue. This place is a must-see for beer travellers: in addition to six draft beers (a rotating collection from Pivovarský dům and the country's regional producers), Pivovarský klub also functions as a rare bottle shop, stocking great brews from around the country and around the world.
ANNUAL OUTPUT: <250 hl.

REGULAR BEERS:
Křižíkova sedmnáctka (5.5%: ★★★/★)
A medium-amber brew with high residual sugar and mineral and honey tastes.

Richter Brewery

Richter Brewery U Bulovky
Bulovka 17
Praha 8–Libeň
T 284 840 650
E richterpub@seznam.cz
www.pivovarubulovky.cz

Founded in 2004, František Richter's lovely brass-and-oak appointed pub was one of the first places in the country to offer both top- and bottom-fermented beers stemming from the owner's experience of brewing both styles in Germany. The house lager, a classic Pilsner-style brew, is always available, as is one or another special, including Richter's takes on Alt, Helles, Dortmunder Export, Bock, Kölsch, wheat beers, ales and even stouts and porters; all are absolutely outstanding. Live music at weekends and a friendly family feel make this a popular destination for beer lovers from around the city and around the world. The deserved winner of 2005's Micro-brewery of the Year award from SPP.

ANNUAL OUTPUT: 250 hl.

REGULAR BEERS:

Richter ležák (5%: ★★★★★)
A dark gold lager with a great malt body balanced by fragrant, florid Saaz hops.

Staropramen (InBev)

Nádražní 84
Praha 5–Smíchov
T 244 018 111
E info@staropramen.cz
www.staropramen.cz

The largest brewery in Prague, Staropramen occupies a significant amount of real estate in Prague 5's Smíchov district. In the late 19th century, much of the area was once home to brewery workers; today it is experiencing a very slow gentrification. It is enough to say that Staropramen is an InBev brand, exported to 34 countries, and despite being superior (though still not that great), the domestic brew is sold alongside the 'premium import', Stella Artois, in the same manner that the world's largest brewer has done around the globe. It would perhaps be too easy to hate Staropramen simply because of its corporate owners. Fortunately, the beers in their current state give us plenty to hate on their own. For what it's worth, tours are available and there is a fun, rowdy pub on site.

ANNUAL OUTPUT: >1,000,000 hl.

REGULAR BEERS:

Staropramen světlé výčepní (4%: ★★/★)
Pale gold and with a chemical aftertaste, the only decent golden beer coming from Smíchov.
Staropramen černý (4.4%: ★★/★)
A dark lager, candy-sugar sweet.
Staropramen Granát (4.8%: ★★★/★)
When it's fresh, not bad: a rich, half-dark lager of a kind that went out of style almost 100 years ago.
Staropramen světlý ležák (5%: ★)
Overwhelmingly unpleasant.

U Fleků

Křemencova 11
Praha 1–Nové Město
T 224 915 118
E ufleku@ufleku.cz
www.ufleku.cz

Okay, they say 'At the Fleks' (or 'Spots') was founded in 1499, and breweries have certainly stood here since then. But it's important to remember that U Fleků's legendary dark lager is just that: a lager, changed over from the older ale recipe about 100 years ago. The dark, chocolaty brew almost makes it worth braving the noisy tour groups, oom-pah! bands and scheming waiters (those shots of Becherovka are *not* complimentary; refuse them). Those are mere caveats. You still have to come here: Flekovské pivo is one of the greatest black lagers in the world.

ANNUAL OUTPUT: >1,000 hl.

REGULAR BEERS:

Flekovský tmavý ležák (4.6%: ★★★★★)
An almost-black, chocolaty and sugary dark lager. One of the world's greats.

U Medvídků

Na Perštýně 7
Praha 1–Staré Město
T 224 211 916
E info@umedvidku.cz
www.umedvidku.cz

Founded in 2005, this brewpub sits inside the legendary 'At the Little Bears', a long-time Budweiser Budvar tap and a city favourite for most of the past 500 years. In addition to the lawsuit-besieged lager from South Bohemia, the almost-hidden upstairs *pivovar* include occasional variations on the strongest beers in the country, brewed at 30° or more, and higher in alcohol than many wines, as well as a standard half-dark lager. In a nod toward the historicity of the locale, all beers are lagered in traditional wooden barrels for a minimum of six weeks for the standard Oldgott, seven months or more for the strong specials. The complex includes a hotel, restaurant and music hall, as well as a beer museum.

ANNUAL OUTPUT: <1,000 hl.

REGULAR BEERS:

Oldgott Barrique (5.2%: ★★★★★)
A glorious, half-dark amber lager with a thick-set head and a lush bittersweet finish.
X-Beer 33° (12.8%: ★★★★★)
Sold in numbered bottles, this special strong beer lagers for most of a year and turns into something approximating a fine Sauternes. Cloudy deep amber with a thick head and tastes of leather, honey, almond and oak, with an extremely complex finish. Outstanding.

Central Bohemia
Středočeský Kraj

POPULATION: **1,154,193**
REGIONAL CAPITAL: **Praha** (1,183,729)
www.kr-stredocesky.cz

THE HIGHEST numbers of both brewpubs and bottlers lie in Central Bohemia, a region whose population would more than double if you were to throw Prague's in with it. Instead, Středočeský kraj sits like a doughnut around the capital, making the breweries here among the most accessible for visitors: two of them, in Chýně and Průhonice, have connections to Prague's public transport system, and none are further than two hours away.

BENEŠOV

Ferdinand

Táborská 306
256 01 Benešov
T 317 722 511
E ferdinand@pivovarferdinand.cz
www.pivovarferdinand.cz

This medium-sized bottler has made some significant innovations in recent years. Like Pilsner Urquell, Staropramen and (to a lesser extent) Krušovice, it has worked to develop themed pubs, such as Prague's Ferdinanda (see Prague Pubs). In common with several other medium-sized brewers, Ferdinand produces a low-cost beer for a supermarket chain: Blanický Rytíř (★★/★) which appears in Plus stores.

Unlike most makers, however, Ferdinand has developed a spiced beer, Sedm Kulí, which is far removed from most beers produced in the country, and one with a remarkable story to its name, to say nothing of its unusual taste. The brewery's hometown of Benešov was once home to Franz Ferdinand, Archduke of Austria-Este, whose assassina-

tion in Sarajevo on 28 June 1914 precipitated World War I. Sedm Kulí, or 'Seven Bullets', gets its name from the number of shots supposedly fired by Franz Ferdinand's assassin, Gavrilo Princip.

It's anyone's guess if Ferdinand would enjoy having a beer named after the means of his murder, let alone an entire brewery bearing his own name. Today, his former residence, the Konopiště castle outside of Benešov, is a museum with a fascinating collection of furniture, weapons and hunting trophies, open for public tours. The brewery, which maintains its own maltings and still uses open fermenters, is also open for tours, and there is a restaurant attached to it. Benešov has good bus and train connections from Prague; the journey takes about an hour.

ANNUAL OUTPUT: >100,000 hl.

REGULAR BEERS:
Golden beer (3.7%)
A golden lager apparently brewed below 10⁰.
Rytíř (3.7%)
Yet another golden lager.
Výčepní pivo světlé (4%)
Still another golden lager.
Ležák tmavý (4.5%: ★★★/★)
Clear dark amber with a sugary, cola-ginger body and a long, sweet finish.
Ležák světlý (4.7%: ★★★)
Clear gold with a cream head and a slightly gassy malt body.
Ležák světlý Premium (5%: ★★★★)
Clear deep gold with very light carbonation and a rich mouthfeel. Slight vanilla notes followed by a lush finish.
Sedm Kulí (5.5%: ★★★)
Deep amber and malty-rich, this special lager has an unusual spicy note.

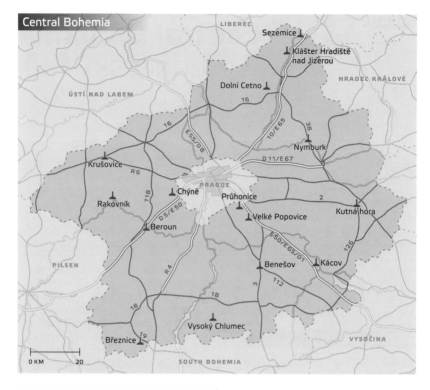

Central Bohemia

BEROUN

Berounský medvěd

Tyršova 135
266 01 Beroun 2
T 311 622 566
E info@berounskymedved.com
www.berounskymedved.com

Set in a salvage yard around the corner from the Beroun train station, the outdoor seating area at the 'Beroun Bear' is an entertaining, if muddly place, overlooking a slew of old armoured personnel carriers, howitzers, tractors and other rusty objects. The pub itself is surprisingly comfortable and even quite sophisticated considering the surroundings, especially when it comes down to its lovely beers. All are unfiltered, unpasteurised yeast beers, available on draught or takeaway in plastic 1.5-litre bottles.

Getting here is not difficult: the town is 20 minutes from Prague on the D5 highway, and frequent commuter trains make the trip quite easy. However, if you really want to work up a thirst, you can follow the Guide's example and walk here over the course of an afternoon, following the beautiful hiking trail from the town of Černošice, just outside Prague.

ANNUAL OUTPUT: 1,000 hl.

REGULAR BEERS:
Berounský medvěd světlý ležák (4%:
★★★★/★)
A beautifully yeasty beer with a pronounced sweet finish and a slight vanilla note. Brewed at 11º.
Berounský medvěd tmavý speciál (4%:
★★★★)
Very dark lager with lasting sweetness and coffee-cream flavours.
Berounský medvěd polotmavý sváteční speciál (5%)
A half-dark special lager brewed only for the holidays.

BŘEZNICE

Herold

Zámecký obvod 31
262 72 Březnice
T 318 682 047
E info@heroldbeer.com
www.heroldbeer.com

In Prague, Herold has long been thought of as a foreign beer, due to its American management and its tendency to appear on draught in English-speaking, expat hangouts. Furthermore, Herold has cultivated its image abroad, reaching out for export markets while its domestic image has suffered. Not infrequently, the few beers found on draught are in bad shape, possibly due to incorrect handling at the pub. But when it is fresh, Herold can be a fine beer, and the innovative wheats were some of the first in the country to break the *světlý/tmavý* hegemony. It uses traditional open fermenters and its own malt. Though it maintains a sizeable brewing and bottling capacity, Herold sadly enters its 501st year operating at significantly lower volumes and, of late, has also reduced the number of beers it produces. In addition to the beers below, it is responsible for the gimmicky, bottled, Pilsner-style beer called **Bastard** (6.1%: ★★★), a perfect gift for that special someone.

ANNUAL OUTPUT: <20,000 hl.

REGULAR BEERS:
Herold Traditional Czech Lager (4.1%)
A golden daily drinker, equivalent to a 10⁰. Lagered for up to a month.
Herold Bohemian Wheat (5.1%: ★★★/★)
One of the first wheat beers to appear in bottles, with a pronounced banana nose and a light, crisp finish.
Herold Bohemian Blond Lager (5.2%: ★★★/★)
A deep gold, Pilsner-style beer with good malt and a pleasantly hoppy finish. Lagered for up to eight weeks.
Herold Bohemian Black Lager (5.3%: ★★★★/★)
An exceptionally rich, extremely dark lager with a warming taste of toasted malt and caramel. Lagered for up to 70 days. Excellent.

Herold Bohemian Granát Lager (5.8%: ★★★★)
A half-dark lager: clear reddish amber with fruity malt sugar in the foreground, followed by a drying, chocolate finish.

CHÝNĚ

Pivovarský dvůr Chýně

Chýně 28
253 01 Hostivice
T 311 670 075
E info@pivovarskydvur.cz
www.pivovarskydvur.cz

This brewery – and Průhonice's U Bezoušků – are nearly close enough to the capital to count as Prague breweries. Both towns are connected to Prague's public transport system – from Prague's Zličín metro station, take bus No. 347 five stops to Chýně-Pivovarský dvůr. Buses leave hourly and take about nine minutes. It is indeed worth the journey: this charming brewpub serves a variety of unfiltered, unpasteurised lagers, along with hearty Czech dishes. If it were in Prague proper, brewer Tomáš Mikulica would probably be elected mayor, if not president of the republic.

ANNUAL OUTPUT: <1,000 hl.

REGULAR BEERS:
Dvorní světlé výčepní (3%: ★★★★★)
Pale gold with a fine white head, a honey note and a moderate bitterness in the finish. Brewed at 10⁰.
Dvorní polotmavá jedenáctka (3.5%: ★★★★)
A half-dark 11⁰ with a thin body, brewed with a wheat adjunct.

Dvorní světlý ležák jedenáctka (3.5%: ★★★★★)
A light 11° beer with a sweet, orange-like malt body and bittersweet finish. Wow.

Dvorní polotmavý ležák (4%: ★★★★/★)
Brewed with Pilsner and caramel malt, this half-dark amber lager has a strong malt body and short sweet finish.

Dvorní speciál černý (5%: ★★★★★)
This dark lager, brewed at 14° from three kinds of malt, has a cold coffee body and light, thirst-quenching bitterness.

Dvorní Starostova 17° (6.5%: ★★★★)
A golden Bock with a sweet finish.

DOLNÍ CETNO

Podkováň

Podkováň 24
294 30 Dolní Cetno
☎ 326 356 231

What a sleeper: this homely bottler makes several excellent lagers, all coming from the tiny village of Podkováň, an outpost of the only marginally larger village of Dolní Cetno. In the area around Mladá Boleslav, some Podkováň beers are available on draught, but anywhere else you're only likely to find the occasional bottle. The brewery does not have a visitors' centre, and there is no restaurant, nor is there one anywhere else in Podkováň proper, and on our visit even the lone pub in Dolní Cetno had closed down. This brewery seems particularly averse to modern technology: at the time of writing, Podkováň had no functioning website, and the old-fashioned, plain-paper labels proudly still bear their traditional Balling numbers.

ANNUAL OUTPUT: >20,000 hl.

REGULAR BEERS:

Podkováňské výčepní světlé 10° (4%: ★★★/★)
A thin malt body with minimal carbonation and a vegetal, slightly grassy hop note.

Podkováňské výčepní tmavé 10° (4%)
A dark lager.

Bednářův truňk 11° (4.7%: ★★★★)
Surprisingly deep gold, very light carbonation and a full malt body with vanilla-plum overtones and a bitter finish.

Podkováň světlý ležák 12° (5%: ★★★/★)
A golden lager with good malt, moderate carbonation and a strong, bitter finish.

Podkováň světlý speciál 14° (6%: ★★★/★)
A very flat, clear golden lager with good malt structure and well-incorporated alcohol.

KÁCOV

Pivovar Kácov

V Podskalí 6
258 09 Kácov
☎ 327 324 693
✉ horejsi@pivovarkacov.cz
www.pivovarkacov.cz

A struggling brewer seemingly overwhelmed by the might of the great brewing corporations, Kácov still makes quality *pivo*, including occasional contract brewing of the Štěpán beer, on draft at Prague's Pivovarský klub. There is a modest taproom at the brewery, located just a few miles off the E50/E65 motorway to Brno, less than an hour from Prague.

ANNUAL OUTPUT: <20,000 hl.

REGULAR BEERS:

Kácovské pivo světlé výčepní 10⁰ (3.8%:
★★★★) *Deep gold with a loose white head,
a sugary body and a bitter, slightly acidic
Saaz hop finish.*
Hubertus Premium 12⁰ (5%: ★★★★/★)
*Deep gold, very slightly cloudy, with thin carbona-
tion and more malt sugar than the 10⁰.*
Malvaz tmavý speciál 13⁰ (5.5%: ★★★★)
*This deep amber lager, made only twice each
year, is malty sweet with a ginger-spice finish.*

KLÁŠTER HRADIŠTĚ NAD JIZEROU

Pivovar Klášter

294 15 Klášter Hradiště nad Jizerou
T 326 771 421
E klaster@iol.cz
www.pivovarklaster.cz

This beautiful brewery is attached to a
historic Benedictine monastery at the top of
a steep hill, smack-dab in the middle of
nowhere, also known as Klášter Hradiště
nad Jizerou. Beer has been brewed here
since 1570. Lagering is done in caves dug 18
m (60 ft) deep into the rock. Unfortunately,
there is no pub nor a visitors' centre on site,
though many restaurants in the area have
Klášter's award-winning beers on draught.

ANNUAL OUTPUT: <100,000 hl.

REGULAR BEERS:
Klášter lehké světlé pivo (2%)
A very low-alcohol golden lager.
Klášter Fitness Beer (2.6%)
A low-alcohol, low-gravity, 'healthy' beer.
Klášter světlé výčepní pivo (4.2%)
The brewery's basic golden lager.
Klášter ležák 11⁰ tmavé pivo (4.3%: ★★★/★)
*Clear deep amber with a tan head and sweet,
cola-ginger flavours.*
Klášter ležák 11⁰ světlé pivo (4.6%: ★★★★)
*A golden lager with rich maltiness. SPP's 11⁰
beer of the year in 2005 and 2006.*
Klášter ležák 12⁰ světlé pivo (5.1%: ★★★/★)
*A clear gold premium lager with a smooth
malt body.*

KRUŠOVICE

Mikropivovar J. Fencl

Krušovice 169
270 53 Krušovice

This home-brewer certainly has a reputation, even though he lacks a public telephone number and web contact information. Regardless, beers from Fencl occasionally show up in half-litre, ceramic-topped 'patent' bottles and crown-capped 0.3-litres. Brewing is done in six or seven batches over the winter months.

ANNUAL OUTPUT: <100 hl.

REGULAR BEERS:
Martin světlé nefiltrované pivo 10⁰
Unfiltered low-gravity golden lager.
Březňák 14⁰
A half-dark higher-gravity lager.

Královský pivovar Krušovice

270 53 Krušovice č. 1
T 313 569 111
E sekretariat@krusovice.cz
www.krusovice.cz

This massive factory is a textbook example of what's gone wrong with Czech brewing. Among the first to switch from traditional open fermenters to cylindro-conical tanks, after privatisation it was sold away to foreign owners, Radeberger, who seem more concerned with high volume than quality beer. We don't know anyone who would say this is their favourite beer now, but we know of many who speak longingly of the lovely Krušovice lagers of old. There is a visitors' centre on site, often filled with truckloads of Russian tourists, and a nearby restaurant which serves the freshest Krušovice in town. That doesn't seem to help matters much.

ANNUAL OUTPUT: >100,000 hl.

REGULAR BEERS:
Radler.cz (2.2%: ★★)
A canned lemonade–lager mixture, made with aspartame, saccharine and other good stuff.
Krušovice světlé (3.8%)
The basic golden lager.

Krušovice černé (3.8%: ★★★)
The dark beer with the highest volume of exports, mostly to Germany. Rich and sugary with an icky sweet finish.
Krušovice Mušketýr (4.5%: ★★★)
The medium-grade golden lager.
Krušovice Jubilejní ležák (4.8%: ★/★)
An unpleasantly bitter golden lager.
Krušovice Imperial (5%: ★★★)
The brewery's slightly fizzy 'premium' lager.

KUTNÁ HORA

Pivovar Kutná Hora

U Lorce 1
284 14 Kutná Hora
T 327 513 801
E du@drinksunion.cz
www.drinksunion.cz

Less than two hours by train from the capital, the UNESCO-listed town of Kutná Hora is a beautiful day-trip destination, featuring medieval streets, a museum of mining, a bone church and a Gothic cathedral, St. Barbara's, whose spires rise so far above they seem to pierce the sky. The town has an ancient history of silver mines, as well as a tradition of alchemy, and there is a small alchemy museum here today. The brewery has no restaurant on site, but several pubs and restaurants in Kutná Hora have the beer on draught.

ANNUAL OUTPUT: >100,000 hl.

REGULAR BEERS:
Dačické světlé (4.1%: ★★★/★)
Clear deep gold, brewed at 10⁰.
Dačické tmavé (4.1%: ★★★/★)
Deep amber with a solid malt body.
Dačický světlý ležák
(5.1%: ★★★/★)
Golden amber with rich malt and a bitter finish.
Lorec speciální světlé pivo
(6.1%: ★★★)
A former 5.2% strong lager, now brewed at higher strength.

Dačický

Rakova 8, 284 01 Kutná Hora

T 327 512 248   www.dacicky.com

Named after local hero Mikuláš Dačický z Heslova, this comfortable pub is one of the few places to serve the local Kutná Hora brew, also called Dačicky, as well as Pilsner Urquell, Budvar and InBev's Hoegaarden, all on draught. Very hearty Czech meals, good service and a lovely, tree-covered beer garden (with ninepins) make this the premiere destination in the UNESCO-listed centre of Kutná Hora, not far from St Barbara's Cathedral and the shocking Sedlec Ossuary, containing about 40,000 human skeletons whose bones have been grouped into chandeliers, coats-of-arms and other church furnishings. An excellent day-trip from Prague. *Sun–Thu 11–23, Fri & Sat 11–midnight.*

NYMBURK

Pivovar Nymburk

Pražská 581
288 25 Nymburk

T 325 517 200

E nymburk@postriziny.cz

www.postriziny.cz

In yet another name game, this brewery is technically called Pivovar Nymburk, though it often goes by 'Postřižinské Pivo', after the Postřižiny ('Cutting it Short') story by Bohumil Hrabal, a beloved Czech author who was raised on the brewery grounds, the stepson of a brewery manager. (Confusingly, the film was actually shot at the Dalešice brewery in Moravia, and today both breweries try to claim a bit of the Hrabalian glow, though only Nymburk goes so far as to put Hrabal's mug on their bottles.)

The beers themselves have third names, also taken from Hrabalian lore, making keeping track even more difficult. The brewery is easy to reach from Prague, but there is no brewery pub, nor is there a visitors' centre, just a simple bottle shop and table where locals enjoy the beer. The brewery maintains its own maltings.

ANNUAL OUTPUT: >100,000 hl.

REGULAR BEERS:

Doktorova 8° (3.1%)
A low-gravity beer in a style rarely seen anymore.

Gold Bohemia Beer (3.5%)
A golden lager produced for the export market.

Nymburk Lager Beer (3.5%)
Another golden lager, also produced for export.

Postřižinské výčepní (3.5%: ★★★)
A light lager with a gentle bitter finish.

Pepinova desítka (4.1%: ★★★★)
A golden lager with a solid maltiness and light residual sugar finish.

Tmavý ležák (4.5%: ★★★/★)
Dark amber with a rich coffee-maple-molasses flavour despite a relatively thin body, followed by a chocolate finish.

Zlatovar (4.7%: ★★★★)
Deep gold with gorgeous malt flavour and very mild hop bitterness.

Francinův ležák (5.1%: ★★★/★)
Clear gold with a thick-set head, solid malt body and very mild astringency.

Bogan (5.5%: ★★★/★)
Rich and creamy, this special golden lager has more malt, less hops and higher alcohol with good balance.

PRŮHONICE

U Bezoušků

Květnové náměstí 5
252 43 Průhonice

T 267 750 551

E ubezousku@seznam.cz

www.ubezousku.cz

Just outside of Prague – and becoming more of a suburb everyday – the quiet village of Průhonice is home to a lovely castle and sprawling Botanical Garden and Park, covering some 250 ha (618 acres) and showcasing over 1,200 tree and shrub species from around the world. Directly on the village square is the restaurant, hotel and brewpub U Bezoušků, which serves three standard lagers. Several buses leave Prague's Opatov metro station every hour, and the trip takes about 15 minutes, depositing travellers virtually at the brewery's door.

ANNUAL OUTPUT: <1,000 hl.

REGULAR BEERS:

Pantátová desítka (4.3%: ★★★)
A crisp golden lager brewed at 10º.

Malvaz (5%: ★★★/★)
Orange-gold with a strong bittersweet finish brewed at 12º.

Bizon (6.5%)
A strong special brewed at 16º.

RAKOVNÍK

Rakovník

Havlíčkova 69
269 01 Rakovník
T 313 512 314
E info@rakovnikbeer.cz
www.rakovnikbeer.cz

This once-proud brewer fell on hard times in the 1990s and even stopped production for several years. Though brewing has resumed under new ownership, most of the pubs in Rakovník's hometown still serve Pilsner Urquell, rather than the local boy.

It's a sad story for such a traditional beer maker. Founded in 1454, the brewery claims that its Latin motto – 'Unus papa Romae, unus portus Anconae, una turris Cremonae, una ceres Raconae' – dates from the 15th century. (That should mean something akin to 'One pope in Rome, one harbour in Ancona, one tower in Cremona, one beer in Rakovník.' Latin scholars have not been able to explain to us why it is 'ceres', or 'grain', and not 'cerevisia', for beer. But we digress.)

So are things here getting back on track? The updated website announces that the brewery will start tours soon, and in 2006 Rakovník won several gold medals at competitions in Russia. Production is still well below capacity, and it is hard to find the beers outside of the region. The brewery is located just behind the main square of this rather scenic town halfway from Prague to Plzeň, and there are frequent rail connections to both cities.

ANNUAL OUTPUT: <20,000 hl.

REGULAR BEERS:

Bakalář pivo světlé výčepní (3.6%)
A golden session beer, brewed at 10º.

Bakalář tmavý ležák (4.8%: ★★★/★)
Clear dark amber with a thick sandy head and a café-au-lait nose. Sugary malt blast in the mouth with a toffee finish.

Bakalář světlý ležák (5%: ★★★/★)
Clear gold with very light carbonation and a slight slickness in the mouth; a taste of malt sugar and honey followed by a short dry finish.

SEZEMICE

K&N Private Brewery

Sezemice 35
294 11 p. Loukov
T 602 422 302
www.pivovarek-sezemice.com

This home brewery, housed in a restored barn, opens on Monday evenings to serve the neighbours. Traditional open fermenters are used, and just two beers are currently produced, though more are said to be forthcoming.

ANNUAL OUTPUT: <100 hl.

REGULAR BEERS:

Sezemický černokněžník
A dark lager brewed at 12°.
Millenium ze Sezemic
A half-dark lager brewed at 14°.

VELKÉ POPOVICE

Velkopopovický Kozel (SAB-Miller)

Ringhofferova 1
251 69 Velké Popovice
T 323 683 111
E pilsner@dmms.cz
www.kozel.cz

This massive bottler is a good second choice among Pilsner Urquell brands, offering better quality and more typically Bohemian flavours than high-volume Gambrinus, especially with the Kozel medium, premium and dark, and the Kozel line often costs less than Gambáč to boot. That said, Kozel ('the Goat') also produces cheap, mass-market lagers like Primus and Klasik for the supermarket aisle. The brewery dominates the town of Velké Popovice, just a half hour down the Brno motorway from Prague. Tours are available, and there is a restaurant on the premises.

ANNUAL OUTPUT: >1,000,000 hl.

REGULAR BEERS:

Klasik (3.6%)
A cheap golden lager.
Velkopopovický Kozel tmavé výčepní (3.8%: ★★/★)
Deep amber with a sugary rush and strong root-beer flavours.
Velkopopovický Kozel světlé výčepní (4%: ★★/★)
Pale gold with a thick head and thin malt body overpowered by hoppy bitterness.
Primus (4.2%)
A cheap golden lager.
Velkopopovický Kozel medium (4.6%: ★★/★)
An uninspired entry into the gold 11° market.
Velkopopovický Kozel Premium (5%: ★★★)
Clear gold and slightly gassy with a thin body and hoppy finish.

VYSOKÝ CHLUMEC

Lobkowicz

Vysoký Chlumec 29
262 52 Vysoký Chlumec
T 318 401 311
E pivovar@lobkowicz.cz
www.lobkowicz.cz

On the southern edge of Central Bohemia, this ancient brewery is back in the possession of the Lobkowicz family, one of the oldest noble families in the Czech lands and the owners of the property since the 15th century. Although they still use traditional methods, including open fermenters and the brewery's own malt, production hovers close to 100,000 hectolitres. Unfortunately, there is no pub or restaurant on site, and tours are not available. Lobkowicz beers are relatively easy to find in bottles, however, and some Prague pubs carry the beers on draught.

ANNUAL OUTPUT: <100,000 hl.

REGULAR BEERS:

Lobkowicz Princ (4%: ★★★)
A 10° golden lager.
Lobkowicz Vévoda (4.5%: ★★★/★)
A golden lager brewed at 11°.
Lobkowicz Baron (4.7%: ★★★/★)
A dark lager, brewed at 12°, with caramel and chocolate notes.
Lobkowicz Kníže (5%: ★★★)
The brewery's premium golden lager.
Démon (5.2%: ★★★/★)
A half-dark lager brewed at 13°.

South Bohemia
Jihočeský Kraj

POPULATION: **627,766**
REGIONAL CAPITAL: **České Budějovice** (94,622)
www.kraj-jihocesky.cz

THOUGH PILSEN has far more renown internationally, many Czechs think of South Bohemia as the real home of great beer. Partly this is due to names such as Budvar, which are also hailed abroad; other long-time favourites, such as Regent, Nektar and Platan, would not be familiar to most non-Czechs, though they do have a certain prominence here. The region is a favourite holiday destination for Praguers, with the nostalgic allure of old farmhouses, rolling hills, apple trees, fish ponds and great lagers, and the Šumava forest especially, to the region's southwest, has been a major holiday spot since Celtic times.

Virtually nothing in South Bohemia is further than four hours from Prague by car, and there are many railway lines and bus connections from the capital. Austrians and backpackers have taken to the stunning, UNESCO-listed medieval city of Český Krumlov, one of the country's can't-miss sights, and a second UNESCO World Heritage Site is Holašovice, a preserved village filled with Southern Bohemian folk architecture just 18 km (11 miles) west of the region's chief draw: the brewery town once known as Budweis.

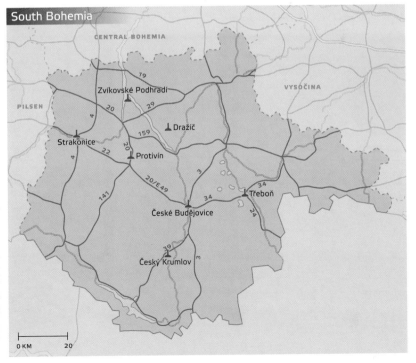

South Bohemia

77

ČESKÉ BUDĚJOVICE

Budějovický Budvar

Karolíny Světlé 4
370 21 České Budějovice
T 387 705 111
E budvar@budvar.cz
www.budvar.cz

Czech national property and an international hero, Budějovický Budvar wears a custom-cut David costume in a well-known Goliath story, for years battling the world's third largest brewer, Anheuser-Busch, over the rights to the name 'Budweiser'. At least literally, this term should indicate something or someone from Budweis, aka the city of České Budějovice, giving some weight to the Czech claim, rather than the one from St Louis.

In fact, it's not quite so clear-cut: Budějovický Budvar was founded after A-B started to use the name 'Budweiser', and 'Budweiser' itself is a German name, not a Czech one. Given Budějovický Budvar's founding during the Czech National Awakening as a Czech-owned brewery in response to the older, German-owned brewery in town, fighting over a Teutonic moniker today seems somewhat inappropriate, if not opportunistic. Moreover, virtually no one in the Czech lands will ever call this beer anything other than 'Budvar'.

Regardless of how you say it, Budvar is one of the best high-production beers in the country, if not the world. And though it should be able to go by whatever name it prefers, especially given the geographic origins involved, 'Budvar' is a strong enough indication of quality today to stand on its own – St Louis be damned. Despite its status as national property, many Czechs might tell you it is not their favourite. Because of its deeper fermentation, it is known to cause headaches and worse in the uninitiated. But as a Czech doctor once advised: 'If Budvar makes you ill, just drink one Budvar every day for two weeks, and then you'll be cured forever.' *Na zdraví.*

Tours are available, but there is no restaurant on site. Instead, try the Budvarka pub (inside Hotel Malý Pivovar, Karla IV 8), just off the town's main square.

Annual output: >1,000,000 hl.

Regular beers:

Budweiser Budvar světlé výčepní pivo
(4%: ★★★★★) *At its best, an absolutely incredible beer of extremely low carbonation and beautifully balanced sweetness and bitterness.*

Budweiser Budvar tmavý ležák (4.7%: ★★★★)
This dark lager is deep amber with a sandy head, cold java and moderate malt sugar.

Budweiser Budvar světlý ležák (5%: ★★★★)
With slightly more fizz than Budvar's 10°, this premium brew is a blend of clear gold malt and fragrant Saaz hop scent that approaches orange blossom.

Budweiser Budvar kroužkovaný ležák
(5%: ★★★★) *A clear yeast-beer variant on Budvar's premium lager: clear gold with a heightened hop bitterness.*

Bud Super Strong (7.6%: ★★★/★)
Brewed at 16° and only available in 0.3-litre bottles, this strong beer has a good malt body and a slight Budvar hop presence.

Pardál (3.8%: ★★)
This new arrival from Budvar is a low-flavour, low-alcohol, high-volume drinker which smells like bear urine and tastes not much better. A bad idea.

...and now they're Buds

It has always been a tangled web of linguistics, eponyms, national history, economies of scale and dates and places of foundation. But in early 2007, the long, bitter fight between Anheuser-Busch and Budvar got even more convoluted when it was announced that A-B, the makers of the American Budweiser, had signed an American distribution deal with Budvar, which many around the world – and certainly most Czechs – regard as the real Budweiser. This, after almost 100 years and about as many lawsuits over who gets to call their beer 'Budweiser' (and where).

Unfortunately, this doesn't actually mean that A-B has finally ceded the name to a more appropriate owner. In fact, A-B will only distribute the Southern Bohemian lager if it is wearing its non-disputed 'Czechvar' costume. It is, definitely, a step in the right direction, and the Czech brewer and American fans of real beer should certainly benefit from access to A-B's network of 600 wholesale distributors in the States. But it's far from a complete ceasefire, and both sides say that the legal battles over the rights to the Budweiser name will continue.

Budějovický Měšťanský Pivovar (Samson)

Lidická 51
370 03 České Budějovice
T 386 708 120
E info@budweiser1795.com
www.budweiser1795.com

Ah yes, the *other* other Budweiser. While the Budvar brewery is better known as the 'real' Budweiser to many, the brewery usually called 'Samson' has an even clearer claim to the name: it was founded earlier, before both Budvar and Anheuser-Busch got around to usurping its name. Lately it has taken to calling itself 'Budweiser 1795' as a means of reinforcing its pride of place in chronology, if not in brewing, and, confusingly, the name 'Budweiser Bürgerbräu' still floats around there as well. This is the older, formerly exclusively German brewery that got the increasingly self-aware Czechs in the late

19th century to build their own brewery, thank you very much, just as they built their own opera and concert halls in Prague and elsewhere at the same time. Despite the chronology, Samson, Budweiser Bürgerbräu, Budějovický Měšťanský Pivovar, Budweiser 1795 or whatever you'd call it are usually second-place finishers after Budvar. Tours are available with advance notice and there is a bottle and paraphernalia shop, but there is no pub on site.

ANNUAL OUTPUT: >100,000 hl.

REGULAR BEERS:

Samson Budweiser Bier černý (3.6%: ★★★/★)
Clear amber with a long-lasting creamy head and a delicious toasted-malt note.

Samson Budweiser Bier světlé pivo
(3.8%: ★★★/★)
A good, if light golden lager. Brewed at 10°.

1795 Budweiser Bier (4.7%)
Another 12°, Pilsner-style beer. Or is it just the same beer under a different name?

Samson Budweiser Bier premium
(4.9%: ★★★★) *Clear gold and nicely malty, the top Pilsner-style beer from the Samson line.*

B.B. Budweiser Bier (5%: ★★★★)
Clear gold with a pronounced citrus-blossom nose. In the mouth, a rich malt body and a fragrant and bitter hop finish. Surprisingly good.

Budvarka Malý pivovar

Karla IV. 8–10, 370 01 České Budějovice
T 386 360 471   **www.malypivovar.cz**
BEER: **Budějovický Budvar**

Part of the Budvarka mini-chain, the 'Small Brewery' pub, restaurant and hotel is the place to taste Budvar in České Budějovice. Located just off the main square (náměstí Přemysla Otakara II) in the Old Town, the place is filled with oompah music, German tour groups and locals. One of the few places in the country to serve Budvar's yeast beer, here called *kroužkovaný ležák*.

ČESKÝ KRUMLOV

Eggenberg

Latrán 27
381 15 Český Krumlov
T 380 711 426
E pivovar@eggenberg.cz
www.eggenberg.cz

Set in a hairpin curve of the Vltava, the historic town of Český Krumlov is an astonishingly beautiful UNESCO World Heritage Site. There is an enormous castle with an original Baroque theatre, dating from 1766, a museum dedicated to the artist Egon Schiele who lived here, and one of Bohemia's oldest monasteries just outside the town. The Eggenberg brewery is very much a part of the city's heritage: In 1347, Petr I z Rožmberka (Peter I von Rosenberg) granted the city its first 'Mile Right' and breweries have stood on or near the current location since at least 1459. The current brewery was built by Vilém z Rožmberka (Wilhelm von Rosenberg) in 1560. Originally, the brewery produced both barley and wheat beers before barley production was temporarily terminated in 1800. It began to produce Bavarian-style lager beers again in 1837, then converting over to Pilsner-style brews in the latter half of the 19th century.

BREWERIES · SOUTH BOHEMIA

After privatisation, the brewery switched to CCTs and increased production accordingly. It was badly damaged in the floods of August 2002, but it has since recovered, with production remaining at around half the highest level it achieved in the late 1990s. Eggenberg beers are available in many pubs and restaurants in Český Krumlov and around South Bohemia, and there is a colourful restaurant and beer hall on site. In bottles, it also produces a generic **světlé výčepní pivo** (3.7%) for the Aro supermarket chain. Despite the name, this brewery has no business connection with the Eggenberg brewery in Austria. It is fully owned by Dionex of Český Krumlov, and like the Austrian brewery, it takes its name from the Eggenberg noble family who inherited the brewery when the Rožmberk line died out in 1611.

ANNUAL OUTPUT: <100,000 hl.

REGULAR BEERS:

Světlé výčepní Kristián (3.7%)
A 10° golden lager, only available in bottles.

Světlé výčepní (4%)
The basic draft lager, available on draft and in bottles.

Tmavý ležák (4.2%: ★★)
Clear deep amber, this dark lager has good coffee bitterness, but it feels quite thin in the mouth and has a suspiciously chemical sweet touch.

Světlý ležák (5%: ★★★)
Clear gold with a loose white head and thinnish malt body.

Svatováclavské pivo (5%: ★★★★)
This cloudy, honey-coloured yeast beer has a rich malt structure and refreshing, yeasty finish.

DRAŽÍČ

Pivovarský dvůr Lipan

Dražíč 50
375 01 Týn nad Vltavou
T 382 588 828
E info@pivovarlipan.cz
www.pivovarlipan.cz

Call it one-stop shopping: the Brewery Court Lipan offers food, beer, lodging and guided tours on the Vltava river, as well as berry-picking trips through the forest, among other essential services. Founded in 1998, it is one of the most charmingly rustic brewery-hotels in the region, yet extremely modest – prices in 2006 were listed at 310 Kč (less than £8) per person, which might explain why it always seems fully booked. The unpasteurised yeast lagers are brewed at 12° and are occasionally seen on draft in restaurants in Písek and Bechyně. As if that weren't enough, there is also an on-site distillery which makes *slivovice* and other brandies.

ANNUAL OUTPUT: <1,000 hl.

REGULAR BEERS:

Světlé pivo Lipan (5.25%: ★★★★★)
A cloudy, golden yeast beer with fine carbonation, full of fruitiness and fruitcake flavours and finishing with rich malt. Served cold, and deliciously so.

Tmavé pivo Lipan (5.25%: ★★★★)
A deep amber, dark yeast lager, purple-black, with a sandy head, flat carbonation and loads of rich coffee-cola notes.

PROTIVÍN

Platan

Pivovarská 168
398 11 Protivín
T 382 733 111
E kovaricek@pivo-platan.cz
www.pivo-platan.cz

Perhaps the most beautiful drive in all of Bohemia is the eponymous plane-lined lane leading up to the Platan brewery. During Communist times, Protivín was nationalised and grouped together with all South Bohemian breweries. It was sold after the revolution in 1992. From that time it was owned by the city of Protivín until November of 2000, when it was acquired by a group of businessmen from Liberec who profess respect for the brewery's traditional methods – it still maintains its own maltings – while expressing a desire to develop the business side further. The grounds retain a feel of public property – cyclists congregate among the plane trees after trips out from nearby Písek, and the citizens of Protivín use the lane as a promenade. There is a lovely restaurant on site, but it can have unusual opening hours if there was a party here the night before, so be sure to call ahead. With advance notice, tours of the brewery are available for groups.

ANNUAL OUTPUT: >100,000 hl.

REGULAR BEERS:

Platan Protivín (4%: ★★★)
A slightly fizzy golden lager.

Platan Granát (4.6%: ★★★/★)
A clear dark amber beer with a moderately sweet malt body and a cocoa finish.

Platan Jedenáct (4.9%)
An 11° golden lager.

Platan Premium (5%: ★★★/★)
Clear pale gold with a slightly fruity nose and light malt body.

Prácheňská perla (6%: ★★★★/★)
This clear, golden special, brewed at 14°, has a head so thick you could build houses out of it. Rich and sweet, it has a syrupy, maple-like finish. Impressive.

Platan Knížecí 21 (10.6%: ★★★)
An amber-coloured high-gravity beer of remarkable strength. It is a malty aperitif-like drink of lasting hop bitterness.

STRAKONICE

Nektar

Podskalská 324
386 01 Strakonice
T 383 312 411
E k.seknicka@pivovarnektar.cz
www.pivovarnektar.cz

This is one brewery that claims no outlandishly ancient year of foundation. The town of Strakonice has made beer since at least 1308, yet this brewery modestly states that it only dates from 1649, when it was founded in town building No. 47 (of 158). After dozens of ownership changes over the centuries, including nationalisation and grouping within the Communist-era South Bohemian brewing collective, the brewery is today owned by the city of Strakonice. Unfortunately, it has no restaurant on the premises, and there is no fancy visitors' centre. However, many pubs and restaurants in town serve Dudek and Nektar on draught, and bottles can be purchased in local shops and at the brewery.

ANNUAL OUTPUT: <100,000 hl.

REGULAR BEERS:

Silver Nektar 9⁰ (3.6%)
A low-alcohol, low-hop daily drinker.

Měšťanská desítka (4.3%)
A standard 10⁰ golden lager.

Strakonický Nektar 11⁰ (4.5%: ★★★/★)
Clear gold, a malty nose and body with a relatively rich Saaz hop finish.

Tmavý ležák Dudák (4.8%: ★★/★)
Clear deep ruby, almost half-dark in colour, with an overwhelmingly sugary finish.

Strakonický Dudák 12⁰ (5%: ★★★/★)
Clear gold with a thick cream head, a solid malt body and pleasantly flat carbonation.

Kvasnicové 12⁰ (5%: ★★/★)
Clear gold, this yeast beer has a good maltiness and a fresh, yeasty aftertaste. Also available as a 10⁰.

TŘEBOŇ

Regent

Trocnovské nám. 124
379 01 Třeboň
T 384 721 319
E fstasek@pivovar-regent.cz
www.pivovar-regent.cz

This historic brewery is a rare beauty: situated in the centre of Třeboň, right next to the local chateau, it was built in 1886 with ornate crenellations and castle motifs. After the Velvet Revolution, Regent was often considered one of the best beers from South Bohemia, even eclipsing Budvar as a favourite among many, but the brewery stumbled in the late 1990s and almost completely disappeared. Today it has returned, making beers using cylindro-conical tanks and other novelties, and unsurprisingly, it seems to have lost some of its earlier magic. The brewery does offer tours and there is a smoky *pivnice* on site, though you might have to seek out a local restaurant for something to eat. The town itself is quite worth seeing, especially the stately tomb of the noble Schwarzenberg family, the charming town square (just steps from the brewery) and the large fish ponds where trout and carp have been farmed since medieval times.

ANNUAL OUTPUT: <100,000 hl.

REGULAR BEERS:
Bohemia Regent schwarzenberské vyčepní pivo (3.4%)
A lower-alcohol, low-gravity beer, only available in bottles.
Bohemia Regent vyčepní pivo (3.9%: ★★/★)
Clear light gold with slight hop bitterness and the taste of a barley fizz.
Bohemia Regent premium tmavý ležák (4.4%: ★★/★)
Deep ruby with a caramel head and coffee-toffee flavours in the mouth.
Bohemia Regent jedenáctka (4.6%: ★★★)
Clear gold with extremely flat carbonation and a taste somewhere between Pilsner Urquell and Budvar. Slightly short on hops in the finish.

Bohemia Regent premium světlý ležák (5%: ★★/★)
Clear gold but with a thinner body than previously, and a bit too bitter in the finish.
Bohemia Regent Petr Vok 13⁰ (5.5%: ★★★/★)
Clear amber with deep malt flavour and a bitter-sweet finish. Very nice. Only available on draught.
Bohemia Regent Prezident (6%)
A pale special lager, brewed at 14⁰.

ZVÍKOVSKÉ PODHRADÍ

Zlatá Labuť

Zvíkovské Podhradí 92
397 01 Písek
T 382 285 660
E pivovar.zvikov@seznam.cz
www.pivovar-zvikov.cz

Not actually in Písek but near it, the hamlet of Zvíkovské Podhradí ('under Zvíkov Castle') stands below a stout, early-Gothic fortification dating back to its founding by King Václav I in 1234 and standing on an inaccessible promontory at the confluence of the Vltava and Oltava rivers. Here the Gold Swan hotel, restaurant and brewpub offers lodging and fortitude for visitors, including excellent lagers and some of the first top-fermented beers to appear in the country. It's worth calling ahead before dropping by: not all beers are always available, plus Zlatá Labuť has limited opening hours during the off-season.

ANNUAL OUTPUT: <1,000 hl.

REGULAR BEERS:
Zlatá labuť kvasnicové pivo 11⁰ (4.7%: ★★★★)
A cloudy gold yeast beer with a flight floral hop bitterness.
Zlatá labuť kvasnicové pivo 12⁰ (4.9%)
A top-fermented ale, only available occasionally.
Zlatá labuť speciál tmavý 13⁰ (5.3%: ★★★★/★)
One of the darkest beers in the country, very flat, with a rare Saaz hop aroma for a dark beer.
Zlatá labuť kvasnicové pivo 14⁰ (5.5%)
Another infrequently served, top-fermented ale.

Pilsen Region
Plzeňský Kraj

POPULATION: **549,678**
REGIONAL CAPITAL: **Plzeň** (164,180)
www.kr-plzensky.cz

FOR MOST VISITORS, the Alpha and the Omega of Czech brewing lie a couple of hours west of Prague: Plzeň, where Pilsner Urquell revolutionised brewing in 1842 and which – despite being bought and sold and sold again after the Velvet Revolution – remains the gold standard for Czech beers some 165 years later. Because of Pilsner Urquell's high production volumes and extreme popularity, only one other bottler, Chodovar, remains in the region, and the remaining breweries are either small brewpubs or have kegged beer with very limited distribution.

In addition to tours at Pilsner Urquell, Plzeň also has a fascinating brewery museum, and the town's history includes a unique coda to the liberation of Czechoslovakia by the Russians. Although the Red Army freed the rest of the country, Plzeň and this part of western Bohemia were liberated by General Patton's 3rd Army, whose left-behind Harley-Davidson motorcycles gave birth to the first Czech group of Hell's Angels. Plzeň is home to a yearly liberation festival each May, where those motorcycles and vintage jeeps cruise under the soaring spires of St Bartholomew's, the tallest church tower in the country, and the Great Synagogue, the third-largest synagogue in the world. Plzeň's main institute of higher learning, the University of West Bohemia, attracts some 17,000 students to the town.

To the south of the region, the Šumava forest has been a holiday hotspot since Celtic times, when the ancient Boii tribe used the word 'Syumawa' to mean a holiday, retreat or time away. It is excellent hiking and biking country, and includes the Šumava National Park and Protected Landscape as well as a UNESCO Biosphere Reserve. Plzeň is extremely easy to reach from Prague, with multiple daily coach and rail connections, and a location directly on the main D5/E50 motorway from Nuremberg. To explore the more remote parts of Plzeňský kraj, however, including the thick, hilly Šumava, you'll definitely need a car.

CHODOVÁ PLANÁ

Chodovar

Pivovarská 107
348 13 Chodová Planá
T 374 794 181
E chodovar@chodovar.cz
www.chodovar.cz

This large, family-owned brewery is just about the only thing happening in the tiny village of Chodová Plana. It operates its own maltings, the brewery, a second line of mineral waters and fizzy drinks, a restaurant (and brewery museum) and a small hotel. As if that weren't enough, in 2006 Chodovar also started offering therapeutic beer baths in the cellar of the hotel, allowing visitors to get soaked, both literally and figuratively. The brewery also hosts an annual beer festival with rock concerts and a barrel-rolling competition that attracts teams from around the globe.

ANNUAL OUTPUT: <100,000 hl.

REGULAR BEERS:
Klasik (2.4%: ★★★)
  Low-alcohol, pale gold, clear and fizzy with a watery body and good malt flavour.
Chodovar desítka (4%)
  A standard 10° light lager.

Černá desítka (4.2%: ★★★)
Clear deep amber with a thin, root-beer body and a sweet malt finish.

Zlatá jedenáctka (4.5%)
An 11° light lager.

President (5%: ★★★/★)
Deep gold, a good malt body and a slightly bitter hop finish.

Kvasnicový Skalní ležák (5%: ★★★/★)
Clear deep gold with a thin head and a slight vanilla-cream flavour.

Zámecký ležák speciál (5.1%: ★★★/★)
Clear gold with a good bittersweet balance and well-incorporated alcohol.

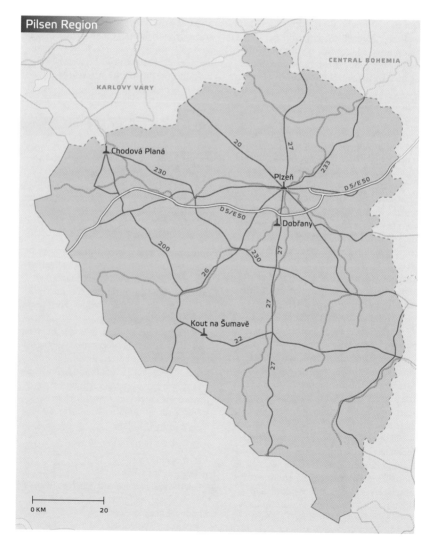

Pilsen Region

Getting soaked

Western Bohemia is well known for its bathing culture, having attracted international celebrities, European royals and the very, very wealthy to spa towns such as Karlovy Vary (aka Carlsbad), Mariánské Lázně (Marienbad) and Františkovy Lázně (Franzenbad) for most of the past 300 years. The region, composed of Plzeňský kraj and Karlovarský kraj, is also the fountainhead of Czech brewing. Naturally, at some point the two had to meet.

That seems to have happened first at Chodovar, the family-owned brewery in Chodová Planá. While other beer baths appeared earlier in Germany and Austria, Chodovar is the first to employ a professional balneologist, a reflection upon the area's curative history.

In the warm, brick-lined cellar of the brewery's 90-bed hotel, Chodovar fills a half-dozen spacious steel tubs – large enough for full-size blokes – with a 50:50 mix of the company's Il-sano mineral water and a specially brewed, low-alcohol bathing beer. The result is a murky, semi-clear amber liquid that smells strongly of malt.

Once you step in, the bath, at a temperature of 34 °C (93.2 °F), is immeasurably relaxing. As are the aromatic Žatec hop aromas rising up from the tub. As is the small glass of light Chodovar lager you are served as you bathe. And as is the second.

After a half-hour or so of almost meta-physical relaxation, you're wrapped in a crisp white sheet and led to a *chaise-longue* in a darkened room not far away. There, the sticky-sweet smell of malt and spicy Czech hops rising from your skin only increases as you tumble deeper and deeper towards sleep. Full-body and partial massages are available for even greater heights of hedonism.

While it may not be an experience to suit everyone, the prices are hardly designed to keep out the hoi polloi. In 2007, the charges at bath time were:

> One person (20-minute bath, 20-minute relaxation plus 2 x 0.3-litre Chodovar lagers): 550 Kč (£13)
> Double bath for two: 950 Kč (£22)
> Partial massage: 220 Kč (£5)
> Full massage: 400 Kč (£9.50)

It is rare for a Czech service to beat those in neighbouring countries, but first-hand experience says that Chodovar's beer baths are better than the Austrian equivalent by a factor of ten. With careful planning on **www.idos.cz**, it's possible to take a train from Prague in the morning, enjoy a beer bath and slow lunch at the brewery restaurant before returning to the capital, relaxed and refreshed, in time for supper. You'll bring back with you the story of a soak that should last a lifetime.

DOBŘANY

Modrá Hvězda

Nám. TGM 159
334 41 Dobřany
T 377 973 770
E pivovar@modra-hvezda.cz
www.modra-hvezda.cz

One of the first brewery-hotels in the west of the country, the Blue Star started brewing in 1998, making just 70 hectolitres. Current production stands at about 210 hectolitres, with six types available, as well as a surprisingly smooth *pivní pálenka*, a clear, *slivovice*-like brandy distilled from beer. Barring the sour-cherry lager, all the drinks here are outstanding, and the hotel offers nice, clean and relatively spacious rooms at very moderate prices.

ANNUAL OUTPUT: <1,000 hl.

REGULAR BEERS:

Dobřanská desítka 10⁰ (4%: ★★★★★)
Pale gold with a thick cream head. Pineapple nose. A moderately sweet, relatively thick malt body with a fruity finish. Exceptional.

Modrá Hvězda 12⁰ (4.5%: ★★★★)
Deep gold with a cream head, pronounced bitterness and more-obvious alcohol.

Modrá Hvězda višňové (4.8%: ★)
An amber sour-cherry lager that, at its best, tastes like cough medicine. Vile.

Modrá Hvězda tmavý speciál 14⁰ (5%: ★★★★)
Deep amber with a sandy head and rich ginger and coffee-caramel flavours.

Dobřanský dragoun 16⁰ (6.5%: ★★★/★)
This half-dark amber lager has long-lasting sugary, coffee and malt flavours.

Dobřanský sekáč 17⁰ (7%: ★★★★)
Cloudy gold with a rich white head and a strawberries-and-cream finish.

KLATOVY

Modré Abbé

Dobrovského 150, 339 01 Klatovy 2
T 373 728 048   www.modryabbe.wz.cz

Not far from the German border is the historic Šumava town of Klatovy, famous for carnations, as well as its Gothic Black Tower dating from 1555, the Baroque 'White Unicorn' pharmacy (now a museum) and this self-styled 'beer studio', the Blue Abbot pub. Located in Klatovy's Old Town, Modrý Abbé serves mostly independent beers from around the country, all of which are on draught. In early 2007, the list included five beers from Platan (10⁰ and 12⁰ světlé nefiltrované, 11⁰ světlý ležák⁰, 11⁰ tmavý ležák and the wonderful 14⁰ Prácheňská Perla strong golden special), Chodovar's 11⁰, 12⁰ and 13⁰, as well as the 10⁰ světlý výčepní from the newly reopened brewery in nearby Kout na Šumavě. Very popular, with reservations a necessity. CLOSED SATURDAY. *Sun–Fri* 16–22.

KOUT NA ŠUMAVĚ

Pivovar Kout na Šumavě

Kout na Šumavě 2, 345 02 Kout na Šumavě
T 379 789 370   **E** janskala@email.cz

A late addition: originally founded in 1826, the only remaining brewery in the Šumava region reopened in 2006 during the course of writing this Guide and thus remains unvisited. Despite its newness, the beer is said to be available at several pubs in Kout and the nearby towns of Domažlice and Horšovský Týn, and management has plans to extend the 5,000-hectolitre annual production up to 30,000 hectolitres.

ANNUAL OUTPUT: <20,000 hl.

REGULAR BEERS:

Koutská desítka světlá (4%)
A 10⁰ pale, Pilsner-style lager.

Koutský ležák světlý (5%)
A 12⁰ lager in the Pilsner style.

Koutský tmavý speciál (6%)
A dark special lager.

Koutský tmavý super special (9%)
A high-alcohol dark lager.

PLZEŇ

Pilsner Urquell/Gambrinus
(SAB-Miller)

U Prazdroje 7
304 97 Plzeň
T 377 061 111
E info@prazdroj.cz
www.prazdroj.cz

Forget the nationalist angle. As a Czech enterprise initially employing a Bavarian brewer, Josef Groll, Pilsner Urquell is hardly a purely Bohemian invention. Rather, it was a cross-cultural hybrid which came along at the right place and at the right time – in a town with exceptionally low-sulphite, low-carbonate water, close to areas that produce some of the world's best hops (Saaz, today's Žatec) and malt (the Haná region near Prostějov), at the time of the mid-19th-century

arrival of cheap, industrial glassware (rather than expensive crystal) which highlighted the beer's shockingly clear and golden appearance. The result was a firestorm which spread across Europe, decimating the older styles of beers, including all of the once-famous wheat beers of Bohemia and most of the old top-fermented brews of Germany.

Today, Pilsner Urquell is no less rapacious, doubling its total production to nearly 8 million hectolitres since the merger of South African Brewing and Miller USA to form SAB-Miller in 2002. Across the country, small bottling brewers and micro-breweries can hardly keep up with Urquell's economies of scale and advertising wallop, and in many regions of the country, Pilsner Urquell and Gambrinus is all you're going to find. The idea of Pilsner Urquell being a product from a certain place has been mocked as well, with management's controversial decision to start brewing Pilsner Urquell in Poland

(though none of this Polish, not-so-Ur-brau is supposed to be imported to the Czech Republic, nor should it be exported anywhere beyond Poland's borders). With all that, you'd be forgiven for thinking Pilsner Urquell might have lost some of its original sparkle, and yet it is Pilsner Urquell which remains the country's favourite beer. They might drink more Gambrinus, but Czechs will put Pilsner Urquell on the table for Christmas dinner. Why? Because it's delicious, for one thing, despite losing more and more of the malt richness and hoppy bite as volume soars. Nonetheless, Czechs consistently rate it the country's best beer in terms of overall quality. Gambrinus, on the other hand, is more of a high-volume guzzler, without Urquell's luscious malt and bitter hops. Or as one expert at the Czech Institute of Malting and Brewing put it: by the standards of Czech brewing, Gambrinus is a German beer.

ANNUAL OUTPUT: >1,000,000 hl.

REGULAR BEERS:

Gambrinus světlé (4.1%: ★★★)
A thin body, not unlike a German Pils, with correspondingly reduced bitter hops.

Pilsner Urquell (4.4%: ★★★★/★)
When it's good, it's fantastic: a clear golden lager with solid malt heart and a sharp bittersweet finish. Best unpasteurised in 'tank' pubs (see Prague Pubs).

Gambrinus Premium (5%: ★★★)
Still thinnish in the body and occasionally unpleasant, but often quite good.

U rytíře Lochoty

Karlovarská 103
300 00 Plzeň
☎ 377 540 946

Facing a busy dual carriageway, this modest brewpub and restaurant functions as a community centre, wedding reception hall and sports bar, depending on the crowd and time of day. The meals here are merely decent, but the beers more than make up for any shortcomings in the kitchen. It's a bit out of the way, far from the centre and not at all close to the Pilsner Urquell brewer, making a cab ride a necessity.

ANNUAL OUTPUT: <1,000 hl.

REGULAR BEERS:

12º Kvasnicové (★★★★/★)
Nearly approaching a garnet, this yeast beer has an amber body, tan head and is thick and malty with moderate, champagne-like carbonation and a refreshing sourness.

14º Amber (★★★★)
Similar maltiness as the 12º, but with more carbonation and less balance in the finish. Nonetheless, an excellent beer by all standards.

Pilsner Unique Bar

Prešovská 16, 301 00 Plzeň
☎ 377 221 131   www.thepubworld.com
BEER: **Pilsner Urquell**

Opened in August of 2005, this tank pub serves unpasteurised Pilsner Urquell with a twist: tableside taps mean visitors can serve themselves and pay by volume. Still no cure for cancer. Understandably, the Pilsner Unique Bar (or PUB) looks set to expand the concept around the country, with individual franchises planned in České Budějovice, Hradec Králové and Tábor, and four in-the-works branches said to be coming to the capital.
Mon–Thu 11–1, Fri 11–4, Sat 13–4, Sun 13–1.

Na Parkáně

Veleslavínova 4, 301 14 Plzeň
☎ 377 324 485
BEER: **Kvasnicový Pilsner Urquell**

Right next to Plzeň's Brewery Museum, the Na Parkáně pub is believed to be the only place in the world to serve a *kvasnicové pivo* from Pilsner Urquell. As if that weren't enough of a draw, Na Parkáně is a pleasant, spacious bar and restaurant with excellent goulash and *uzené* (smoked pork). In warm weather, head to the back for the pleasant covered patio and tiny beer garden.
Mon–Thu 11–23, Fri & Sat 11–1, Sun 11–22.

Karlovy Vary Region
Karlovarský Kraj

POPULATION: **303,874**
REGIONAL CAPITAL: **Karlovy Vary** (53,404)
www.kr-karlovarsky.cz

IF ANY CITY IN THE Czech Republic has more opulence than ever-richer Prague, it is Karlovy Vary, also known as Carlsbad. Year-round, the town's historic mineral springs, scenic promenades along the Teplá river and therapeutic baths and resorts draw visitors from around the world, including a sizeable and permanent Russian émigré community. Every summer the Karlovy Vary International Film Festival brings Hollywood celebrities to town for a week of screenings and award-giving, virtually eliminating any remaining vacancies in town, from the plushest 5-star suites to simple family rooms.

But it is not just the capital of Karlovský kraj that has something to offer: other towns such as Mariánské Lázně (formerly Marienbad) and Františkovy Lázně have lower-profile spas with more therapy and less luxury. The mineral springs appear among the area's rocky hills, lush forests and mountains such as the Krušné hory (Erzgebirge, or Ore Mountains) and the volcanic Doupovské hory. Much of the region historically had a German population and culture, and even today the area feels most comfortable with German as a second language, rather than English. It is the Czech region closest to Bavaria's Upper Franconia, which perhaps explains the excellent brews here – or is it the other way around?

Getting to Karlovarský kraj is relatively easy, with multiple train and bus connections from Prague. By car, it is about two hours from the Czech capital to Karlovy Vary, also accessible from Germany via Nuremberg and Bayreuth. Due to its proximity to Plzeň, the only remaining local breweries are non-bottling brewpubs with limited distribution, usually only on-site. But the good news? Two of the four breweries here opened in 2006.

CHEB

Hradní krčma

Chebský hrad
Dobrovského 15/16
350 02 Cheb
T 602 830 094

The Czech town of Cheb was once the German town of Eger, and then Cheb, and then Eger and then Cheb again. The town retains its cross-cultural feel, although its beer is a decidedly Bohemian (rather than Bavarian) brew, with all the hop and malt flavours that entails. Situated in a rustic cellar at Cheb Castle, the tiny brewpub serves grilled ribs and other rustic fare to go along with its world-class lagers. Lagering is done in the old stone cellars, and open fermenters are used. It was in the castle's banqueting room that the officers of Austrian general Wallenstein were murdered in 1634 while he himself was dispatched into the afterlife in the town hall.

ANNUAL OUTPUT: <1,000 hl.

REGULAR BEERS:
11⁰ chebské světlé (4.7%: ★★★★/★)
  Clear deep gold with an almond nose and slightly fizzy carbonation. Modelled on the 10⁰ Pilsner Urquell of yore. Excellent.
12⁰ světlé (5.3%: ★★★/★)
  Clear gold with an extremely thick head. Very good.
12⁰ kvasnicové (5.4%: ★★★/★)
  Perfectly clear gold with a slight apple note in the finish.
14⁰ tmavé (6.1%: ★★★)
  Very deep amber, almost black, with a sandy head, a gingery, cola-like flavour and a long finish.

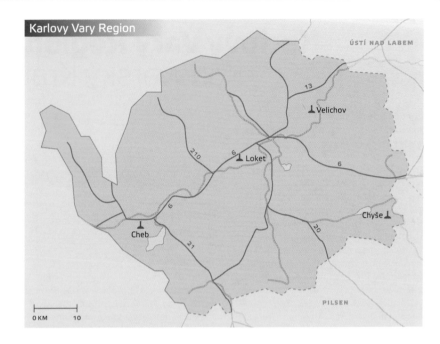

Karlovy Vary Region

CHYŠE

Zámecký Pivovar

Zámek Chyše
364 53 Chyše
T 728 948 868
E pivovar@chyse.com
www.chyse.com

In 1996, Vladimír Lažanský repurchased his family's ancestral home, restoring it over the next several years. The brewpub and beer-hall first opened in the spring of 2006, right on the ground floor of one of the main chateau buildings. Two large showpiece kettles stand at the edge of the dining area. This gloriously restored manse and park also houses an exhibit dedicated to the science-fiction writer Karel Čapek, who served as a tutor for the noble Lažanský family for five months in 1917 and who invented the word 'robot'. Chyše makes for a wonderful day trip, especially during warmer weather. It is easily accessible by train from Prague or Plzeň.

ANNUAL OUTPUT: <1,000 hl.

REGULAR BEERS:
Prokop 11° světlé (4%: ★★/★)
Yellow-gold and cloudy with a doughy nose, some fizziness and a slightly sour finish.
Prokop 12° jantar (4.2%: ★★/★)
Deep amber, fine carbonation, but somewhat lacking in body.
Prokop 12° tmavé (4.2%: ★★)
Dark amber with a caramel head and a slightly medicinal aftertaste.

LOKET

Svatý Florián

Hotel Císař Ferdinand
TGM 136
357 33 Loket
T 352 327 130

What a star: the beauty of this fairy-tale town, gracefully perched on a mountain ridge with the river Ohre surrounding it on three sides, its 13th-century castle earned it a small cameo role in *Casino Royale*, the most recent Bond film. The castle, including the dungeons,

is now open to the public. In the former post office, a hotel and brewery-restaurant opened in mid-2006 with at least moral support from the brewmaster at Velichov. Worth a trip, and several return trips after that, both for its natural beauty and the wonderful amber lager.

ANNUAL OUTPUT: <250 hl.

REGULAR BEERS:
13⁰ Florian (4.3%: ★★★★/★)
This half-dark lager is a cloudy deep amber with almost no carbonation and a refreshing sour finish. Gorgeous.

VELICHOV

Forman

Velichov 84
363 01 Ostrov

Most visitors will probably never come here, and even if they did, they'd never stumble across this smoky mini-brewpub that looks like a converted garage, hidden behind a (shut-down? still functioning?) Mexican restaurant and with no telephone number of its own. If you could possibly make your way here, and asked what kind of beer they had on draught, the locals would likely tell you 'Gambrinus'. If they do sell Gambáč, it only serves to heighten the superiority of the local brew: Velichovský Forman, one of the country's unrecognised masterpieces. While the amount of alcohol is listed as a set figure, this beer is a living organism, and strength can increase slightly over time.

ANNUAL OUTPUT: <1,000 hl.

REGULAR BEERS:
Forman (3.7%: ★★★★★)
A golden yeast beer with a thin body, moderate carbonation and an orangey finish. Outstanding.

Ústí Nad Labem Region
Ústecký Kraj

POPULATION: **823,173**
REGIONAL CAPITAL: **Ústí nad Labem** (94,204)
www.kr-ustecky.cz

UP IN THE northeast corner of the country, Ústecký kraj is the legendary home of the Czech nation, where, in times immemorial, Praotec ('Forefather') Čech delivered his people out of the land of Croats to a settlement on Říp mountain, just to the southeast of today's Litoměřice, a place 'full of deer and birds, abounded with milk and honey'.

Life in today's Ústecký kraj is substantially less sweet: post-industrial towns, such as Most and Ústi nad Labem, suffer from chronic unemployment, and the region is a frequent setting for Czech films of the oh-God-I'm-depressed variety. Tourism, especially beer tourism, looks set to pick things up. The town of Žatec (Saaz, in German) is embracing its history as the home of the greatest of Czech hops, hosting a yearly hop festival in late August or early September (see 'Beer Tourism') and making a show of the local crop, with hop bines permanently planted on the town's main square. In late summer it's not unusual to see villagers riding by with huge garlands of hops piled on the backs of bicycles, later to be turned into pillows or decorations for the hearth. (Of course, this could probably be considered stealing, but they've got the stuff coming out of their ears around here.)

Ústecký kraj has no brewpubs and just four bottlers, three of which are owned by the Drinks Union chain, although the area is the historic home of countless older breweries, many of which have been shuttered for centuries. Anheuser-Busch may be best known for 'borrowing' a name from a famous South Bohemian brewing town, but just outside of Žatec you will find another, less-celebrated example: the once-great brewing town of Měcholupy, known in German as Michelob…

LOUNY

Pivovar Louny

Beneše z Loun 139
T 415 629 111
E du@drinksunion.cz
www.drinksunion.cz

Owned by the Drinks Union mini-chain, which also produces liqueurs. The brewery is located just outside the town walls, and the brewery today maintains its own maltings. There is no restaurant on site, and tours are not available.

ANNUAL OUTPUT: >100,000 hl.

REGULAR BEERS:
Louny Klasik (3.3%)
  A low-gravity golden lager only available in bottles.
Louny světlé výčepní (4.1%: ★★★★)
  Clear light gold with a thick white head, a slightly watery body with apricot notes and a bittersweet finish.
Louny tmavé výčepní (4.1%)
  A dark lager.
Louny světlý ležák (5.1%: ★★★/★)
  A clear gold lager brewed at 12°. Some fruit and a good malt flavour.
Louny tmavý ležák (5.1%: ★★★/★)
  Only available in bottles, this dark lager has a stewed-prune nose, a fruity malt body and lasting coffee-like finish.

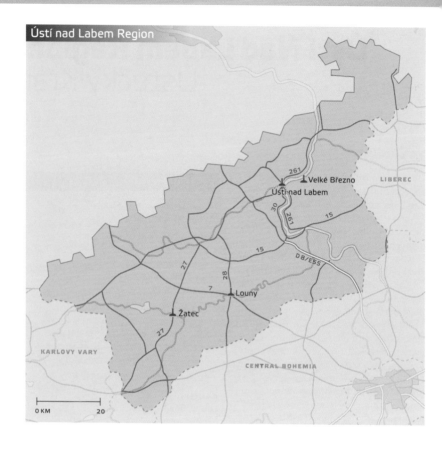

Ústí nad Labem Region

ÚSTÍ NAD LABEM

Zlatopramen

Drážďanská 80
400 07 Ústí nad Labem
T 472 703 111
E du@drinksunion.cz
www.drinksunion.cz

Another Drinks Union brewery whose Zlatopramen 11° single-handedly kicked off the country's recent craze for medium-bodied golden lagers, though the rich 12° is very nearly as good. Although the town is largely industrial, with open-cast mining and chemical industries based here, its location on the Elbe river makes for attractive countryside nearby. There are also some romantic castle ruins, the stunningly modern Mariánský Bridge and a lavish Neo-Romanesque baths complex to see.

ANNUAL OUTPUT: >100,000 hl.

REGULAR BEERS:

Zlatopramen světlé výčepní pivo (4.1%)
A daily-drinking golden 10° lager.

Zlatopramen 11° (4.9%: ★★★★)
A golden beer with a solid malt flavour and hop balance lacking the heft of a 12°.

Zlatopramen 11° tmavé (4.9%: ★★★/★)
Clear deep amber with a moderate smoky note followed by a lasting, dry sweetness.

Zlatopramen 12° (5.1%: ★★★/★)
Clear light gold with a rich malt rush followed by an orange-blossom hop finish.

VELKÉ BŘEZNO

Březňák

Pivovarská 116, 403 23 Velké Březno
T 475 309 111
E du@drinksunion.cz
www.drinksunion.cz

With three breweries out of four, the Drinks Union group dominates the Ústi nad Labem region. This is not necessarily a bad thing. At Velké Březno, Jana Rostová is one of the country's few lady brewers, though she distinguishes herself not so much for that as for her excellent lagers, traditional brewing methods and the SPP prize for Brewer of the Year in 2005. The brewery still uses open fermenters, and lagering can be lengthy: the 12° golden rests for at least 50 days and sometimes as long as 70; the 14° can spend as much as four months in aging. The brewery does offer tours, and its beers are available throughout the region.

ANNUAL OUTPUT: >100,000 hl.

REGULAR BEERS:

Březňák 10⁰ (★★★★)
A nice hop nose, light carbonation and moderately sweet finish on this clear golden lager

Březňák tmavý (★★/★)
Also brewed at 10°, this dark lager is deep amber with a coffee-cola flavour and a note of added sugar.

Březňák 12⁰ (★★★/★)
Deep gold with a creamy head and cascades of tiny bubbles. A malt body with a sweet and slightly sour finish.

Březňák světlý vyčepní 14⁰ (★★★★)
Golden amber with a thick, creamy head and very fine carbonation; a solid maltiness and well-incorporated alcohol.

Do you know this man?

When historians finally discovered the name behind this portrait, they solved one of the greatest mysteries of Czech beer lore. The iconic face of Březňák beer was first registered as the brewery's trademark in 1906, appearing on millions of bottles annually, and yet until recently no one remembered exactly who he was. Previously called just 'Zippich', he was thought to be a former postmaster in Velké Březno, a town just outside of Ústí nad Labem.

In fact, 100 years after the trademark was registered, researchers identified the man as Victor Cibich, the town's late 19th-century railway stationmaster. Soon after the discovery, Czech media were filled with stories about the life of 'pan Březňák'. Born in house No. 92 in Hustopeče, South Moravia, on 11 November 1856, he was the son of financial inspector Johann Cibich and his wife Klára, née Galinová, who came from Lipník nad Bečvou. After joining the railways, Victor Cibich married Augusta Bunzelová in Prague on 24 June 1884, and the couple had two sons: Bruno, born in 1886, and Paul, born in 1889.

The Cibich family moved to Velké Březno on 12 March 1891, and lived in an apartment in one of the railway buildings, where Victor worked as a conductor and rented out a bit of train station space to start a small business selling coal, eventually becoming a railway controller in 1901.

A gregarious and friendly figure, Victor Cibich became a beloved member of the town's largely German social circle, and legend has it that he received a lifelong payment of 30 bottles of beer per day in exchange for the use of his image. The confusion about his identity seems to have come from his son Paul, who became a postmaster in Velké Březno only to lose his job with the Austrian imperial post due to the family's German-Jewish roots. Though Victor Cibich was just 59 when he died of a heart attack in 1916, his afterlife as 'Mr. Březňák' looks set to last forever.

ŽATEC

Žatecký pivovar

Žižkovo nám. 81
438 01 Žatec
T 415 710 781
E lejsek@zateckypivovar.cz
www.zateckypivovar.cz

The brewers of Žatec were first granted the right to brew beer in 1261, but it's a shame: the only brewery today in the city of Czech hops is apparently blocked out of its own market by the Big Three! The Žatec brewery is located right off the town's main square, yet only a few of the neighbouring pubs and restaurants stock Žatec beer, opting instead for stuff from České Budějovice, Prague and Plzeň. The brewery was or is owned by absentee landlords in Cyprus, and production has dipped from earlier levels, far below capacity. It still uses open fermenting vessels, and its beers continue to enjoy a reputation among cognoscenti. Unfortunately, without more of a push in terms of marketing and distribution, it's doubtful Žatec will ever return to its previous production levels. There is no restaurant, pub or visitors' centre on site,

tours do not seem to be available, and bottles are rarely seen outside of the region.

Annual output: >20,000 hl.

Regular beers:

Žatec Světlé (4.1%)
A golden lager.

Lučan Premium tmavé (4.3%: ★★★★)
Less a dark beer than a slice of Sachertorte: a full-bodied, chocolaty dark lager with a pronounced fruitiness and a jam-like intense finish.

Žatec Premium (4.9%: ★★★★/★)
A gorgeous golden lager with an intense, citrus-like hop aroma married to a refined malt body. A showpiece for Saaz.

Žatec Export (5.1%: ★★★★)
Less hoppy in the nose, with more malt sugar.

Baronka (5.3%: ★★★★)
A new golden lager from 2005, with almost as much hop nose as the Premium.

Liberec Region
Liberecký Kraj

POPULATION: **428,291**
REGIONAL CAPITAL: **Liberec** (97,400)
www.kraj-lbc.cz

STRETCHING from the Lusatian Mountains through the Jizera Mountains to the edge of the Krkonoše, Liberecký kraj occupies the heart of the Sudeten geographical region, a series of peaks that defines Bohemia's northern border with Germany and Poland. It is strange, then, to see more licence plates here from Holland than from either of the

Czech Republic's two neighbouring countries, but the Dutch have discovered North Bohemia in a big way, and they seem to holiday here in ever-increasing numbers, driving their cars, caravans and campers through these scenic mountains practically year-round. It might be the natural beauty that has drawn them in, though the inexpensive, well-made beers – with nary a foreign-owned mega-brewery in sight – might have played a part too.

There are no major airports for international flights here. You'll want to drive in from Prague on the E65 through Mladá Boleslav; a trip to Liberec should be under three hours. Frequent buses for Liberec leave Prague's Černý Most station just about every hour.

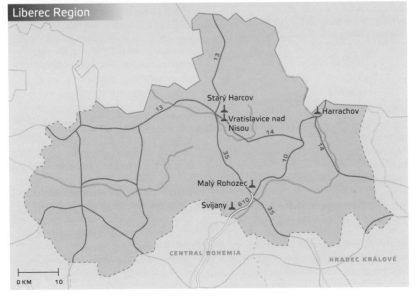

Liberec Region

Starý Harcov
Vratislavice nad Nisou
Harrachov
Malý Rohozec
Svijany

CENTRAL BOHEMIA

HRADEC KRÁLOVÉ

0 KM   10

HARRACHOV

Novosad a syn sklárna a minipivovar

Harrachov 95
512 46 Harrachov
T 481 528 141
E obchod@sklarnaharrachov.cz
www.sklarnaharrachov.cz

The Novosad glassworks, originally founded under a different name in 1712, have housed a brewpub since 2002, partly to satisfy employee demand: glass-blowers toil year-round in temperatures of around 49 ºC (120 ºF), and being Czechs, they consume a lot of low-alcohol beer to cool off during their shifts, and plenty more regular-grade lager after work as well. All brews here are unpasteurised and unfiltered, made with local spring water drawn from an exclusive forest well in the nearby Krkonoše mountains. Beers here have between one and three full months of lagering, and the result is absolutely delicious. The glassworks produce mainly drinking and decorative glasses, as well as crystal chandeliers. There is a museum and a shop, and tours are available, and you can watch glass-blowers work up a thirst from the slightly cooler enclave of the brewpub's mezzanine. The adjoining restaurant serves dishes made with beer.

ANNUAL OUTPUT: <1,000 hl.

REGULAR BEERS:

Huťské vyčepní 8º (3.5%: ★★★★)
This thin, watery, low-gravity, low-alcohol brew is meant to be drunk by glass-workers in need of rehydration. Even so, more malty and flavoursome than most mass-produced 12º brews.

Františkův světlý ležák 12º (5%: ★★★★/★)
Cloudy, pale gold with a creamy white head and an orange-blossom Saaz hop scent. Delicious.

Černý ležák 12º (5%: ★★★★)
A pale-sand head and deep amber body, not so sugary with only a touch of caramel. Reminiscent of a thin porter.

MALÝ ROHOZEC

Pivovar Rohozec

Malý Rohozec 29
511 01 Turnov
T 481 321 219
E pivorohozec@pivorohozec.cz
www.pivorohozec.cz

The kind of place where old Zetor tractors pass by almost as often as cars do, Malý Rohozec lies just outside of Turnov, surrounded by acres of farmland, making it a favourite stop for weekend cyclists. There's plenty of outdoor seating and a large bicycle parking area, too.

ANNUAL OUTPUT: >20,000 hl.

REGULAR BEERS:
Podskalák (4.2%: ★★★)
A pale gold lager of extra-light carbonation, thin body and bitter finish. Equivalent to a 10⁰.
Skalák světlý ležák (5%: ★★★/★)
Slightly deeper gold with more carbonation: a typical Czech beer, a shade ahead of most large-production lagers.

Skalák světlý ležák premium (5.3%: ★★★/★)
Clear gold with a light malt body and gentle hoppiness.
Skalák tmavé speciální pivo (5.9%: ★★★★)
Extremely dark amber with a coffee nose and a complex palate followed by a refreshing light sourness. Exceptional.
Skalák světlé speciální pivo (6%: ★★★★)
A golden special lager with a light, citrusy hop bouquet and moderate malt body.

STARÝ HARCOV

Vendelín

Lukášovská 43
460 15 Liberec – Starý Harcov
T 485 163 096

Three rough-hewn picnic tables along the road next to Vendelín Krkoška's house turn his front yard into an impromptu pub fuelled by his wonderful *kvasnicové pivo*. Not available in bottles or anywhere else, and hailed by connoisseurs from here to Honduras (where Mr Krkoška set up a similar brewery at an

island hotel run by Czech émigrés), the beer is remarkably fruity and refreshing. Brewing capacity is one hectolitre per day, and the beer is almost exclusively available at Mr. Krkoška's pub, converted from his former barn. The partially coal-fired brewing takes place over eight hours in a nearby shed, and lagering can last for up to three months.

ANNUAL OUTPUT: <250 hl

REGULAR BEERS:

Vendelín světlý ležák (5%: ★★★★★)
A honey-coloured, slightly cloudy lager with a fragrant nose reminiscent of apricots and yeasty dough. In the mouth, extremely low carbonation with a sugary, fruity finish. Spectacular.

SVIJANY

Pivovar Svijany

Svijany 25, 463 46 Příšovice

T 485 177 141

E obchod@pivovarsvijany.cz

www.pivovarsvijany.cz

This largish independent bottler boasts a bustling bottle and paraphernalia shop, a sports pub and an acacia-covered patio, offering *kvasnicové pivo* and five other brews

on draft. All beers are unpasteurised. Svijany won the SPP's award for Brewery of the Year in 2006, and though they can be hard to find, several of its beers are available on draft in Prague (see Prague Pubs).

ANNUAL OUTPUT: >100,000 hl.

REGULAR BEERS:

Svijanská Desítka (4%)
A 10° golden lager. Unpasteurised.

Svijanský Máz 11° (4.8%: ★★★)
Clear, light carbonation and a thin head with a decent malt body.

Svijanský Rytíř 12° (5%: ★★★★)
The brewery's premium Pilsner-style beer: clear gold with a yeasty nose and a rich fruitiness in the mouth.

Svijanská Kněžna 13° (5.2%: ★★★/★)
A dark special: clear amber with a taste of toasty malt.

Svijanský Kníže 13° (5.6%: ★★★★)
A special golden lager with a fragrant nose, a sugary malt body and a bitter hop finish.

Kvasničák 12.5° (6%: ★★★)
This yeast beer is a cloudy light amber with light carbonation and a flat, semi-sweet finish that can occasionally approach the medicinal.

Baron 15° (6.5%: ★★★)
Clear gold with a full body, noticeable alcohol and a very bitter finish.

VRATISLAVICE NAD NISOU

Pivovar Konrad

Tanvaldská 163, 463 11 Liberec 30
T 485 393 122
E konrad@hols.cz
www.pivo-konrad.cz

Though it was founded in 1872, the Konrad brewery today feels more like 1972, with a kind of dark, post-Prague-Spring atmosphere of 'normalisation' and authoritarian repression. There is no pub or restaurant on site and visitors don't seem to be terribly welcome. Worse, all beers are made with added sugar and all are pasteurised. In a few years, it will probably be fixed up and turned into an exclusive 'beer tourist' destination, with a fancy hotel and restaurant on site to entertain busloads of tourists. But for now, it's pretty grim. Despite appearances, several of the beers, especially the half-dark Eso, show real quality.

ANNUAL OUTPUT: >20,000 hl.

REGULAR BEERS:

Konrad 10⁰ (4%)
The standard low-gravity, golden lager.

Konrad tmavý 11⁰ (4.4%)
A dark 11° lager.

Eso (4.7%: ★★★★)
Clear amber with a loose white head, this 11° half-dark has a candy-malt sweet body and a delicious sour-sweet finish.

Konrad 11⁰ (4.8%)
A standard gold lager of medium gravity.

Konrad 12⁰ (5.4%: ★★★)
A 'premium' gold lager: clear and sugary with a bitter finish.

Jocker (6%: ★★★/★)
Brewed at 14° with an adjunct of wheat that results in a lighter body and crisp finish.

Červený Král (5%: ★★/★)
This special lager, brewed for the holidays, is as red as watermelon juice and slightly bitter. And not necessarily in the good way.

Hradec Králové Region
Královéhradecký Kraj

POPULATION: 554,348
REGIONAL CAPITAL: **Hradec Králové** (161,844)
www.kr-kralovehradecky.cz

PERHAPS THE LEAST homogeneous of the country's regions, Královéhradecký kraj in Bohemia shares much of the Krkonoše mountains with Liberecký kraj, and it includes high ranges in the eastern Orlické hory as well, although the regional capital of Hradec Králové lies far to the south and west, and at a much lower height. The contrasts can be astounding: while the mountain regions are rustic and quaint, Hradec Králové is a surprisingly urbane city, with lots of remarkable modern architecture, much of it by the Cubist master Josef Gočár, blending well with earlier buildings from the Baroque and Gothic periods. In fact, the town is one of the oldest settlements in Bohemia; its name,

meaning 'Castle of the Queen', dates from its designation as one of the dowry towns which were given to Eliška Rejčka (Elizabeth of Poland) by her husband, Václav II of Bohemia (Wenceslas), upon their marriage in 1300. Today it is home to several university faculties and hosts events as diverse as May's Air Ambulance Show to one of Europe's biggest hip-hop festivals each August. The area to the region's northwest, near Dětenice and Jičín, is a natural preserve so renowned for its beauty that its name is Český ráj – Bohemian Paradise. An old sandstone plateau, it is indeed an unspoilt eden of rocky outcrops, river valleys and dense pine forests.

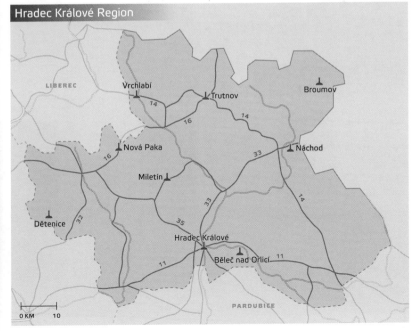

Hradec Králové Region

BĚLEČ NAD ORLICÍ

U Hušků

Běleč nad Orlicí 58
T 495 593 738
E balounek@centrum.cz
www.biapivo.com

Using the term 'brewpub' here might be stretching it: U Hušků is more like a 'brew garden', with outdoor seating in warm weather the big attraction, while the dim, dingy pub lacks the showy (read 'clean') décor and glowing kettles of the places most people would actually like to visit. In fact, the brewing seems to be done off-site, so it's more like a garden, plain and simple. That said, the three unpasteurised lagers are excellent, and although the food menu is limited to grilled sausage or chicken, if there's anything to eat available at all, the beers make this smoky dive more than worth a stop if you're passing through nearby Hradec Králové.

ANNUAL OUTPUT: <250 hl.

REGULAR BEERS:

Bělečský Car kvasnicový ležák 12⁰
(4.8%: ★★★★/★)
Deep gold, this yeast beer has a thick white head, a yeasty nose and relatively flat carbonation.

Bělečský Car medový 12⁰ (4.8%: ★★★★/★)
This deep gold lager is made with honey, which adds a lasting sweetness to the finish.

Bělečský Car tmavý 12⁰ (4.8%: ★★★★)
A medium-amber dark lager with a honey nose and a coffee-cola flavour, akin to Kofola, the Czech cola drink.

BROUMOV

Pivovar Broumov

Tř. Osvobození 55, 550 01 Broumov
T 491 523 779
E pivovar@pivovarbroumov.cz
www.pivovarbroumov.cz

Get ready for a longer journey: Broumov is so far from Central Bohemia and so close to the Polish border that many Praguers will have trouble understanding the local dialect, let alone finding the place to begin with. (The brewery is actually in the neighbouring village of Olivětín.) In fact, there's not much reason to travel up here, as the beautiful brewery has no pub on site, and most of the local pubs serve trucked-in beers from the national brands. Broumov beer can sometimes be found in shops around the country, however. The brewery itself is often referred to simply as *'Opat'* (abbot), the name of its line of lagers; it is also responsible for the Rampuš and Novic beers produced for regional Coop and Tesco stores.

ANNUAL OUTPUT: 20,000 hl.

REGULAR BEERS:

Opat tmavé (3.5%)
A dark lager of moderate alcohol.

Opat 10⁰ (3.8%)
A well-regarded golden lager.

Opat 12⁰ (5%: ★★★★)
A rich and malty golden lager with a sweet fruity finish, the winner of an SPP award in 2005.

Opat speciál 13⁰ (5.5%: ★★★★)
Pale gold, with a thick white head and a lovely apricot nose, a lush malt body and a fruity finish.

Sváteční speciál 17⁰ (6.6%: ★★★★)
A clear amber holiday beer with candied sugar and caramel notes.

DĚTENICE

Zámecký pivovar Dětenice

Zámek Dětenice
T 493 596 132
E info@detenice.cz
www.krcmadetenice.cz

Founded in 1822, but only renewed and reopened in 2003, Chateau Dětenice now houses a medieval-themed restaurant, where rustic food is served peasant-style (no silverware) by gruff-speaking wenches and lads in character. Along with the grilled meats and dense loaves come two lagers, light and dark, said to be brewed in oak barrels.

Tours of the brewery are available, and there is a small brewery museum on site. Dětenice lies in the westernmost part of Královéhradecký kraj, less than 90 minutes away from Prague by car. With connections in Nymburk and Kopidlno, travellers can get here by train in just over two hours.

ANNUAL OUTPUT: 1,000 hl.

REGULAR BEERS:

Světlé dětenické pivo (4%: ★★★★/★)
Pale gold with an orange-blossom nose, a moderate honey flavour and a bright, hoppy finish.

Tmavé dětenické pivo (4%: ★★)
A deep-amber dark lager without much character.

HRADEC KRÁLOVÉ

Rambousek

Velké nám. 130
500 03 Hradec Králové
T 603 730 816
www.rambousek.wz.cz

Milan Rambousek is a gifted home-brewer who has long deserved a larger venue: while he makes excellent, unusual lagers, at the time of writing there is no pub which stocks them regularly, and they are not available in bottles. Not open to the public, his brewery currently occupies just 14 sq m (150 sq ft). The beers have shown up on draught at the Pivovarský klub in Prague, but they remain extremely rare. This lamentable state should change in late 2007, however, when Mr. Rambousek opens a new brewpub in the administrative building of the old Hradec Králové brewery, right on the town's main square, where he will serve three standard brews and occasional specials.

ANNUAL OUTPUT: <250 hl.

REGULAR BEERS:

Eliščino královské pivo tmavé (4.6%)
A dark lager.

Eliščino královské pivo světlé (4.6%)
A golden lager.

Rambousek kaštanomedový ležák
(5.5%: ★★★★/★)

Deep amber, with a chestnut nose and a touch of smoke in the rich malt body. Made with chestnut honey.

Jubilee 16⁰ (6.4%)
A special dark lager brewed at a higher original gravity.

NÁCHOD

Primátor

Dobrošovská 130
547 40 Náchod
T 491 407 111
E marketing@primator.cz
www.primator.cz

One of the few state-owned Czech breweries remaining (think Budvar), Primátor is owned by the city of Náchod, contributing significantly to the municipality's coffers. It is also one of the few breweries to stick with its original open fermenters. It brews an unusual line of beers, including several remarkable high-gravity beers, as well as the first English-style pale ale and one of the first wheat beers to appear in bottles in the Czech Republic. The brewery is located in the centre of the scenic mountain town of Náchod, and tours are available.

ANNUAL OUTPUT: >100,000 hl.

REGULAR BEERS:

Primátor Světlý (4%)
The brewery's basic golden lager.

Primátor Premium Dark (4.8%: ★★★/★)
Almost black, this dark lager has a malty nose and coffee, cola and ginger notes in the mouth.

Primátor Premium (5%: ★★★★)
A clear gold lager with a rich, toasted-malt body and a grassy hop finish.

Primátor Weizenbier (5%: ★★★★)
A clove-scented Hefeweizen (yeast wheat beer). In bottles, it comes with significant yeast sediment.

Primátor English Pale Ale (5%: ★★★★/★)
Clear amber with a lasting white head and Belgian lace. Notes of vanilla and oak with a lasting, grassy hop finish.

Primátor Polotmavý 13⁰ (5.5%: ★★★)
Clear amber, slightly fizzy with a sweet malt

finish. SPP's half-dark lager of the year 2006.

Primátor Exklusiv 16⁰ (7%: ★★★★)
A sweet, low-carbonated strong lager with a pronounced caramel finish.

Primátor Rytířský 21⁰ (9%: ★★★/★)
A strong amber lager with the taste of added sugar.

Primátor Double 24⁰ (10%: ★★★/★)
Excellent with food, this wine-like, rich dark lager has peppery, spicy hop notes.

NOVÁ PAKA

Pivovar Nová Paka

Pivovarská 400
509 01 Nová Paka
T 493 721 031
E broucek@novopackepivo.cz
www.novopackepivo.cz

Nová Paka is one of the quiet, hidden gems of Czech brewing, slowly soldiering on with tradition while the bigger names quickly adopt new technologies in order to grab market share. Scenically set above a duck pond, the brewery today looks much as it did when it was founded in 1872. It still uses open fermenters and maintains its own maltings, and its water comes from a 100-m (328-ft) deep Artesian well on the premises. But Nová Paka isn't hamstrung by tradition: newer beers include a remarkable lager brewed with hemp extract, which puts into relief the connection between cannabis and the hop plant. Guided tours of the brewery are available for groups of ten or more with advance reservations, and there is a restaurant on site. Reservations are recommended.

ANNUAL OUTPUT: >20,000 hl.

REGULAR BEERS:

Brouček (4%: ★★★)
Clear gold with a loose head and an unusual smoky flavour in the mouth. Rather fizzy, but not bad.

Kryštof (4.3%: ★★★/★)
Clear gold, loose white head like most beers from this brewery. Small bubbles, slightly fizzy with a decent hop finish.

Hemp Valley Beer (4.5%: ★★★/★)
*Deep gold, clear, with a moderate hop-like bite
in the nose. Fairly fizzy, nice sweetness and good
bitter 'hop' finish. A great Pilsner, made with
Swiss hemp extract.*

Kumburák (5%: ★★★★)
*A slightly longer-lasting loose head, clear deep
gold, with a lightly fruity nose. Good malt body,
nice hop finish. This brewery's best beer.*

Granát (5%: ★★★/★)
*Deep amber with a moderate sandy head.
Moderately fizzy. Made with added sugar,
with some candied sugar aftertaste.*

Podkrkonošský Speciál Dark (6.3%: ★★★/★)
*This dark beer has a sandy head with coffee and
chocolate notes in the mouth, with a lasting
taste of added sugar.*

Podkrkonošský speciál světlý (6.3%: ★★★)
*Deep gold, with small-bubble carbonation.
Strong malt nose and sugary body with a
slightly bitter, lasting hop finish.*

Valdštejn (7%: ★★★)
*Clear deep gold, fine carbonation and micro-
foam head, with a malt nose and maltose rush
with a slightly unbalanced alcoholic back-bite
and redeeming dry finish.*

MILETÍN

Sousedský dům

Nám. K. J. Erbena 98
507 71 Miletín
☎ 493 693 419

This smoky pub mostly serves Gambrinus to
the gang of regulars, though you can have
one of the house brews if you ask for it. You
should, as they are far better than the second
brew from Plzeň. The pub, called 'Neighbour
House', is located directly on the main square
in Miletín. In warmer months it expands to
include a beer garden.

ANNUAL OUTPUT: <250 hl.

REGULAR BEERS:
Chmelka 10⁰ (★★★★)
*Clear amber with mild carbonation and an
almond bitterness in the mouth followed by a
lasting sweet finish.*

Pytlák 12⁰
*A rare Pilsner-style beer served only at weekends
in the beer garden.*

TRUTNOV

Krakonoš

Křižíkova 486
541 01 Trutnov
T 499 840 114
E krakonos@pivovar-krakonos.cz
www.pivovar-krakonos.cz

The Krakonoš brewery takes its name from a local giant who is said to dwell in the Krkonoše, or Giant Mountains. This range, forming the border between Bohemia and Polish Silesia, is home to many ski resorts and holiday homes. There is a national park straddling the border, and the Labe (Elbe) river rises here too. The area has an almost alpine feel that seems quite far removed from urban Prague. The brewery, a medium-sized bottler, sells much of its production abroad; on-site there is a recently renovated restaurant and newly opened hotel, one of the country's only brewery-hotels that is not connected to a brewpub. Nonetheless, the restaurant here does serve a brewpub-like *kvasnicové pivo*.

ANNUAL OUTPUT: <100,000 hl.

REGULAR BEERS:

Krakonoš světlé výčepní 10⁰ (3.9%)
A gold lager of moderate original gravity.

Krakonoš tmavé výčepní 10⁰ (3.9%)
A dark lager of moderate original gravity.

Krakonoš světlý ležák 11⁰ (4.3%)
A medium-gravity Czech lager.

Krakonoš světlý ležák 12⁰ (5.1%: ★★★/★)
Clear gold, a hoppy nose, solid malt body and bittersweet finish.

Krakonoš kvasnicové (5.1%: ★★★/★)
Deep gold with a light malty aroma and a moderately bittersweet taste.

Krakonoš speciál 14⁰ (5.8%: ★★★)
A higher-gravity Christmas brew: clear gold, almost amber, with a slight vegetal (or mineral?) taste underneath the malt body.

VRCHLABÍ

Pivovarská bašta

Horská 198
543 02 Vrchlabí
T 499 421 272
E hotelbasta@hotelbasta.cz
www.hotelbasta.cz

Up in the ski country of the Krkonoše mountains, this hotel and brewpub sits right atop the 295 motorway in Hořejší (Upper) Vrchlabí on the way to Špindlerův mlýn, making it a favourite for the powder crowd.

The hotel's 'Krkonoše Bear' beers can vary from good to double-plus ungood. By no means should you have the sour-cherry beer, flavoured with sour-cherry extract, and the large industrial-size jug of food colouring near the brewing kettles gives little support to the strange-tasting dark lager. The regular brews almost redeem the brewery, however, and some bottles and kegs occasionally turn up in Prague.

ANNUAL OUTPUT: >1,000 hl.

REGULAR BEERS:

Krkonošský Medvěd 10⁰ (3.5%)
A Czech light lager of lower original gravity.

Krkonošský Medvěd světlý ležák 12⁰
(4.5%: ★★★★)
Pale gold, this Pilsner-style lager has an unctuous, buttery mouth feel and rich malt body.

Krkonošský Medvěd tmavý ležák 12⁰ (4.5%: ★)
An off-tasting dark beer apparently made with food colouring.

Krkonošský Medvěd světlé kvasnicové
(4.5%: ★★★★)
A clear yeast beer with a nice sweet-acid balance and a slight vegetal taste in the finish.

Krkonošský Medvěd višňové (4.5%: ★)
An amber lager flavoured with sour-cherry extract, or children's cough medicine?

Krkonošský Medvěd medové (4.5%: ★★)
An amber lager flavoured with honey.

Krkonošský Medvěd veselé pivo (6%: ★★★/★)
A strong gold lager brewed at 14⁰. Clear gold and nicely malty, but lacking in balance.

Pardubice Region
Pardubický Kraj

POPULATION: **506,128**
REGIONAL CAPITAL: **Pardubice** (89,725)
www.pardubickykraj.cz

PARDUBICE, home to the great and notoriously tough Pardubice Steeplechase (Velká Pardubická), is one of the largest cities close to Prague, about 90 minutes away by car, or 1 hour 40 minutes on a normal train; the high-speed Pendolino and Intercity trains cover this distance in less than an hour. The cities have been tied together since Arnošt of Pardubice was elected the first archbishop of Prague in the 14th century, yet even today this modest distance is still enough to create a feeling of being well outside Central Bohemia. Nonetheless, Pardubický kraj is hardly a homogenous region, with the areas to the north and east being more like Královéhradecký kraj's mountainous border region, and the southern edge clearly tied to the Vysočina highlands.

The essential sight here is Litomyšl, a UNESCO World Heritage Site and home to most of the great thinkers of the 19th-century Czech National Awakening, which worked to cast off the shackles of Austrian control. Perhaps more to the point, Litomyšl is also the birthplace of composer Bedřich Smetana, whose best-known works are the Vltava cycle and the comic opera *The Bartered Bride*. Smetana, son of the town brewmaster, was born at the town's brewery. Unfortunately (and typically), that brewery is now defunct.

Pardubický kraj is still home to three medium-sized bottlers, as well as two brewpubs, one of which sells a few beers in bottles. If you're here in race season, come for the Steeplechase, as fans have since 1874. At any other time, come for the beer alone.

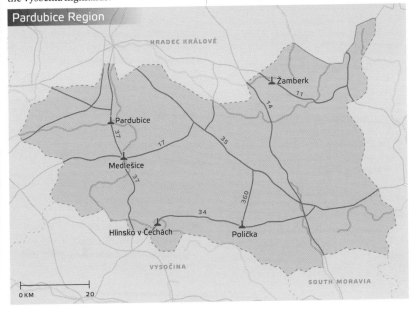

Pardubice Region

Beer and the bride

In terms of High Culture, *pivo's* star turn probably takes place in Bedřich Smetana's beloved comic opera *The Bartered Bride (Prodaná nevěsta)*. In the libretto by Karel Sabina, beer is given a central role, with the second act opening up at the pub where the chorus sings:

> *To pivečko, to věru je nebeský dar,*
> *vše psoty a trampoty vede na zmar*
> *a sílí a dává kuráže!*
> *Ejchuchu!*
> *Bez piva by člověk smutný byl zde host;*
> *jeť starostí na světě beztoho dost –*
> *a blázen, kdo na ně se váže!*
> *Ejchuchu!*

Translations of the libretto in English and German often change the meaning slightly for the sake of rhyme and singing. (In one version, 'beer' becomes 'ale', an unusual term in the Czech lands.) A more literal translation might be:

> Beer, no doubt, is a heavenly gift,
> tearing all evil and troubles apart,
> and giving strength and courage!
> Hooray!
> Without beer a man would be unhappy
>   to be a guest here,
> there's enough trouble in the world
>   without it already
> and only a fool would be tied to that!
> Hooray!

The main character, Jeník, disagrees, declaring that love is superior (rendered in English as 'Good fellows, that's your view, now listen to mine. True love is far better than all beer or wine.') In most productions, it is quite clear that no one in the chorus believes him.

HLINSKO V ČECHÁCH

Rychtář

Resslova 260
539 01 Hlinsko v Čechách
T 469 311 609
E pivo@rychar.cz
www.rychtar.cz

The town and ski resort of 'Hlinsko in Bohemia' is very much located in the Vysočina, or Highlands, at least spiritually: politically it remains within the Pardubický region's borders. Inside Hlinsko itself is an historic village, Betlém, which is part of the much larger Open-Air Museum of Folk Architecture and Handicrafts, extending over several villages. Betlém is composed of a number of timbered houses, farm buildings and workshops (of potters, weavers, cobblers and a toymaker, for example) dating from the 19th century, some of which have been converted into pubs, cafés and hotels today.

Both Hlinsko v Čechách and Medlešice lie on the main rail route from Pardubice to Havlíčkův Brod, making a four-brewery trip relatively easy to plan (although neighbouring Polička is less reachable). In general, Rychtář makes excellent beers for a large brewer, displaying the pronounced maltiness most characteristic of the Czech Pilsner style, but there is no permanent pub or restaurant on the brewery grounds. Naturally, many pubs in the city have the beer on tap, and the brewery hosts open-air rock concerts throughout July, August and September.

ANNUAL OUTPUT: <100,000 hl.

REGULAR BEERS:
Klasik 10⁰ (4%)
 A basic golden lager, the brewery's daily drinker.
Standard 11⁰ (4.5%: ★★★/★)
 A clear gold lager with the brewery's typical emphasis on malt.
Malvaz 12⁰ (4.5%: ★★★★)
 A dark lager made with added sugar, as are many Czech darks. A medium malt body with a pronounced cola flavour and extremely flat carbonation.

Natur 12⁰ (4.9%: ★★★/★)
This clear gold yeast beer has a slightly sour finish. Only available on draught.

Premium 12⁰ (5%: ★★★★)
A solid malt body bolstered by added sugar: clear gold with very modest carbonation and a crisp hop finish.

Hejtman 12⁰ (5%: ★★★/★)
A half-dark lager also made with added sugar: clear amber with a thin, sandy head, a good malt body and light, slightly vegetal, Saaz-hop finish.

Speciál 15⁰ (6.5%: ★★★)
Clear gold with a pure white head of fine foam. Also with added sugar. Very thin carbonation punctuates a rich malt body and bitter finish.

MEDLEŠICE

Pivovar Medlešice

Medlešice 2
538 31 Medlešice (okres Chrudim)
T 469 688 884
E pivovar.medlesice@seznam.cz
www.medlesice.cz

Claiming a history dating back to 1673, today's Medlešice brewery is a slightly-larger-than-a-hobby-style affair which nonetheless makes two very good yeast beers. There is a pub on site, which functions as a kind of community centre: on the Guide's recent visit, a costume party for children was taking place, with little cowboys and Indians running around the pub. The beer does not seem to be available anywhere else, making a trip (and a call ahead) a necessity. The town is located 20 minutes to the south of Pardubice, just north of Chrudim.

ANNUAL OUTPUT: <1,000 hl.

REGULAR BEERS:

12⁰ Medlešický ležák světlý (★★★★/★)
A cloudy yellow lager with a thick head, a thin body and a citrus-peel aftertaste, followed by a lambic-like sour finish. Unusual.

12⁰ Medlešický ležák černý (★★★★)
This dark lager is a cloudy deep amber with a pronounced malt body and sugary finish.

PARDUBICE

Pernštejn

Palackého 250
530 33 Pardubice
T 466 511 321
E pivovar@pernstejn.cz
www.pernstejn.cz

Another of the country's heroically hard-working mid-sized bottlers, Pernštejn confusingly shares its name with a different town and famous castle, but it was named after Vilém Pernštejn, the 'richest man in the country' who settled here. It is located in the very heart of the historical city centre of Pardubice, a short walk from the city's train station. The brewery maintains its own maltings, and like many others in the country, Pernštejn has a second line of fruit sodas and other non-alcoholic beverages. Its beers are all accomplished examples of Czech standards, with one rare exception: the 8% alcohol porter, one of the sole

remaining examples of the Baltic porter style in this country, brewed here since 1890. The brewery has an excellent restaurant and pub on site, with a bottle and paraphernalia store next door, and hosts a number of 'witch nights' and 'beer days' throughout the year.

ANNUAL OUTPUT: <100,000 hl.

REGULAR BEERS:
Pernštejn Kovář (3.5%)
A golden draught lager.
Pernštejn světlé výčepní (4%)
A slightly more serious golden draught lager.
Pernštejn polotmavé výčepní (4%: ★★★/★)
Clear dark amber with a sandy head. A thin, watery body with a slight caramel aftertaste.
Pernštejn jedenáctka (4.7%: ★★★)
Clear pale gold with weak carbonation and a thin body.
Pernštejn světlý ležák (5.2%: ★★★/★)
Clear deep gold with a good white head and rich malt body.
Pernštejn Granát (5.7%: ★★★)
Deep amber with a thick tan head and a rich, sugary body.
Pardubický Porter (8%: ★★★/★)
An unusual, bottom-fermented porter roughly in the Baltic style: clear deep amber with a loose tan head, cola and spice notes with a sugary cold coffee finish.

POLIČKA

Pivovarská 151

572 14 Polička
T 461 725 575
E pivovar@pivovar-policka.cz
www.pivovar-policka.cz

Another Czech musical town, Polička is known as the home of composer Bohuslav Martinů, who was born in the church bell tower here in 1890. It is also one of the few walled towns to retain most of its original stone fortifications, measuring 1,220 m (4,002 ft) long and 10 m (33 ft) high and dating back to the 14th century. The town itself was founded even earlier, in 1265, by King Otakar II of Bohemia. Though Polička has only 9,128 inhabitants, the brewery cranks out an amazing 15 million pints annually, with distribution throughout the region and bottles and kegs even appearing sporadically in Prague. Unfortunately, the brewery has no pub or restaurant on site and does not offer tours in English.

ANNUAL OUTPUT: <100,000 hl.

REGULAR BEERS:

10⁰ Hradební tmavé výčepní (3.7%: ★★★/★)
Clear dark amber with a reddish hue and a chocolate-mocha body.

10⁰ Hradební světlé výčepní (3.9%: ★★★★)
Very clear pale gold with visibly light carbonation and malt aroma. In the mouth, caramel malt flavours with a very moderate hop finish.

11⁰ Otakar světlý ležák (4.2%: ★★★/★)
Clear gold with a strawberries-and-cream aroma, slightly thin malt body and flat carbonation.

11⁰ Otakar světlý kvasnicový (4.2%: ★★★/★)
Cloudy pale gold, this yeast beer has a slight fizziness and rich malt with a fruity hop balance.

12⁰ Záviš světlý ležák (5%: ★★★)
Clear gold with slightly more carbonation, a thick malt body and a slightly overpowering hop bitterness.

12⁰ Záviš světlý kvasnicový (5%: ★★★★)
Slightly deeper gold than the 12⁰, this yeast lager has complex apricot and melon tastes in the mouth.

ŽAMBERK

Minipivovar Žamberk

Havlenova 10
564 01 Žamberk
T 465 611 918
E intero@intero.cz

Way out in the east of the Pardubický kraj, Žamberk feels more like a part of the neighbouring Královéhradecký region, located high up in the Orlické mountains where snow gets so thick that 4x4 clubs come over from Poland to rip things up here. This tiny micro-brewery serves 'Žamberk Boar' beers, also available in bottles, but it's more of a brewpub in size and feel, with dim lighting, heavy hardwood tables and a warm,

neighbourly atmosphere. Only a few light dishes are available for meals as of writing the Guide, so you might want to plan your dinner elsewhere before trying out the pub's excellent draughts. Other than skiing, snowshoeing or driving your jeep around in the snow in winter, or hiking, fishing and cycling in the summer, not much else will draw you to Žamberk, but that – and the beers – are enough.

ANNUAL OUTPUT: <1,000 hl.

REGULAR BEERS:

Žamberecký Kanec 10⁰ (3.8%: ★★★★/★)
A slightly cloudy deep gold with a note of apricot jam.

Žamberecký Kanec 12⁰ (4%: ★★★/★)
A flat gold lager with a thick head and a touch of sourness that goes chutney-strong by the finish.

Žamberecký Kanec 13⁰ (4.6%: ★★★★/★)
A cloudy deep gold with a rich malt body and a honey-pear flavour.

Žamberecký Kanec 14⁰ (6%★★★★)
Deep amber with a thick sandy head. In the mouth, well-balanced alcohol, notes of sour cherries and stone fruit with a sweet finish.

Kraj Vysočina

POPULATION: **510,032**
REGIONAL CAPITAL: **Jihlava** (50,676)
www.kr-vysocina.cz

THE VYSOČINA, or highlands, have some of the most beautiful rolling hills in the Czech Republic, bridging the vast open spaces of South Bohemia and the vineyards of South Moravia. The Vysočina has three sites on the UNESCO World Heritage list: the town of Telč, founded in the mid-14th century, home to a massive medieval square and castle; the preserved Jewish quarter and nearby St. Procopius' Basilica in the town of Třebíč; and the ornate Pilgrimage Church of St. John of Nepomuk at Zelená Hora in Žďár nad Sázavou, where the maverick architect Jan Santini Aichel combined Baroque and Gothic elements with an arcane numerical symbolism that defies description. All three are must-sees for travellers and can easily be reached by car from a base such as the charming hotel and brewpub Jelínkova Vila.

Perhaps because of its isolated position far from the various bases of SAB-Miller, InBev, Heineken and Budvar, the area's four independent, medium-sized bottlers carry on, and in certain cases, even thrive. With two excellent brewpubs, a fish-out-of-water monastery brewery, and historic and architectural settings of great significance for European culture, the Vysočina would make for an excellent road trip of five to seven days. The D1/E50/E65 motorway bisects it neatly, and the first stop, Humpolec, can be reached in about two hours from Prague by car or bus.

left: The graveyard and pilgrims' quarters at the church of St John of Nepomuk at Zelená Hora.

DALEŠICE

Dalešice

Dalešice 71
T 568 860 942
E sladek@pivovar-dalesice.cz
www.pivovar-dalesice.cz

This storied brewery, now operating as a brewpub, lies in the Vysočina region, although it feels closer to South Bohemia and the second city of Brno. It was once owned by Austrian brewing great Anton Dreher the Younger, his first enterprise in the Czech lands, and reverted to a co-operative in 1925. After the arrival of socialism, it was nationalised and made a part of the South Bohemian Breweries, brewing continuously until its closure in 1977. It is perhaps most famous for being the site where the 1980 movie *Postřižiny* ('Cutting it Short') was filmed, based on the novel by Bohumil Hrabal and directed by Oscar-winner Jiří Menzel. (Confusingly, the setting for *Postřižiny* is actually the brewery in Nymburk, which today uses Hrabal's likeness on its beer labels.) The pub has great atmosphere and excellent beers, as well as a very small 'museum' dedicated to Austro-Hungarian brewing.

ANNUAL OUTPUT: <20,000 hl.

REGULAR BEERS:
11⁰ kvasnicové (4.2%: ★★★★/★)
A cloudy gold yeast beer with a nose of cooked strawberries and a slight vanilla flavour.
11⁰ filtrované (4.2%: ★★★★)
A filtered Pilsner-style lager with a similar strawberry jam nose and a berries-and-cream note in the mouth.

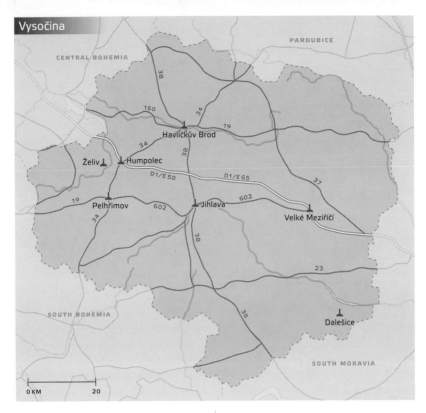

12⁰ polotmavé (4.8%: ★★★/★)
This half-dark lager is a cloudy medium amber with a sauerkraut nose and a very sour finish.

13⁰ kvasnicové světlé (5.3%: ★★★★/★)
Cloudy gold with a thick head that melts slowly, like ice cream. Malty in nose and body with a bitter hop bite.

13⁰ kvasnicové tmavé (5.3%)
A yeasty dark special lager.

HAVLÍČKŮV BROD

Rebel

Dobrovského 2027
Havlíčkův Brod
T 569 495 111
E rebel@hbrebel.cz
www.hbrebel.cz

Today's town of Havlíčkův Brod was known as Německý Brod (German Ford) from 1310, named after the German silver miners who were invited to work here by the Bohemian nobleman Smil of Lichtenburk. The silver mines declined, and the town was sacked in the Hussite wars because of the people's support for King Sigismund. It was later revitalised with the establishment of the textile industry in the 19th century. The brewery, just uphill from the well-preserved main square, has a brand-new restaurant and pub in the former Augustinian Latin school. It was here that 19th-century Czech nationalist Karel Havlíček Borovský was educated. Borovský is regarded as the first Czech journalist, and the town was renamed in his honour after 1945, when the remaining German population was expelled because of their support for the Nazi occupation. The brewery, Rebel, also takes its name from this

national hero, who was charged several times with dissent, subjected to censorship and eventually exiled to Austria. Rebel beers are substantially less controversial, with good maltiness and generous hop flavours.

ANNUAL OUTPUT: <100,000 hl.

REGULAR BEERS:

Rebel Tradiční (3.9%: ★★★★)
Brewed at 10° Balling, this clear-gold lager is light in body with a fruity citrus taste and a fragrant hop finish.

Tudor (4.2%)
A 10° gold lager designed to bridge the European and Bohemian styles.

Haškův Rebel (4.2%)
A Pilsner-style beer with increased alcohol relative to its lower OG.

Rebel Zlatý/Czech Rebel Beer (4.4%: ★★★)
Slightly cloudy gold with very light carbonation and big malt taste for an 11°.

Rebel Černý (4.7%: ★★★/★)
Dark amber and clear with a lacy tan head and slight cola and ginger flavours.

Rebel Originál Premium (4.8%: ★★★/★)
A clear Pilsner-style lager with excellent maltiness. Some slickness in the mouth. Dry hop finish.

Rebel Kvasnicový (4.8%: ★★★)
Slightly cloudy gold with grapey fruitiness. Not available in bottles.

HUMPOLEC

Bernard

Ul. 5. května 1
Humpolec
T 565 532 407
E pivovar@bernard.cz
www.bernard.cz

One of this Guide's favourite beers, Bernard proves that small brewers can survive, and indeed thrive, despite the continuing exclusionary and anti-competitive practices of the Big Three. In Bernard's case, success has come by producing beers that are full of character, usually with pronounced maltiness and a balancing hop bitterness reminiscent of the greatest Pilsner-style beers of old. These are not innocuous beers designed to please the mainstream – many beer lovers find Bernard's lagers too rich or too bitter, especially if they are used to the thinner German style of Pils. But the characteristically rich Bernard lagers have earned much recognition for the brewery, with owner Stanislav Bernard currently starring in advertisements for a national bank, and a number of other small producers starting to echo Bernard's 'unpasteurised' angle (beers sold domestically are micro-filtered but unpasteurised, though apparently pasteurisation is used for exports). Belgian family brewer Duvel made a 50 per cent strategic investment in the company, which allowed it to start a relatively aggressive advertising campaign. In another connection with tradition, it is one of the few breweries to maintain its own maltings, and lagering can last 40 days. Tours are available with advance notice. There is no restaurant or pub on site, though the beers are everywhere in the region and can frequently be found at discriminating outlets in Prague and elsewhere.

ANNUAL OUTPUT: >100,000 hl.

REGULAR BEERS:

10⁰ světlé (3.8%: ★★★★)
Clear gold with a light body and a sharply bitter finish. SPP's 10⁰ of the year in 2006.

11⁰ světlé (4.5%: ★★★/★)
Clear gold with very flat carbonation and a slightly minty hop finish.

11⁰ polotmavé (4.5%: ★★★★)
A clear deep amber, nearly as dark as many 'black' lagers, with a rich malt body and beautiful bittersweet balance.

12⁰ světlý ležák (4.7%: ★★★★/★)
A rich golden lager with a pronounced maltiness.

12⁰ svateční ležák (5%: ★★★★/★)
The special golden lager, bottled with an addition of fresh yeast.

Speciální černý ležák 13⁰ (5.1%: ★★★★★)
A chocolate blend of five malts in one rich, deep dark brew. SPP's dark beer of the year when introduced in 2005.

OX 14⁰ (5.8%: ★★★/★)
An unusual new lager made with highly modified malt, uncommon at the brewery, and using deep fermentation at 14⁰, resulting in a lighter body and more alcohol.

JIHLAVA

Ježek

Vrchlického 2
Jihlava
T 567 564 111
E info@pivovar-jihlava.cz
www.pivovar-jihlava.cz

Sitting right at the main western entrance to the town of Jihlava, the Ježek (hedgehog) brewery has a pleasant summer beer garden, complete with children's playground and musical stage, as well as a spacious on-site restaurant and beer hall. Today, everything is noticeably run-down; the restaurant only stocks half the beers produced by the brewery, though a separate bottle shop on site sells most of the line. Worth a stop,

although the beers seem to have lost much of their earlier character, barring the 18°, high-alcohol Jihlavský Grand.

ANNUAL OUTPUT: 100,000 hl.

REGULAR BEERS:

Ježek 8° (3.5%)
One of the last remaining 8° lagers. Perfect for breakfast.

Ježek 10° Formanské světlé (4.1%: ★★★)
Pale yellow with a thin body and decent bittersweet balance.

Ježek 10° tmavý (4.1%: ★★★)
A dark lager with rich coffee and caramel notes and a strong sugary finish.

Pivoj 10° (4.1%)
A clear light lager only available in bottles.

Ježek 11° Stříbrný (4.5%: ★★/★)
A clear gold brew well on its way to becoming a standard Eurolager.

Ježek 11° kvasnicové (4.5%: ★★★)
Cloudy gold with a cinnamon-spice nose, decent malt body and thin finish.

Ježek světlý 12° (5%: ★★)
A clear gold lager with a loose head and an unpleasant fizz.

Ježek světlý 14° (6.1%)
A clear special lager of higher original gravity and alcohol.

Jihlavský Grand (8.1%: ★★★/★)
Brewed at a remarkable 18°. Clear honey-gold with a thick micro-foam head, rich maltiness and slight grassy, hemp-like hop notes.

PELHŘIMOV

Poutník

Pivovarská 856
Pelhřimov
T 565 323 231
E pivovar@dup.cz
www.pivovarpoutnik.cz

The middle-sized 'Pilgrim' brewery hides in the centre of the quaint hillside town of Pelhřimov. There is no pub or restaurant on site, but Poutník beers are available throughout the region, and can occasionally be found in bottles in Prague and elsewhere.

ANNUAL OUTPUT: >20,000 hl.

REGULAR BEERS:

Poutník světlé výčepní pivo 10° (3.8%)
The brewery's light golden lager.

Poutník světlý ležák premium (5%: ★★★)
Clear gold with a solid malt body and a balanced bitter finish.

Poutník Speciál 14° (5.8%: ★★★★)
Clear gold, this special lager has extremely light carbonation, a rich malt body and notes of stone fruit in the mouth.

VELKÉ MEZIŘÍČÍ

Jelínkova Vila/ Malostránský pivovar

Třebíčska 342/10
Velké Meziříčí
T 566 502 205
E hotel@jelinkovavila.cz
www.jelinkovavila.cz

One of the area's nicest hotels for the price, the Jelínkova Vila boasts the added bonus of a very good brewpub downstairs, which serves three great lagers and a large number of fresh fish, including tench, eel, trout, catfish, carp, pike and zander. Though the town itself has the requisite chateau, town gate, towers, synagogue and churches, the main destination seems to be Jelínkova Vila's terrace overlooking the river, where locals gather to visit and sample the excellent *pivo*. Brewing takes place in the pub's two large showpiece kettles, with lagering of up to 70 days. All beers here are unpasteurised and unfiltered. The deserving winner of SPP's award for the Best Small Brewery of 2006.

ANNUAL OUTPUT: 1,000 hl.

REGULAR BEERS:
Světlý ležák (5.2%: ★★★★/★)
Cloudy deep gold with a thick-set white foam and a honey-like sweet-sour finish.
Tmavý ležák (5.2%: ★★★★/★)
Almost black, with excellent cold-coffee taste and aroma.
Speciál 14⁰ (6%: ★★★★)
Deep amber with thick light foam and a sugary, candy-like rush in the mouth and slightly more apparent alcohol.

ŽELIV

Klášterní pivovar Želiv

Želiv 1
T 565 581 074
E info@pivovar.zeliv.cz
www.pivovar.zeliv.cz

Talk about a rare bird: the three-year-old Želiv Monastery Brewery makes its beer at an ancient Premonstratensian (Norbertine) monastery, founded here in 1139, and the monks today take part in the production, making the beers roughly akin to Trappist ales. In fact, they are all modelled on Belgian ales, made with top-fermenting yeast, a rarity in the Czech Republic. All are bottle-conditioned and all are named after notable abbots and monks. The monastery is just a few minutes south of the main motorway between Prague and Brno, not far from Humpolec, and is easily accessible by car on a day trip from Prague. Rooms for overnight accommodation are also available at modest prices, though the lodging facilities closed temporarily for reconstruction in mid-2006. Tours of the brewery are available with advance notice.

ANNUAL OUTPUT: <20,000 hl.

REGULAR BEERS:
Siard Falco (5.2%: ★★★/★)
A cloudy amber ale with significant yeast sediment in the bottle and a mild sour-cherry flavour from added extract.
Gottschalk (6.5%: ★★★/★)
An amber Belgian-style ale with a sweet body and no measurable carbonation. A slightly sour finish.
Castulus (6.5%: ★★★)
Made with an adjunct of mead, this deep amber ale has a significant honey note.

South Moravia
Jihomoravský Kraj

POPULATION: **1,170,897**
REGIONAL CAPITAL: **Brno** (366,661)
www.kr-jihomoravsky.cz

SOUTH MORAVIA IS wine country, sitting directly across the border from and on the same *terroir* as some of the best Austrian Rieslings and Grüner Veltliners. Most visitors coming here are up for wine tastings in Mikulov, Velké Pavlovice and Valtice, whose English-style Baroque gardens earned a listing on the UNESCO World Heritage list. Despite the víno, South Moravia remains a great destination for beer lovers as well, home to excellent small brewpubs with a wide variety of styles, as well as one remarkable independent brewer, and two massive factories from international concerns.

Getting to the regional capital Brno by car is a straight run down the E50/E65 motorway from Prague, which should take about four hours in a 20-year-old Škoda 120L running on three cylinders, or slightly faster if you feel the need to travel in a more expensive vehicle. Many direct bus and train connections also link the two largest Czech cities. Currently, Ryanair flies to Brno's Tuřany airport from Stansted, Czech Airlines ties the city to Prague, and Cirrus Airlines has daily connections between Brno and Munich. It can also be reached within two hours on the E461 motorway from Vienna, or roughly the same amount of time from Bratislava on the E65. Both of the neighbouring capitals have frequent bus and rail connections to Brno, making a day trip or weekend quite

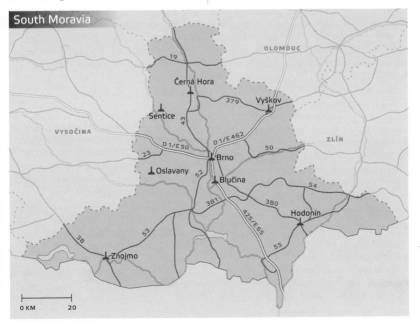

feasible. To get around to outlying areas (and breweries) of the region, however, you will need a car.

Despite the great variety of beers available, a trip to South Moravia doesn't have to be all about brewing. Brno itself is a haven for Functionalist architecture, as the International Modern is termed here, with examples like Bohuslav Fuchs' stunning Zemanova Kavárna and Hotel Avion backing up the high shrine of Modernism in the Czech lands, Mies van der Rohe's Villa Tugendhat, another UNESCO World Heritage site (and worth a tour every time you return to Brno).

BLUČINA

Pivovar Xaver

Měnínská 74
664 56 Blučina
T 547 235 075
E stravas@volny.cz

About a half hour south of Brno by car, the village of Blučina is home to this unique brewery scarcely larger than many homebrewing operations. Owner Svatopluk Strava expresses disdain for weak and sweet beers, aiming instead to produce bitter lagers using a remarkable 19–20 kg (42–44 lbs) of malt per hectolitre, while larger breweries often get by with just 17 kg (37 lbs). The brewery's standard Pilsner-style beer is rarely made. Xaver's special beers lager for 80–90 days and are both made with an adjunct of herbs and spices directly added to the wort, rather than an adjunct of flavouring syrup after brewing. Brewing is done off-site, meaning tours are not available, though the restaurant does have modest lodging facilities.

ANNUAL OUTPUT: <250 hl.

REGULAR BEERS:
Xaver Original (5%)
 A rarely made 12° Pilsner-style lager.
František 15° (5.6%)
 A strong half-dark brewed with just Munich malt and an addition of vanilla.

Oldřich 18° (6.5%: ★★★★/★)
 Cloudy, thick, mud-coloured beer brewed with Munich, caramel and dark malt, as well as cardamom. Slight cardamom nose and malt body with a bitter herbal note and a slight, pleasant sourness to the finish.

BRNO

Pegas Hotel and Microbrewery

Jakubská 4
602 00 Brno
T 542 210 104
E hotelpegas@hotelpegas.cz
www.hotelpegas.cz

Brno's best choice for beer and lodging, in that order, is the Pegas hotel and micro-brewery. They serve big crowds nightly, so be sure to make reservations. The crowds are certainly not drawn in by the dinner menu (a standard selection of roast pork and grilled chicken which is merely okay), but rather by the great beers, including one of the country's best wheat brews. It's right in the middle of Brno's pedestrian Old Town, not far from the opera, making this an ideal base for exploring a very interesting second city, with the notorious Baroque prison fortress of Špilberk Castle and the Cathedral of St. Peter and Paul among its principal attractions.

ANNUAL OUTPUT: >1,000 hl.

REGULAR BEERS:
Světlý ležák kvasnicový (5%: ★★★★/★)
 This cloudy yeast beer has mild citrus and linden-blossom notes. Excellent.
Tmavý ležák kvasnicový (5%: ★★★)
 Clear deep amber, this dark yeast beer has cold coffee notes with a sugary malt finish.
Pšeničné (5%: ★★★★/★)
 With a sugary nose, this wheat beer is a cloudy gold with a thin body and a slightly sour finish.
16° speciál (6.5-7%: ★★★★/★)
 This rusty coloured special lager smells of strawberry compote and has a lush maltiness in the mouth. Well-balanced.

Starobrno (Heineken)

Hlinky 12
661 47 Brno
T 543 516 111
E starobrno@starobrno.cz
www.starobrno.cz

Heineken's main beachhead in the Czech
lands is this historic brewery next door to
Brno's Augustinian Abbey of St Thomas and
the pea garden of Gregor Mendel (1822–84),
father of modern genetics, on the grounds
there. The name, Starobrno, means 'Old
Brno', but many Czechs prefer the nickname
of Starobláto, or 'Old Mud', although that
might be unfair as the beer seems to have
improved in recent years. A recent facelift of
the premises cleared away the old dirt and
smoke, resulting in a very pleasant pub, café
and restaurant on-site. Locals lament the
changes, though, and it doesn't help matters
that the upper level of the restaurant is a
dedicated Heineken bar: yet again, a foreign
company foisting an inferior, mass-produced
Pilsner-style lager upon the country which
invented Pilsner. Thank God, that hardly
looks set to catch on. On the Guide's visit,
the Heineken bar was distinctly empty. The
on-site pub also serves **Starobrno kvasnicové**
(★★/★), but it's hardly worth seeking out.

ANNUAL OUTPUT: >100,000 hl.

REGULAR BEERS:
Osma (3.2%)
  Low-alcohol, low-gravity lager.
Černé (3.8%: ★★★)
  *Clear dark amber and thick tan head. Relatively
  flat with notes of coffee and residual sugar.*
Tradiční (4%)
  Traditional 10° Czech golden lager.
Řezák (4%)
  A half-dark lager.
Medium (4.5%: ★/★)
  *A watery Eurolager with a chemical finish.
  Better than Radegast.*
Ležák (5%: ★★)
  *Clear gold with flat carbonation and an
  unpleasant 'factory' taste.*
Black Drak (5.5%: ★★★)
  *Clear dark amber with light carbonation and
  molasses-coffee notes, the 'Black Dragon' beer
  is only available in bottles.*

Baron Trenck (6%: ★★★/★)
  *Clear gold with a lacy head, flat body and
  well-incorporated alcohol for a strong beer.
  A slightly sugary finish.*
Červený Drak (6%: ★★)
  *Ruby-red and clear, the 'Red Dragon' lager
  has a candy-sugar body with vague medicinal
  tastes in the finish. Brewed at 15° Balling.
  Only available in 0.3-litre bottles.*

U Richarda

Ríšova 12
641 00 Brno-Žebětín
T 546 217 715
E info@ekoprodukt.cz

The Brno suburb of Žebětín still feels like the small village it once was, and the cosiest place for a cold one here is the brewpub and restaurant U Richarda, opened in mid-2004. Inside is a cheery room and bar with three craft lagers, including the country's best sour-cherry beer, along with full lunch and dinner menus. Special beers are occasionally prepared for the holidays, including a half-dark, 16° lager brewed with an adjunct of honey.

ANNUAL OUTPUT: <1,000 hl.

REGULAR BEERS:
Světlé kvasnicové (5%: ★★★★)
  Relatively clear gold, slightly thin body with an even-balanced bittersweet finish.
Višňové (5%: ★★★/★)
  Reddish-gold, this sour-cherry beer has a uniquely non-medicinal taste. Served with preserved sour cherries in the bottom of the glass.
Pšeničné (5%: ★★★★)
  A wheat beer with an usual complexity to the nose and a nice sour finish.

ČERNÁ HORA

Pivovar Černá Hora

Černá Hora 3/5
679 21 Černá Hora
T 516 482 411
E pivovarch@pivovarch.cz
www.pivovarch.cz

Straight up the E461 motorway about an hour north of Brno, this remarkable bottler practically overwhelms the village of Černá Hora, or 'Black Mountain'. Sitting right in the middle of the main road into town, the brewery maintains a significantly large production and is found on draught even as far away as Prague. In addition to its very good beers, the brewery also produces a large amount of soft drinks, including one made from malt, Grena (★★★/★). Tours of the premises are available, and the facilities here include a restaurant, beer hall, 24-hour bottle store, outdoor dining and drinking areas and the brewery's own bowling alley. Fun. Černá Hora itself and surroundings are regarded as the Czech Republic's second best skiing areas.

ANNUAL OUTPUT: >100,000 hl.

REGULAR BEERS:
Tas (4%)
  A 10° golden lager, available both on draught and in bottles.
Moravské sklepní nefiltrované (4%: ★★★★)
  An unfiltered 10° lager: cloudy gold with a thin body and a lingering malt-sugar finish. Only on draught.
Kern (4%: ★★★/★)
  This half-dark lager is a light amber with a malty nose and a thin malt body with a refreshingly crisp finish.
Páter (4.6%: ★★★)
  Clear gold, this 11° lager has a rich malt body and strong bitter finish.
Ležák (4.8%: ★★★★)
  Deep gold with big malt flavour and a hint of vanilla in the mouth.

Granát (4.8%: ★★★)

Clear dark amber with a caramel head, a nose of malt and plum with a plum compote flavour followed by a sugary finish.

Black Hill (5.5%: ★★★/★)

This clear amber lager has very moderate carbonation and would be an excellent pairing with game and other hearty Central European recipes. It is brewed with herbal extracts and has distinct spicy notes and a pronounced bitter finish. Only sold in bottles.

Kvasar (5.7%: ★★★/★)

This 14°, brewed with honey, is inspired by the Kvasar brewery in Sentice. Clear deep gold with a thick, long-lasting head and slightly unbalanced alcohol.

1530 (6.3%: ★★★/★)

First brewed in 2006, this 15.30° golden special has a thick micro-foam head that settles to a loose cream. Low carbonation and a fruity nose with a moderate malt body and a dry finish. In bottles only.

HODONÍN

Kunc

Národní třída 10
695 01 Hodonín
T 518 343 446

Call it a paradox: Hodonín isn't the most happening city in the republic by any means, but *minipivovar* Kunc is the most happening place in all of Hodonín. On any given night you'll find a fleet of customers of all ages dropping by here for food, cigarettes and rambling conversations, as well as the 'the beers of our fathers'. (Apparently, our fathers drank ginger-flavoured lagers.) Bustling indoors and out, with a nice non-smoking section for people who actually want to taste what they're eating and drinking.

ANNUAL OUTPUT: <1,000 hl.

REGULAR BEERS:
Zázvorové pivo (4%: ★★)
   Ginger beer, deep gold with a clear ginger nose followed by a sharply bitter finish. To be honest, it's kind of yucky.
Světlý ležák (4%: ★★★)
   Cloudy, deep gold with a sharp malt nose and a pleasantly bitter finish.
Tmavé pivo (4.5%: ★★★)
   This dark beer is a clear, deep amber of almost black with a cream head and a coffee nose.

Budvarka Hodonín

Měšťanská 10, 695 00 Hodonín
T 518 340 324
www.budvarka-hodonin.cz
BEER: **Budějovický Budvar**

In this part of South Moravia, the Kunc brewpub is the major attraction for beer lovers. But Kunc has no hotel. Enter the local branch of the Budvarka chain, which offers modest doubles starting at less than £20. Did we forget to mention that there's a pub attached, one of the few in the country to serve *kroužkovaný ležák*, the South Bohemian take on yeast beer? Good meals, lots of room and a pleasant beer garden in the back too.

OSLAVANY

Zámecký Pivovar Oslavany

Zámek 1
664 12 Oslavany
T 546 418 900
E tomeking@quick.cz
www.zamek-oslavany.com

This tiny brewery-cum-restaurant-cum-print-shop-cum-fitness-centre hides out in the old Oslavany castle, about 30 km (17 miles) to the southwest of Brno. Finding it is easy: just keep the windows open and follow the scent of rich malt and bitter hops. If you get lost, ask for the *zámek*, or castle, or listen for the sighs of extremely contented lager-lovers.

ANNUAL OUTPUT: <1,000 hl.

REGULAR BEERS:
10⁰ (4.2%: ★★★★★)
   A cloudy gold with a bready, yeasty nose. In the mouth: sweetness followed by a burst of sour and a bitter finish.
12⁰ (4.9%: ★★★★★)
   Malt and yeast in the nose, followed by a spicy, skunky hop taste and a lasting bitter finish.
13⁰ (5.4%: ★★★★/★)
   Deep amber and slightly cloudy with a caramel nose. A sweet malt rush in the mouth, followed by a long, dry finish.

SENTICE

Kvasar

Sentice 13
Sentice u Tišnova
T 549 416 117
E kvasar.pivo@tiscali.cz
www.kvasar.vyrobce.cz

This tiny home-brewer/micro-brewer should hand out awards of merit (and free bottles) for customers who can actually find the place, as the village of Sentice uses the medieval technology of house numbers rather than street addresses. (It's less a question of location than it is a sense of chronological order: generally, the lower the number, the older the house.) Our suggestion? Once you get to Sentice, just south of the town of Tišnov to the northwest of the city of Brno, head uphill (west?) until it smells of honey (a principal ingredient in all of Kvasar's brews), at which point you should turn right (which is to the north, or perhaps east, or maybe south). There is no pub, and beers are only available to take away in plastic 1.5-litre bottles. If you do make it, buy as many as you can carry, especially of the delicious XV, a 15° light lager with a remarkable honey flavour.

ANNUAL OUTPUT: <1,000 hl.

REGULAR BEERS:

Výčepní světlé pivo X (3.8%: ★★★★/★)
Cloudy gold with a white head. Some sediment in the bottle. A burst of honey in the mouth followed by a sweet finish.

Světlý ležák XII (4.8%: ★★★★)
Thick white head, cloudy gold colour with a yeasty nose. In the mouth: even, fine carbonation, a rich body and a slightly bitter finish.

Speciální tmavé pivo XIII (5.1%: ★★★★)
Dark amber in colour, a caramel-sweet body with a slightly bittersweet finish.

Speciální světlé pivo XV (6%: ★★★★/★)
This deep gold special lager has extremely fine carbonation, a smooth malt body and a pronounced honey finish.

VYŠKOV

Pivovar Vyškov

Čsl. armády 116/4
682 01 Vyškov
T 517 326 411
E info@pivovyskov.cz
www.pivovyskov.cz

Right in the centre of the walled town of
Vyškov, this large bottling brewery has a
popular old-style (read: smoky and grimy)
beer hall on-site, where only the Džbán
and Řezák are available on draught. It is
absolutely worth a trip, if only to stock up on
the excellent Jubiler, perhaps the country's
best strong lager. However, the standard
line can be found throughout the region.

ANNUAL OUTPUT: <100,000 hl.

REGULAR BEERS:
Atlet (3.3%)
  *A golden, low-alcohol beer brewed at a very low
  original gravity.*

144

Desítka (4.2%)
A 10° golden lager.

Řezák (4.5%: ★★★/★)
*A half-dark 11° of clear light amber with a
malty nose and molasses flavours,
an excellent accompaniment for food.*

Havran (4.5%: ★★★)
*Brewed at 11°, a dark lager with good
chocolate and malt notes, somewhat
hindered by an artificially sweet finish.*

Džbán (4.7%: ★★★)
*A Pilsner-style lager: clear yellow with a
chemically white head, thin sweet body
and short finish.*

Bira (4.7%)
*A standard Pilsner-style lager produced
for the low-price market.*

Exportní (5%)
*A golden lager produced for the American
market, brewed at 12° Balling and lagered for
60 days.*

Březňák (5.2%: ★★★/★)
*Clear gold with a light body and a refreshingly
grassy hop finish.*

Generál (6%: ★★★★/★)
*Brewed at 14°, this golden special has a rich
maltiness and a pronounced, Saaz-hop bitter
finish.*

Jubiler (7.5%: ★★★★/★)
*Brewed at 16.8o Balling in memory of the year
of the brewery's founding. Clear deep gold with
a loose, lacy head, solid malt body and a mild,
German Märzen-like, sugary malt finish.*

ZNOJMO

Hostan (Heineken)

Hradní 2
669 28 Znojmo
T 515 226 651
E info@hostan.cz
www.hostan.cz

Heineken's second outpost in Moravia is
the low-budget Hostan, way out in Znojmo,
a town more famous for its pickles than its
beer. These high-volume brews are common-
place in Southern Moravia, though you'd
be better off looking for something else.
In a show of remarkable cheek, the brewery
renamed its 10° lager 'Naše Pivko',
the same name as a well-known beer award.
Avoidable.

ANNUAL OUTPUT: >100,000 hl.

REGULAR BEERS:
Hostan Naše Pivko (4%)
A low-gravity Eurobrew.

Hostan Hradní (4.7%)
A standard Pilsner-style lager.

Hostan Zámecké (5.6%)
A golden special lager.

Zlín Region
Zlínský Kraj

POPULATION: **595,010**
REGIONAL CAPITAL: **Zlín** (78,599)
www.kr-zlinsky.cz

ONCE FAMOUS FOR ITS SHOES – as in the international footwear chain Baťa, founded in the capital of Zlín in 1894 – Zlínský kraj is just one short step away from the wine region of South Moravia. Perhaps it is because of that oenological association, that it is tied with Karlovarský kraj as the region with the fewest breweries: four, including just one bottler, Janáček, of a medium size. The area is easy to reach from Brno, continuing by car on the E462 and 47, a route which will take you straight to the beautiful medieval town of Kroměříž, whose Archbishop's castle and sculpted gardens constitute yet another UNESCO World Heritage site. The capital Zlín itself is known for its urban architecture, exemplifying the principles of the Garden City (by Ebenezer Howard) and functional urban modernity (by Le Corbusier), much of it constructed by Tomáš Baťa (1876–1932) in the interwar years.

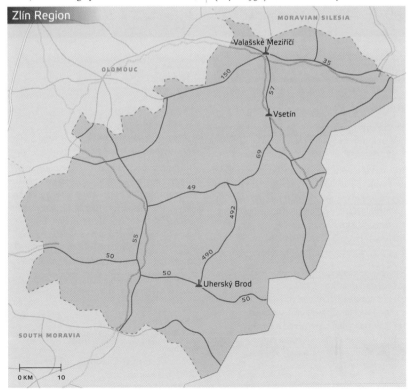

Zlín Region

MORAVIAN SILESIA

Valašské Meziříčí

OLOMOUC

150

35

57

Vsetín

69

49

492

55

50

490

50

Uherský Brod

50

SOUTH MORAVIA

0 KM   10

UHERSKÝ BROD

Balkán

Na dlouhých 218
688 01 Uherský Brod
T 572 637 658

This modest restaurant and micro-brewery overlooks a park just on the other side of the city centre from the motorway. Fried chicken schnitzel (řízek) and pork with dumplings are as good as it gets on the food menu. Fortunately, the beers are a bit better.

ANNUAL OUTPUT: <1,000 hl.

REGULAR BEERS:
10⁰ Havran desítka (★★★)
   A clear gold with very light carbonation and a bitter finish in the Budvar mould.
12⁰ Havran kvasnicové pivo (★★★/★)
   An opaque gold with almost no visible carbonation and a malty body which turns thin in the finish.

Janáček

Neradice 369
688 16 Uherský Brod
T 572 632 461
E info@pivovar-janacek.cz
www.pivovar-janacek.cz

This largish bottler is just off the main road entrance to Uherský Brod. There is no pub on site, but there's a bottle shop where you can pick up the classics, which is a strange way to describe their 'Beerberry', a new-fangled beer-pop made with berries, spices, lemon and cola. (What on earth did they leave out?) Unfortunately (fortunately?) Janáček beers are rarely seen outside of the region.

ANNUAL OUTPUT: <100,000 hl.

REGULAR BEERS:
Janáček Olšavan (3.7%)
   A golden lager with a pronounced bitter finish.
Beerberry (3.9%)
   A bottled beverage flavoured with blueberries, ginger, lemon and cola.

Janáček Prima (4.0%)
A second golden lager with more malt.

Janáček světlé kvasnicové pivo (4%)
A golden yeast beer, available in bottles as well as on draught.

Janáček tmavé výčepní (4.1%)
The brewery's dark lager.

Janáček Patriot (4.6%)
Yet another golden lager.

Janáček Extra (5%: ★★★/★)
The brewery's premium brew: clear deep gold with a fluffy white cloud for a head. A malty nose and supple body followed by a smooth, lasting finish.

Comenius Speciál (6%: ★★/★)
A golden special lager. In the mouth, stiff, as if it were made out of cardboard, and somewhat unbalanced. Said to improve with age.

VALAŠSKÉ MEZIŘÍČÍ

Bon

Žerotínova 20
757 01 Valašské Meziříčí
T 571 613 486
E info@pivovarbon.cz
www.pivovarbon.cz

This is the real David vs Goliath: a small maker of high-grade lagers trying to find distribution in a land dominated by giants, including those giants which are national property. This tiny brewery has no pub on site, nor any visitors' centre. Only some addresses in the Olomouc region seem to carry it.

ANNUAL OUTPUT: 20,000 hl.

REGULAR BEERS:
Bon světlá desítka (4%: ★★★★)
A pale gold 10° with a sweet taste of pear cider. Unusual.

Bon světlá dvanactka (4.2%: ★★★★)
Deep gold with a loose head and a sweet fruit-cocktail finish.

Bon tmavá čtrnactka (5.2%: ★★★/★)
A clear dark amber with a thick caramel head and the scent of strawberry jam. In the mouth, a sour-sweet cola note.

VSETÍN

Valášek

Dolní Jasenka 169
755 01 Vsetín
T 571 459 170
E provozni@minipivovar.com
www.minipivovar.com

Not far from the Slovak and Austrian borders, this wood-panelled brewpub in the Dolní Jasenka area, just north of Vsetín's centre, serves hearty, inexpensive meals. (At the time of writing, the weekday lunch specials even included a free small beer.) The best natural reserves in the Beskydy mountains are just minutes from the bar.

ANNUAL OUTPUT: <1,000 hl.

REGULAR BEERS:
Světlý ležák (4.8%: ★★★/★)
A slightly cloudy deep gold yeast lager with a loose, long-lasting head and an apple-juice nose. A surprisingly bitter finish.

Tmavý ležák (4.7%: ★★★)
A clear deep amber with little carbonation, a thin body and a distinct, ginger-ale flavour.

Olomouc Region
Olomoucký Kraj

POPULATION: **635,126**
REGIONAL CAPITAL: **Olomouc** (224,296)
www.kr-olomoucky.cz

OTHER FAMOUS CZECH BEER regions are household names: everyone knows Plzeň (Pilsen), České Budějovice (Budweis) and Žatec (Saaz). And yet the Haná valley of the Olomouc region remains uncelebrated, despite being the ancestral home of some of the world's best two-row barley and the source of the most desirous Moravian malt today. But there are other aspects of Olomoucký kraj to celebrate: the Jeseníky and Orlické mountain ranges, an incredibly stinky cheese (Olomoucké tvarůžky) and amazing sights such as the Column of the Holy Trinity, included on the UNESCO World Heritage list.

Getting here from Prague is easy, arriving directly by car on the E462 via Brno, although it's worth noting that the roads here are small, which suits the slowed-down pace of the region. Regular direct buses and trains also connect Prague to Olomouc, including the new, high-speed Pendolino, which entered service in December 2005, and which completes the 250-km (155-mile) trek in just 2 hours 25 minutes. With a return Pendolino leaving Olomouc at 10:49 pm, a day trip is entirely possible.

HANUŠOVICE

Holba

Pivovarská 261
788 33 Hanušovice
T 583 300 900
E pivovarholba@holba.cz
www.holba.cz

Up in the far north of Olomoucký kraj, this massive factory brewer sits in a depressing town that reminds local visitors of the dismally grey 1980s. The surrounding valley contains elements of real beauty, however, with soaring mountains and verdant forests that belie the area's Communist-era industrial exploitation. Though the drive here might be enjoyable, the Holba brewery has no pub on site, and its large-volume beers are not the real treasures of the region. For determined visitors, tours are available with advance reservation.

ANNUAL OUTPUT: >100,000 hl.

REGULAR BEERS:
Classic 10° (4.2%: ★★/★)
Clear gold, slightly gassy. Thin malt, but nice hoppy notes in the finish.
Holba Šerák 11° (4.7%: ★★★)
Slightly more malt than a German Pils, though less than the Czech standard.
Premium 12° (5.2%: ★★/★)
Gassy lager with just a touch too much alcohol in the mouth.

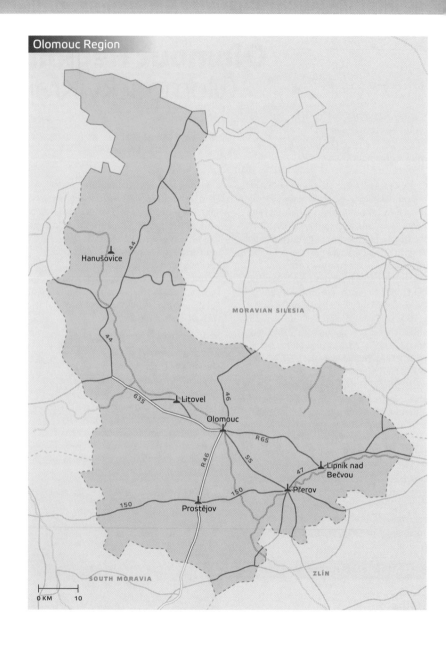

Olomouc Region

Hanušovice

MORAVIAN SILESIA

Litovel

Olomouc

Lipník nad
Bečvou

Přerov

Prostějov

SOUTH MORAVIA

ZLÍN

0 KM   10

LIPNÍK NAD BEČVOU

První soukromý pivovar společenský v Lipníku nad Bečvou

28 října 20/6
751 31 Lipník nad Bečvou
T 581 773 798
E radeksekanina@seznam.cz
E pavlikadamek@seznam.cz

What a surprise: this bustling village, with its share of historic buildings and Baroque fountains, to the northeast of industrial Přerov, has its own micro-brewery – micro as in truly tiny – right off the main square. Though the 'First Private Social Brewery in Lipník nad Bečvou', as the unwieldy name translates, makes just 100 hectolitres annually, it brews them all very well indeed. Just one type of yeast beer is available, served only in this tiny sports bar with just a handful of seats.

ANNUAL OUTPUT: <250 hl.

REGULAR BEERS:
11⁰ Lipnický ležák (4.8: ★★★★/★)
An unfiltered, cloudy orange-yellow brew with a light body and a sweet, melon-scented finish. Remarkable.

LITOVEL

Pivovar Litovel

Palackého 934
784 01 Litovel
T 585 493 111
E pivo@litovel.cz
www.litovel.cz

A sizeable factory brewer that manages to make a couple of very good beers, Litovel sits right on the main road into town from the E442 motorway. A friendly pub and beer garden greet visitors with a flowing fountain constructed from an old pony keg and a can of Litovel beer. It's an attractive place to sample the brewery's excellent yeast beer, or try the Maestro, one of the best of the mixed-gas breeds. The main sights in town are the Plague Column, dating from 1724, and the Czech Republic's third-oldest stone bridge, the 1592 Bridge of St John, crossing the Morava River. There is also a museum displaying costumes and embroidery from the Haná Valley.

ANNUAL OUTPUT: >100,000 hl.

REGULAR BEERS:
Dark (3.8%: ★★★)
This dark lager has a loose chalk head and a typical cold coffee taste with a sour finish.
Maestro (4.1%: ★★★★)
An excellent deep-gold mixed-gas beer with a creamy, long-lasting head and rich malt body.
Classic (4.3%)
A clear golden lager, roughly equivalent to 10⁰.

153

Kvasnicové pivo (4.8%: ★★★★)

An excellent yeast beer for a big brewer, with stewed stone fruit in the nose and an aftertaste of pure Saaz hops.

Moravan (4.8%: ★★/★)

An unfortunately bland Pilsner-style lager with fine carbonation and bitter finish.

OLOMOUC

Svatováclavský pivovar

Riegrova 22

779 00 Olomouc

☎ 585 203 641

Just steps from the main square of Olomouc and its attendant Column of the Holy Trinity (a UNESCO World Heritage Site dating from 1754), this new brewpub opened in mid-2006 to rave reviews. Multi-level and spacious, with rather good pub food to match the fine beers, Svatováclavsky pivovar has a capacity of up to 1,000 litres (2,113 pints) daily, though both the annual output and the alcoholic capacity of their beers remain unmeasured. A university town with an exceptionally rich cultural heritage, Olomouc is worth a trip in its own right. The stylish 'St Wenceslas Brewery' is situated in the historical centre of the city, near the Town Hall. A second brewpub, Moritz (see Future Breweries, page TK), recently appeared in the basement of a burgher home, not far from the Theresian Gate.

ANNUAL OUTPUT: NA

REGULAR BEERS:

Vašek 10⁰ (★★★/★)
Slightly cloudy with a thick white head and a thin body.

Svatováclavské 12⁰ (★★★★)
A relatively clear deep gold with a creamy malt body and a lasting sour-sweet finish.

Černé pivo 13⁰ (★★★/★)
Almost black, this dark lager has fine coffee flavours with a vanilla note in the finish.

Weißbier/pšeničné 13⁰ (★★★★)
Opaque with a beautifully thick-set head, this wheat beer has a slight banana note and a peppery Saaz finish.

PROSTĚJOV

U Krále Ječmínka

Újezd 4a
796 01 Prostějov
T 582 346 401
E marlon@seznam.cz

Truly legendary, the eight-year-old 'At the Barley King' celebrates the great grain right in the heart of the Haná valley. A brewpub with four stellar standard beers, U Krále Ječmínka also makes a series of beloved seasonal brews at Christmas, Easter and throughout the year. It's not terribly hard to find, located just to the east of the old town, a few steps from the Hotel Avion and the city theatre. You'd like to think it was all up to the lager, but the outstanding roast pork knuckle (*koleno*) and bustling atmosphere both mean that reservations here are highly recommended. SPP Micro-brewery of the Year for 2004.

ANNUAL OUTPUT: <1,000 hl.

REGULAR BEERS:

10⁰ (4.2%: ★★★★)
Light, clear gold with a bittersweet finish. A great summer quencher.

12⁰ ječmenný ležák (4.8%: ★★★/★)
A head like half-melted ice cream tops this very good, Pilsner-style lager.

13⁰ tmavé pivo (5.9%: ★★★★/★)
Clear dark amber with fine, Champagne-like carbonation and a sweet vanilla finish.

13⁰ Weißbier (5.8%: ★★★★)
This wheat beer is cloudy gold with a loose white head, sharp clove scent and a lovely spicy backbite.

PŘEROV

Zubr

Komenského 35
751 52 Přerov
T 581 270 111
E zubr@zubr.cz
www.zubr.cz

A big, industrial brewer in a big, industrial town, Zubr ('Bison') comes in last among the marques of the Litovel group. There are no tours available, but there is a nice restaurant on site, with several pleasant, wood-furnished rooms right next to the brewery's main entrance. They once served a yeast beer here, but it wasn't stocked on the Guide's visit, and our waitress added that it didn't sell particularly well. Worth seeing in Přerov, on Hradisko Hill, is an archaeological site dating back to the early Stone Age.

ANNUAL OUTPUT: >100,000 hl.

REGULAR BEERS:

Classic 10⁰ light (4.1%)
Zubr's basic Pilsner-style beer.

Classic 10⁰ dark (4.1%: ★★/★)
Deep clear amber with a thick head and a fizzy drink-like malt body.

Zubr Gold 11⁰ (4.6%: ★/★)
Thin, character-free, international lager with a slightly hoppy finish.

Zubr Premium 12⁰ (5.1%: ★★)
Slightly more malt in the body, though no real flavour. Harmless.

Moravian Silesia
Moravskoslezký Kraj

POPULATION: **1,255,910**
REGIONAL CAPITAL: **Ostrava** (312,254)
www.kr-moravskoslezsky.cz

THE EXTREME EASTERN END of the country is, naturally enough, the hardest to reach for most travellers coming from the west – a trip from Prague will take several hours by car, bus or train, and the only direct international flights currently landing in Ostrava, its regional capital, arrive from nearby Vienna. Thus, Moravian Silesia is not a day-trip destination, but rather a place to wander around, preferably by car, over a long weekend or even several weeks. The area is home to great natural beauty, including the lush Beskydy and Jeseníky mountain ranges, making it a rich resource for summer and winter outdoor

sports, as well as plenty of photogenic villages, churches, mills and farms. The wildlife is spectacular and includes golden eagles, lynxes, wolves and possibly even bears.

The three major breweries in Opava (Zlatovar), Ostrava (Ostravar) and Frýdek-Místek's neighbouring village of Nošovice (Radegast) are, unsurprisingly, the least interesting; lacking restaurants and visitor centres, Radegast and Ostravar can be dismissed completely, and Zlatovar seemingly exists in name only, though there is a restaurant on site. The first four to target are in the tight cluster of Příbor, Kopřivnice, Hukvaldy and

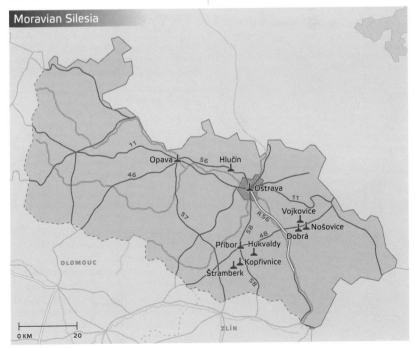

Moravian Silesia

157

lovely Štramberk, which also has a bakery and small hotel. In case you need to work up a thirst, this is excellent mountain-biking territory as well.

DOBRÁ

Arthur's

Na Sýpce restaurant
Dobrá 883
739 54 Frýdek-Místek
T 558 641 254
E kwaczkova@quick.cz
www.nasypce.cz

Arthur's Old Keltic Beer, or Arthur's Impossible-to-Find Yeast Beer as it should be called, is brewed and sold at the Na Sýpce restaurant and hotel in Frýdek-Místek's neighbouring village of Dobrá. (That's not a euphemism: the only address, above, is a house number, not a street number, so you will probably have to ask for directions, barring extremely good luck. It's on a nameless lane south of and parallel to the main road coming into town, two blocks north and one block west of the train station, roughly speaking.)

Having said that, it's definitely worth seeking out, especially compared to the noxious swill coming from Radegast just down the road. There is a restaurant and a guesthouse with sauna in the former granary.

ANNUAL OUTPUT: <250 hl.

REGULAR BEERS:
Arthur's Old Keltic Beer (4.5% : ★★★★)
   This kvasnicové pivo is a cloudy amber with a loose white foam and a spicy, pumpkin-pie flavour.

HLUČÍN

Pivovar Avar
(Hlučínský starý pivovar)

Pode zdí 148, 748 01 Hlučín
T 595 042 165

This brewpub closed for repairs in late 2006 and was said to be ready to open again in 2007.

ANNUAL OUTPUT: NA

REGULAR BEERS:
Dérer dark lager (4.3%)
Avar light lager (5.0%)

HUKVALDY

U zastávky

Dolní Sklenov 19
739 46 Hukvaldy
T 558 699 215
E pivovar-hukvaldy@atlas.cz
www.pivovar-hukvaldy.cz

Literally 'at the stop', the pub U zastávky sits at the bus stop in the Dolní Sklenov neighbourhood of Hukvaldy, a town best known as the home of one of the Czech Republic's foremost composers, Leoš Janáček, whose music is featured in a festival here each year. A single room with a billiards table and large portraits of the regulars on the walls, U zastávky makes its own excellent lager, though many drinkers seem to prefer far-cheaper Radegast. That is a grave mistake.

ANNUAL OUTPUT: <1,000 hl.

REGULAR BEERS:

12⁰ Kvasnicové hukvaldské pivo
  (5–5.5%: ★★★★★)
  Cloudy gold with a complex bittersweet note,
  akin to a well-made cocktail.

14⁰ Tmavé hukvaldské pivo (★★★)
  Clear deep amber with a sour-sweet finish.

KOPŘIVNICE

Vulkán

Štramberská 389
742 21 Kopřivnice
T 737 485 498

This mini-brewery without a pub sells its fresh *kvasnicové pivo* through only a few addresses in and around the unlovely, post-industrial town of Kopřivnice, birthplace of the athlete Emil Zátopek. The main venue is the sport and beer bar Žába (meaning 'The Frog', sometimes also known as 'U žáby', or 'At the Frog') on the ground floor of the massive, communist-era Hotel Tatra (Záhumenní 1161; **T** 556 821 405). The beer, called Vulkán, is perhaps the only reason to seek the town out, and certainly something you'll have to hunt for once you're here.

ANNUAL OUTPUT: <1,000 hl.

REGULAR BEERS:
Vulkán 12⁰ (4.9%: ★★★★/★)
  Slightly cloudy gold with mild carbonation and a bitter-sour-sweet combination reminiscent of fresh grapefruit.

NOŠOVICE

Radegast (SAB-Miller)

739 51 Nošovice
T 558 602 111
E info@radegast.cz
www.radegast.cz

The fourth Czech brand from SAB-Miller finishes dead last, after Pilsner Urquell, Kozel and (way back) Gambrinus. Looking like it comes straight out of a Communist Central Committee planning meeting, the brewery sells bottles, kegs and paraphernalia on site, but there is no pub, nor any restaurant. No matter: in Moravskoslezký kraj, you can't swing a dead cat without hitting a pub that serves Radegast. So much the worse.

ANNUAL OUTPUT: >1,000,000 hl.

REGULAR BEERS:
Klasik (3.6%: ★)
  As close as Czech beer gets to American Budweiser.
Radegast Originál (4%)
  A standard golden lager, roughly equivalent to a 10⁰.
Radegast Premium 12⁰ (5%: ★★)
  An unpleasant, boring factory lager.

Zlatovar's brewery restaurant, still going strong.

OPAVA

Zlatovar

Pivovarská 6
746 01 Opava
T 553 606 111
E info@zlatovar.cz
www.zlatovar.cz

Technically speaking, is this still a brewery? It certainly once was, at least until a mysterious closure a few years back. Today it looks like a brewery, sits on 'Brewery Street' and has a brewery restaurant on site. Nonetheless, at the time of writing Opava's beers are apparently being made under contract by Litovel, which, by all accounts, doesn't seem to hurt matters much. Management refuses to answer questions, let alone accept telephone calls from nosy guidebook writers.

ANNUAL OUTPUT: NA

REGULAR BEERS:

Axman 10⁰ (4%: ★★★/★)
  A light lager with fine carbonation, a loose head and a light body.

11⁰ kvasnicové pivo (4.5%: ★★★★)
  Medium gold, cloudy, with a chalky head and a bread-like, yeasty nose.

Max 11⁰ (4.5%: ★★★)
  Clear gold with very light carbonation, and a full, slick mouth feel.

Premium 12⁰ (5% : ★★★)
  A slightly cloudy deep gold with a white head and light carbonation.

161

OSTRAVA

Ostravar (InBev)

Hornopolní 57
T 596 650 111
www.staropramen.cz

It's a sad sign that Ostravar, way out in the boondocks of Ostrava, makes a better basic 12° lager than what comes from its high-profile sister in the capital, Staropramen, as well as a stout-like dark beer and the group's other curiosity, the mixed-gas Velvet. That's sad for Prague visitors, that is, though people in Ostrava actually have it pretty nice. Although the brewery is one of the biggest businesses around, there's no pub on site. A beer garden across the street serves the freshest Ostravar in town. Ostrava itself has made its coal seams into a tourist sight, yet it is also surprisingly green, with protected lakes and water meadows within its boundaries.

ANNUAL OUTPUT: >100,000 hl.

REGULAR BEERS:
Ostravar Originál 10° (4.3%)
The basic gold lager.
Kelt (4.8%: ★★★)
The domestic take on Irish stout: a chocolate-malt body, though disappointingly thin.
Ostravar Premium 12° (5.1%: ★★★/★)
A thick head atop a well-made factory lager. Clear gold with a slightly acidic orangey finish.
Velvet (5.3%: ★★★/★)
A mixed-gas beer with a so-called 'avalanche effect', a rich malt body and a nice sour bite.
Ostravar Strong (6%)
The brewery's strong special.

PŘÍBOR

Minipivovar Příbor

U Brány 106
742 58 Příbor
T 608 345 508
E lichtenberg@seznam

Just 150 years ago, this town gave birth to one of the world's greatest thinkers. Today, the main square, a bakery and even the local micro-brewery are all named after Sigmund Freud (1856–1939), father of psychoanalysis, though only a few restaurants and bars in the area sell 'Freudovo pivo', the product of a mini-brewery without a pub. (Two options in town at the time of writing: Oáza Vinárna, upstairs at U Brány 106, and the Mexico restaurant just out of town at Frenštátská 166.) Such dearth is a pity, as the *tmavé pivo* is one of the best, though much less a classic dark lager than a stout by another name. As a town, Příbor remains fairly grim, though the tumbledown main square and Freud connection make it worth a stop, if not a trip of its own, with great access to the nearby Beskydy mountains.

ANNUAL OUTPUT: <250 hl.

REGULAR BEERS:
Světlý ležák 12° (5.2%: ★★★★/★)
Deep gold with a thick micro-foam head with a vanilla-cream finish.
Tmavý ležák 13° (5.2%: ★★★★★)
Incredible micro-foam head atop a rich, coffee-and-cream dark beer followed by a sharply sour finish.

ŠTRAMBERK

Městský pivovar

Náměstí 5
742 66 Štramberk
T 556 813 710
E pivo@truba.cz
www.truba.cz

This antique hilltop village just a few miles from Příbor simply has to be seen. Sitting on the restored main square with pretty 18th- and 19th-century timber-framed houses, and under the eye of the massive watchtower (known as the Trúba, or trumpet) and the ruins of Castle Strallenberg, this charming combination of bakery, brewpub and hotel serves plenty of *štramberské uši*, the local ear-shaped ginger waffle biscuit, as well as two great brews befitting such a pretty locale.

ANNUAL OUTPUT: <1,000 hl.

REGULAR BEERS:
Trubač světlý ležák 12⁰ (4.3 %: ★★★★/★)
Clear, deep gold with light carbonation and a thick, long-lasting cream head.
Troobacz tmavý ležák 12⁰ (4.3% : ★★★★★)
This ultra-black dark beer has a cold-coffee nose and aftertaste.

VOJKOVICE

Hostinec u Koníčka

Vojkovice 10
T 558 651 172
www.minipivovarkonicek.cz

This new brewpub near Frýdek-Místek – with a name that means both 'pony' and 'hobby' – opened during the course of writing this Guide. As such, it remains virgin territory: a possible hidden treasure in the country's far east.

ANNUAL OUTPUT: <1,000 hl.

REGULAR BEERS:
Ryzák 11⁰ světlý (4.3%)
Vraník 12⁰ tmavý (4.3%)

Future Breweries

The future is now: the Czech Republic is such a dynamic young country that it is nearly impossible to formulate a definitive list of all breweries without the extensive use of a time machine. Otherwise, the minute you do compose such a list, two new brewpubs open up. Then you make a new list, and a long-struggling bottler finally closes, while a long-shuttered micro reopens. You write another list, and then, somehow, another great new brewpub shows up in the middle of nowhere.

That's bad news for those of us who are pushing the pencils, but very good news for beer lovers, both foreign and domestic. As this book goes to press, we've heard rumours or indications of new breweries in the following locations:

DOMAŽLICE

Pivovar Domažlice

Komenského 10

Ten years after it was shut down by former owner Plzeňský Prazdroj, the Domažlice town brewery is scheduled to reappear in mid-2007 as a 120-bed hotel, conference centre and brewpub. Rumours of the opening have been around for years, but this time it looks like it's going to actually bear fruit.

Before its closure, Domažlice produced an interesting range of beers:

PAST BEERS:
Písař 8⁰ (světlé lehké)
Radní 10⁰ (světlé výčepní)
Purkmistr 10⁰ (tmavé výčepní)
Purkmistr 12⁰ (tmavý ležák)
Prior (světlý pšeničný kvasnicový ležák)

It's unknown how many of these might reappear in the new brewpub, although the traditional dark lagers and an unfiltered, golden 12° are both fairly good bets. However, given the current popularity of wheat beers and the brewery's earlier tradition with Prior, everything but the lightweight Písař seems quite likely.

HRADEC KRÁLOVÉ

U Anténáka

The identity of the 'antenna man' is a complete mystery to us, though we certainly know Petr Hošek's renown as a home-brewer: it was Anteňák who supposedly gave Žamberk its magical recipe for Imperial Stout, which appeared just as the Guide went to press. Now the man, the myth, the legend himself is rumoured to be opening his own brewpub in the former dowry town of Hradec Králové.

LESKOVEC

Slezan

Leskovec (near Opava)

Officially opening in December 2006, the Slezan brewery just to the south of Opava is scheduled to start producing 11°, 12° and 13° beers with an annual production of 480 hectolitres. In the future, it plans to add dark lagers, wheat beers and high-gravity specials. It was inspired in part by the excellent Freudovo pivo from Příbor.

OLOMOUC

Moritz

Nešverova 2   **T** 585 205 560
www.hostinec-moritz.com

The second beautiful brewpub in Olomouc opened just as this book was being finished. On deadline, we took a high-speed Pendolino out from Prague to find that Moritz is the first completely non-smoking brewpub in the country. That alone would be enough to earn attention. Less than a month after opening, Moritz was so crowded on our visit that they were (graciously) turning away dozens of guests. Make reservations now. And pray that they open another location soon.

REGULAR BEERS:
Světlá 11° (★★★★/★)
A cloudy-gold unfiltered beer of moderate carbonation, light maltiness and a perfectly balanced bitter finish.
Světlá 12° (★★★★★)
Deep gold and slightly cloudy with a moderate malt body and a pronounced hop bitterness. Very flat, strangely reminiscent of British bitter. Gorgeous.
Weissbier (★★★★)
Cloudy gold with a thick white head and body which is strangely rich in malt, lacking in a wheat beer's usual clove and banana aromas and light, citrus-scented body.
Černá Tereza 13° (★★★★)
Cloudy deep amber with a good toasty malt taste and rich, slightly creamy finish.

The new brewpub Moritz in Olomouc.

PLZEŇ

Pivovarský dvůr Plzeň

No information at press time, other than the name, the city and the supposed connection to brewery supplier Lukr Ingeneering. (www.lukr.cz).

POLEPY

Svatý Ján

Polepy 232 Kolín **☎** 321 728 155
www.pivovarek.cz

Martin Karaivanov's 'St John' brewery was a well-regarded hobby brewery, but it closed for relocation while we were researching this Guide. In 2007, it was set to reopen in Polepy, a village just to the south of Kolín in Central Bohemia.

PRAGUE

U Zlatého anděla

Celetná 29, Praha 1

A new brewpub scheduled to appear in mid-2007 in the 'Golden Angel', an ancient Old Town inn which once hosted Mozart and the queens of Denmark and Greece, though not all at the same time, we presume. The brewpub has announced that it will serve 'exclusive beer in exclusive surroundings', whatever that means, and visitors will be able to draught their own half-litres from their own taps at their own tables, paying a slightly higher price for the privilege of serving themselves. In an alternative universe, this all somehow makes sense.

Joe's Garage

Táborská, Praha 4
Bottles of outstanding homebrew with the Joe's Garage label started appearing in Prague just as this book went to press. Speculation and hearsay have it that influential home-brewer Josef Krýsl is looking to open his own brewpub in Prague's Nusle neighbourhood sometime in 2007.

SOKOLOV

Permon

After an absence of 50 years, beers from Sokolov in Karlovarský kraj are ready to reappear under the name of Permon, with a new brewery-restaurant located in the town's former Capuchin monastery.

STŘÍBRO

www.extreme-system.cz

With a brewing history dating back to 1197, the town of Stříbro is long overdue for a new brewery. We have no details other than the website and village location, just to the west of Plzeň, and the statement that this is to be a brewpub, not a big bottler. The former brewery here, Brauerei Mies, was closed by the Communists in 1950; the new brewpub is said to be opening in September of 2007.

Bars and Pubs

Introduction

'I suppose that drinking beer in pubs has got a good influence on the behaviour of Czech society, because beer contains less alcohol than, for example, wine, vodka or whisky and therefore people's political chat in pubs is less crazy.' Václav Havel

Mission impossible

The Czech Republic is the homeland of Pilsner-style brewing, and Prague is the country's capital. It is a city of more than one million inhabitants, all of whom drink a remarkable amount of beer themselves, to say nothing of the many tourists coming to Prague for that purpose. There must be hundreds of great destinations for beer lovers there. Or are there?

Here's the catch. In Prague, you are likely to find beer from just three Czech breweries: Pilsner Urquell (and Gambrinus), Staropramen and Budvar. These are the Big Three, owned by SAB-Miller, InBev and the Czech government, respectively. Together they account for the majority of all the beer consumed in the country, and they are all doing their damnedest to increase production.

The Big Three maintain their dominance of the local market through economies of scale, utilising high-volume production, extensive distribution networks and high-impact marketing. It is their distribution and marketing efforts which occasionally get the Big Three in trouble with anti-trust legislation. Thankfully, it is now illegal for brewers to compel pubs to stock their beers and their beers only. However, many people will tell you that these 'exclusivity agreements' have hardly disappeared: instead, they have turned into oral contracts between distributors and publicans, with a sort of carrot-and-stick approach on the part of the distributors. In exchange for exclusively stocking the brewery's beer, a pub owner will be given free beer taps and pipes, free menus, free coasters (printed with his pub's name, opening hours and address), pavement signs, fancy lights, refrigerators or other prizes that will keep him selling 'Beerovar' and 'Beerovar' only. Naturally, smaller producers lack the purchasing power to offer signs and lamps to every pub owner, locking them out of the most desirous markets. And in many cases, it's far more than a sign or a lamp: in one Central Bohemian town, the main pub carried the local beer until its owner was offered 200,000 Kč to switch to one of the Big Three, ending a 125-year local connection for less than £4,800. As another pub owner once told this Guide, 'I would love to stock an independent beer. But the other guys gave me so much money!'

Thus the challenge: in Prague, you will be very hard-pressed to find draught beers from more than 25 breweries (not counting the city's amazing brewpubs, Prague's saving grace). In the tourist-friendly areas of Prague 1 and Prague 2, you'll be lucky to find beers from more than 10 Czech breweries. You will find Pilsner Urquell, Gambrinus, Staropramen and Budvar in spades. But even just six more would make for a very lucky day indeed.

That means that if you want to taste something other than the Big Three, you will have to get out of the centre. Our pubs are arranged geographically, starting in Staré Město (Old Town) and continuing outwards in a roughly clockwise spiral. In all cases, we have done our best to tell you how to get there. From Charles Bridge, none should be more than an hour away on public transport most can be reached within 30 minutes.

For the sake of clarity, we are calling these establishments 'pubs', though of course not all of them are. Some are pubs, while some are cafés. Some are coffeehouses in the great Central European tradition. Some are fine-dining restaurants with fancy tablecloths and snotty waiters. Some are stands selling *pivo* to lazy people waiting for buses, or pretending that they are waiting for buses, or waiting to steal wallets from people who are waiting for buses. When they are gritty, we say they are gritty (and we might just call them 'dirty'). Pubs that are smoky, dark, dingy and dank are generally listed as such.

In all cases, our only criterion for including a pub on this list was the fact that the establishment served good beer. We even included some pubs serving beers from the Big Three, if that beer or that pub had a special attribute, such as Pilsner Urquell's 'tank' pubs, which serve an amazing, unpasteurised Pilsner Urquell not available outside of the Czech Republic.

These are not the only pubs in Prague – far from it. But as we see it, these are the Prague pubs, restaurants and cafés which will be of the most interest to people who love good beer.

A users' manual

Here's the drill: You walk into the pub. In this country, men walk in first – it is considered impolite for gentlemen to open the door and allow ladies to enter before them, a belief which apparently dates back to the days when the air in a typical Czech pub was filled with squadrons of flying glassware. Most people say *Dobrý den* ('Good Day') when they walk into a room filled with people, and pubs are no different. It is considered normal, as if the pub would get its feelings hurt otherwise.

Naturally, there is nowhere to sit. (But if there is a free table, grab it!) Almost none of the addresses in this listing are places where customers should wait until seated. If a table is reserved, it will probably have a sign or a slip of paper saying '*reservé*' or '*zadáno*'. Check for a time, such as 21.30. Your table might be reserved from a point six hours in the future. Generally speaking, this means it's free until then.

Assuming there is no completely free table, look for one which has a few free seats. '*Je tu volno?*' means 'Is this free?', and it is what you should ask as you point to the chairs with a glance of expected confirmation.

You'll probably get a nod of the head and perhaps an adjustment of body language or personal effects away from the desired chairs. This means you can sit down.

A discussion of the nuances of service in Czech pubs would take far more space than this Guide allows and would entitle the writer to a PhD in the field of applied disinterest. You will probably have to wait for several minutes to get noticed. Your server might be slightly disinterested, very disinterested or aggressively disinterested in your well-being. Try to understand that this is part of the job description, and has nothing to do with you, nor with your server, nor with what your server thinks about you. (Your server does not think about you in any way whatsoever.)

This Guide would be leading you astray if it suggested you should try to speak fluent Czech. However, a little effort in this regard will go a very long way. When your server arrives, repeat the phrase '*Dobrý den*'. If this is as much Czech as you can be bothered to learn, learn it. From here on, you can say 'English menu, please?' or '*Pivo, prosím*', or whatever combination of English, Czech and hand puppetry will get you what you think you would like to eat or drink. Pointing at the menu and nodding should work fine. Remember that you are in a landlocked country of just 10 million inhabitants who have no history of dispossessing native peoples in faraway colonies. Unlike the French, most Czechs understand that not everyone in the world speaks their particular form of the Indo-European tongue. Any efforts you make in this regard will be appreciated, no matter how badly you screw it up.

In most pubs, bars and cafés, your bill will be tallied on a little slip of paper your server will place on your table, perhaps under an ashtray. As it arrives, each beer will usually be noted by a single slash mark; small beers usually get an X. You pay when you are ready to leave by waiting for what seems like hours until your server finally notices you again. '*Zaplatím, prosím*' means 'I will pay, please' and you should say it when you're ready to do so. Your server may return with a computer printout of your bill, or he or she may just add it up at the table. In either case, rounding up to the nearest even figure is customary; a tip of 10 per cent is usually greatly appreciated. Your server will probably make change out of a bulky billfold.

However, before you pay, you should eyeball the bill to the best of your abilities, especially if it is late in the evening and the manager has already left and the waiter looks like he might be hungry. If you don't understand any of the items on the bill, ask for an explanation. No pub in these listings should add *'servis'* charges to the bill. If a restaurant charges for a *'couvert'* (silverware), it must be clearly posted on the menu. (Since the country's EU entry in April 2004, this sort of petty fraud has largely disappeared, but it wouldn't hurt to keep an eye out. Your wallet may thank you.)

What's in a name?

It is enough to drive you to drink: without extensive education in the Czech language, you will probably have trouble understanding the names of pubs. For example, the great *U Zlatého tygra* ('At the Golden Tiger') starts with the word *'u'*, akin to the French *'chez'*. In everyday speech, it might be called *Hospoda* (pub) *u zlatého tygra*, *Výčep* (taproom) *u zlatého tygra*, to say nothing of *Restaurace* (restaurant) or *Hospůdka* (also pub) *u zlatého tygra*. And just as the French might omit the *'chez'* when speaking about a restaurant called *'Chez Marcel'*, many people here will also drop the *'u'*. In Czech this changes the grammatical case of the phrase so that *U Zlatého tygra* becomes just *Zlatý tygr*.

In point of fact, the correct name is *Pivnice* (beer hall) *U Zlatého tygra*. For the sake of our listings (and your sanity), this Guide lists the pub as *'U Zlatého tygra'*. Words such as *pivnice, výčep, hospoda, hospůdka*, restaurant and *restaurace* are omitted in titles whenever possible.

Getting lost

Prague is a very easy city to explore by foot. However, in an attempt to list as many beers as possible, we have included pubs in outlying areas. Wherever possible, we have included instructions on how to get there by public transport, listing the nearest or

easiest tram or metro station when convenient. Prague's public transport system is one of the best in Europe, and serious beer explorers are advised to buy a pass for the length of their stay. The two ticket offices at Prague airport, open 7–22 daily, sell 3-, 7- and 15-day passes; other ticket offices can be found at metro stations Můstek, Muzeum, Nádraží Holešovice and Anděl. Single-use tickets (14 Kč) or transfer tickets (20 Kč) can also be purchased from a newsagent *(trafika)* or from the orange vending machines at many tram stops and metro stations. For more information, see **www.dpp.cz**.

Opening hours

Standard pub times are 11am until 11pm. For the sake of consistency and to avoid misunder-standings, this Guide uses the same 24-hour time that Czech pubs use, listing such hours as 11–23. Most pubs and restaurants are open seven days a week; at weekends they often open later.

The listed opening times are usually fairly accurate. Closing hours, however, tend to fluctuate wildly. If it's well past midnight and everyone's still having a good time, the pub might just keep going, despite a posted closing an hour earlier. If the bar is empty, workers may knock off an hour or two early. In all cases we have made an effort to list the correct operating hours, but as in most cases, reality here can vastly differ from our expecta-tions. *Z technických důvodů zavřeno* means 'closed for technical reasons' and may be used to explain any of the following causes why a pub might not be open: power cut; water shortage; beer delivery didn't arrive; on-site malarial outbreak; death of a beloved customer; manager's hangover; keys to the door lost; bankruptcy; police conducting a crime scene investigation inside; waitress reading a really good book right now; private party has booked the entire pub; bartender holding tickets to a modern dance show tonight; bartender performing in a modern dance show tonight; toilets blocked; fire; failed health inspection; chef quit (again).

Public holidays

The Czech Republic has 12 annual public holidays; fortunately, most of them do not take precedence over beer time (many beloved Prague pubs are open over Christmas). If anything, a holiday *(svátek)* usually serves as an excuse to spend more time in the pub, though opening hours of many other essential services may be affected; public transport will run on less-frequent Sunday schedules.

In the Czech Republic, the public holidays are:

New Year's Day	1st January
Easter Monday	March or April
Labour Day	1st May
Liberation Day	8th May
Saints Cyril and Methodius Day	5th July
Jan Hus Day	6th July
Saint Wenceslas Day	28th September
Independent Czechoslovak State Day	28th October
Struggle for Freedom and Democracy Day	17th November
Christmas Eve	24th December
Christmas Day	25th December
Saint Stephen's Day	26th December

Children in cafés

Most pubs have signs on the door saying that the sale of alcohol is strictly forbidden to individuals under 18 years of age. This is taken about as seriously as any other fairy tale, and many Prague pubs seem to survive on a teenage clientele. Despite the packs of kids guzzling beer, well-behaved younger children who accompany their parents often seem unwelcome in Prague pubs, certainly after nightfall. In a café – which might well serve great beer as well – children are slightly more welcome, and even more so in most restaurants. By and large, however, infants are rarely seen in public here, and certainly not very often in beer halls.

Food

Well, you didn't come here for the food, did you? That said, Czech pub food is hearty, filling, usually inexpensive and often quite good. Most pubs offer at least some kind of beer snacks, usually the ubiquitous *utopence* (thick pickled sausages) or *topinky* (slices of fried bread, usually served with a clove of garlic); many more will serve one main dish such as goulash or roast pork. These listings include everything from basic beer halls to fine-dining restaurants. Where the Guide has first-hand knowledge of the quality of the food, that information is included.

It is worth noting that few pubs are currently non-smoking; very few places even have a non-smoking section. However, it is a little-known fact that smoking is forbidden during lunchtime and dinnertime. Like many others, this law is regularly flouted.

How we chose our pubs

God bless the good folks over at *Good Beer Guide Belgium*. Editor Tim Webb is lucky enough to look for beer cafés that 'list at least 60 different beers'. If we were to hold our pubs to the same standard, we'd have exactly two entries.

In fact, many of our pubs have just one beer on tap. The reason these pubs were chosen is because this beer is something out of the ordinary, a rare bird that is otherwise unknown in the capital or an unfiltered or unpasteurised version of a more familiar beer. We've also included pubs that are of interest as pubs themselves – but always with an eye towards what's in the glass. This list features addresses of interest to tourists and business travellers as well as locals-only haunts out in the suburbs. In all cases, the quest was to create a list that is as varied as possible within the limitations of a city that is dominated by just three brewers.

While we expended plenty of shoe leather on our own, our best resources were the recommendations that came from other beer lovers. Many of the listings in this book arrived from friends or acquaintances who provided tips based on their own experiences. We have checked the important information as carefully as possible and in most cases we have dropped by for anonymous visits ourselves.

If you find a pub serving a great beer beyond the usual suspects, in Prague or in the provinces, please let us know – write to us at **GBGPrague@gmail.com** or through CAMRA Books. *EVAN RAIL*

So where are all the Belgian-style beer cafés?

In Belgium. For a plethora of reasons starting with the Communist takeover of 1948, it is a rare thing indeed to find a Czech pub anywhere that serves more than one brand of beer. In the provinces, the homogeneity is even more pronounced.

In part this is due to the local preference for draught, rather than bottles, as well as the 41 years of collectivisation. Add in cowboy capitalism and the post-revolution phenomenon of tied pubs and you end up with a place where three-quarters of the market is locked up by the three biggest brewers, turning the country's vibrant possibilities into a stultifying grey sameness. And it doesn't make for a particularly good shade of grey, either: the majority of pubs outside of the major Czech cities remain unhappy places where little has changed since Communist times. Most of them serve the same two beers from InBev and SAB-Miller.

This Guide contains chapters for pubs in Prague and Brno, the two largest cities in the country and the two with direct flights to Britain. When we've found good pubs out in the regions, such as the cosy Dačický in Kutná Hora (p. 73) or the wonderful Modrý Abbé in Klatovy (p. 90), we've included listings for them in the appropriate breweries and brewpubs chapters.

Of course, these chapters also list the country's 50-plus brewpubs, which now exist in every corner of the Czech Republic, as well as the 20-plus restaurants and taprooms at bigger breweries. By our reckoning, these are the most recommendable destinations for people who love good beer.

But conditions here are changing fast, and with any luck more places like Prague's Pivovarský klub – 'Beers from six independent breweries on draught? Impossible!' – will start to show up in the regions. They'll never be Belgian beer cafés, of course, but Belgium has to serve some useful purpose. And if you come across a pub that deserves our attention, drop us a line on **GBGPrague@gmail.com**.

Prague Pubs

Budweiser Bürgerbräu (1)

Králodvorská
Praha 1–Staré Město
BEER: **Budweiser Bürgerbräu**

Near metro station Náměstí Republiky, this outdoor beer kiosk along Králodvorská Street, in the shade of the massive Kotva shopping centre, serves the *other* other Budweiser. No telephone, so there's little chance to reserve one of the many wooden tables available here in warm weather.
Daily 11–21.

Duende (2)

Karolíny Světlé 30
Praha 1-Staré Město
T 775 186 077
www.duende.cz
BEER: **Bernard**

Just off the riverbank in Staré Město, Duende is a café for conversationalists where everyone ends up talking to someone else. It also is one of the best choices for draught Bernard, with bottled Pilsner Urquell and Duvel also available. Loads of character, late nights. Nearby tram stops are Karlovy lázně (tram Nos. 17 or 18) and Národní divadlo (tram Nos. 6, 9, 18, 21, 22 or 23).
Daily 11–1.

Kolkovna (3)

V kolkovně 8
Praha 1–Staré Město
T 224 819 701
www.kolkovna.cz
BEER: **Unpasteurised Pilsner Urquell**

This former print shop serves great draught Pilsner Urquell from a tank and good Czech cuisine. Busy, popular with both tourists and locals. The pub stands directly across from the Moorish-style Spanish Synagogue, built in 1868 and reopened in 1998, close to Old Town Square, just off Dlouhá Street.
Daily 9–midnight.

Krušovická pivnice (4)

Národní třída 7
Praha 1–Staré Město
T 224 237 212
BEER: **Krušovice**

Located on 'National' way just steps from the National Theatre and Café Slavia, this spacious hall serves Krušovice yeast beer as well as the brewery's standard lagers. Full lunch and dinner menus are available, including roast pork knee in Krušovice black beer.
Mon–Fri 11–23, *Sat–Sun* noon–22.30.

U Medvídků (5)

Na Perštýně 7
Praha 1–Staré Město
T 224 211 916
www.umedvidku.cz
BEER: **Budvar** and others

Not only does U Medvídků have a spacious ground-floor main beer hall and restaurant

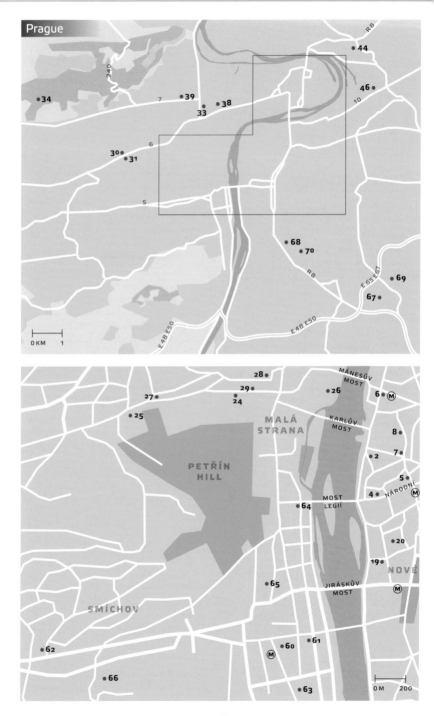

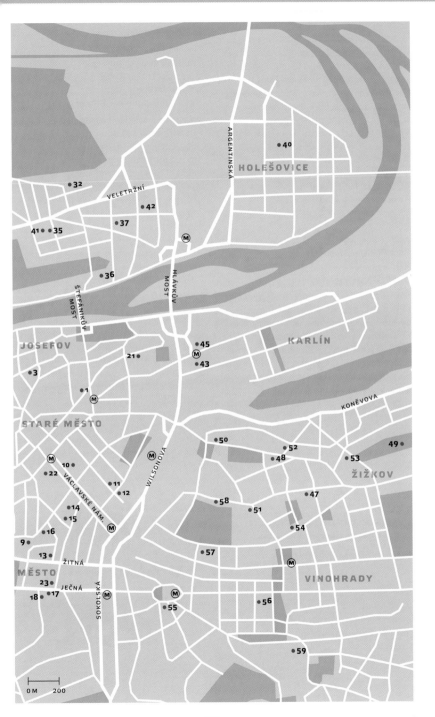

(serving Budvar only), it also has an upstairs 'X-Beer' brewpub (serving its own beer) as well as a separate, ground-floor 'Budweiser Bar' (serving five kinds of Budvar, including yeast beer, and several regional favourites in bottles). The rooms have different opening hours and menus, but they all sit at the same address, making for just one entry here. Very close to Národní třída (metro B or tram Nos. 6, 9, 18, 21, 22 or 23). (See also Breweries and brewpubs – Prague).
Beer hall and X-Beer Brewpub: *daily* 11.30–23.
Budweiser Bar: *daily* 16–3.

U Rudolfina (6)

Křižovnická 10
Praha 1–Staré Město
☎ 222 313 088
BEER: **Unpasteurised Pilsner Urquell**

One of the city's favourite Pilsner Urquell tank pubs, the dirty, dingy and untouched-by-progress U Rudolfina sits just half a block down from the grand Neo-Renaissance Rudolfinum concert hall and metro station Staroměstská in the heart of the Old Town. Skip the boring upstairs area for the crowded cellar and squeeze in somewhere. Groups of three or more would be well-advised to make reservations.
Daily 11–23.

U Zeleného stromu (7)

Betlémské nám. 6
Praha 1–Staré Město
☎ 222 220 228
www.restaurantuzelenehostromu.cz
BEER: **Unpasteurised Pilsner Urquell**

Very near the Bethlehem Chapel, where Jan Hus preached before being excommunicated, is the 'Green Tree's' hidden beer-garden, tank-pub sanctuary. In cold weather, the labyrinthine cellar rooms are an equally popular retreat from the Old Town tourist throngs. Full lunch and dinner menus of Czech classics.
Daily 11–23.30.

U Zlatého tygra (8)

Husova 17
Praha 1–Staré Město
☎ 222 221 111
www.uzlatehotygra.cz
BEER: **Unpasteurised Pilsner Urquell**

This is the real deal: the grandfather, forefather and godfather of all Prague pubs, a celebrated destination known around the world as the favourite local haunt of the Czech novelist and short-story writer Bohumil Hrabal (1914–97) of *Closely Watched Trains* (1965) fame – and also the bane of many a tourist, as virtually every seat is reserved for regulars. The trick is to come early in the day – the 'Golden Tiger' opens at 3 in the afternoon – and have your unpasteurised Pilsner Uquell then. When the *štamgast* (regulars) crowd shows up, you'll probably be forced to skedaddle, but if you're well-behaved, there's a chance you might get to stick around. Is it worth it? Many Praguers think this place serves the best Pilsner Urquell in the city. And of course, the aura is palpable: the 'Golden Tiger' has served brews to Bill Clinton, Madeleine Albright and Václav Havel, and management claims that some of the regulars first stepped foot in here in 1937.
Daily 15–23.

NOVÉ MĚSTO (New Town)

Beograd (9)

Vodičkova 5
Praha 1–Nové Město
☏ 224 946 063
BEER: **Krušovice**

A tank pub serving Krušovice not far from the Nové Město Hall, site of the first Defenestration of Prague on 30 July 1419 (when an angry mob of radical Hussites threw several council members out of the window, thus starting the Hussite Wars, lasting until about 1434). The pub looks similarly dated, though it has only been here for a few years. The beer is about as good as Krušovice gets, with decent meat-and-potatoes fare to back it up.
Daily 11–23.

Billiard centrum (10)

V Cípu 1
Praha 1–Nové Město
☏ 224 009 235
www.billiardcentrum.cz/panska.htm
BEER: **Černá Hora**

The largest pool hall in the capital occupies a sprawling labyrinth just off Panská Street, one big block north of central Wenceslas Square. The main hall has one snooker table, two Russian tables, seven carom billiards tables and 18 pocket tables, as well as bowling and table football; ping-pong tables are somewhere far away upstairs. In addition to the games, this is one of the best sources for Černá Hora beer on draught. Drinks are tallied on your ticket and paid for when you leave. No matter how many you have, do not lose your ticket.
Daily 11–2.

Bredovský Dvůr (11)

Politických vězňů 13
Praha 1–Nové Město
☏ 224 215 428
www.bredovskydvur.unas.cz
BEER: **Unpasteurised Pilsner Urquell**

One of the most modern and civilised of the Pilsner Urquell tank pubs is located just a block north of Wenceslas Square, where incredibly large plates of honey-roasted pork ribs make for a very strong second serve. Large-screen TVs show sports, but this is not a sports pub per se: Bredovský Dvůr attracts beer lovers with the boast that its beer only travels 3 m (10 ft) from the tank to the tap, noting that 'real' beer lovers will know exactly what that means. (Clean pipes and fresh brew, we imagine.)
Mon–Sat 11–midnight, *Sun* 11–23.

Ferdinanda (12)

Opletalova and Politických vězňů
Praha 1–Nové Město
☏ 222 244 302
www.ferdinanda.cz
BEER: **Ferdinand**

SPP's Pub of the Year in 2005, the charming Ferdinanda serves excellent Ferdinand beers from Benešov as well as very good Central European fare, making it an extremely popular destination in the area just north of Wenceslas Square. A weekday lunch special usually includes a small beer. Excellent atmosphere, tasty victuals, attentive service and great beer.
Mon–Fri 8–23, *Sat–Sun* 11–23.

Kolíbka (13)

Řeznická 10
Praha 2–Nové Město
☏ 296 325 555
BEER: **Bernard**

Once upon a time, this was the smokiest café-pub in all of Prague, its dense indoor cloud maintained by a constant student population. Then, in a revelation of almost biblical proportions, it suddenly went smoke-free. Otherwise Kolíbka is constructed along typical Prague proportions: small, dark and intimate, with just one or two types of Bernard available on draught.
Mon–Fri 11–23, *Sat–Sun* 14–23.

Knihkupectví a kavárna Řehoře Samsy (14)

Vodičkova 30
Praha 1–Nové Město
T 224 225 413
www.samsa.psomart.cz
BEER: **Polička**

Tiny bookstore, café and bar in the middle of the Lucerna and U Nováků arcades just off Wenceslas Square, serving very good Polička beer, single malts, wine, coffee, cigars and cigarettes. If the tables all say *reservé*, don't worry: ask nicely and you might find that one is reserved just for you. Closed on weekends.
Mon–Fri 9–21.

Kyvadlo (15)

V Jámě 5
Praha 1–Nové Město
T 224 162 415
www.kyvadlo.com
BEER: **Bernard**

The ever-popular 'Pendulum' restaurant serves good chicken, pork and rabbit dishes with liquid refreshment of up to four kinds of Bernard on draught, just south of Wenceslas Square on the other side of the Lucerna Pasáž arcade.
Mon–Fri 11–midnight, *Sat–Sun* noon–midnight.

Novoměstský pivovar (16)

Vodičkova 20
Praha 1–Nové Město
T 222 232 448
www.npivovar.cz
BEER: **Novoměstské pivo**

This mazelike brewpub can make astonishingly good beers and has the best connections of just about any address in town, with trams Nos. 3, 9, 14 and 24 pulling up just outside the doors at tram stop Vodičkova; metro station Můstek (lines A and B) is about five minutes away by foot. Apart from the main brewhouse there is a Gentlemens' Lounge, and air-conditioned Councillors' Lounge, the Cave (which has good views), the Fermenting Cellar (where you can watch the beer ferment), three (not very) Gothic Halls,

and in summer a terrace and a barn. (See also 'Breweries and brewpubs – Prague')
Mon–Fri 10–23.30, *Sat* 11.30–23.30, *Sun* 12–22.

Pivovarský dům (17)

Lípová 15
Praha 2–Nové Město
T 296 216 666
www.gastroinfo.cz/pivodum
BEER: **Pivovarský dům**

Located in the same building as the Czech Research Institute of Brewing and Malting, this is probably the city's favourite brewpub. An easy-to-find location at tram stop Štěpánská (tram Nos. 4, 6, 10, 16, 22 or 23). Excellent lagers and good, if extremely filling Czech cuisine. (See also 'Breweries and Brewpubs – Prague').
Daily 11–23.30.

Salmovská literární kavárna (18)

Salmovská 16
Praha 2–Nové Město
T 224 919 364
www.salmovska.cz
BEER: **Rebel**

A 'literary café' just around the corner from the great Pivovarský dům (see above), Salmovská is a rollicking performance venue where Czech and Irish musicians share the stage and trade licks – rock, blues, folk, funk, almost anything goes. Frequently crowded, often fun. Rebel beer on draught.
Mon–Thu 15–midnight, *Fri* 17–midnight.

U Bubeníčků (19)

Myslíkova 8
Praha 2–Nové Město
T 224 922 357
www.ububenicku.cz
BEER: **Unpasteurised Pilsner Urquell**

Pub, restaurant and hotel, 'At the Little Drummers' has a reputation for great unpasteurised Pilsner Urquell in a somewhat overlooked New Town location near the Globe bookstore and the Mánes art gallery. Equidistant from metro station Národní třída and Karlovo náměstí (also served by tram Nos. 3, 4, 6, 10, 14, 16, 18, 22 and 23), though even closer to tram stop Jiráskovo náměstí (tram Nos. 17 or 21).
Daily 11–23.

U Fleků (20)

Křemencova 11
Praha 1–Nové Město
T 224 915 118
www.ufleku.cz
BEER: **Flekovské pivo**

This historic brewpub is a tourist trap, but a good one, with an outstanding dark lager brewed in-house. There are eight rooms which can accommodate 1,200 guests in Gothic vaulted halls with long tables, as well as a cabaret dance-show with a programme ranging from Czech polka and Baroque through to Latin rhythms. The nearest metro station is Národní třída on the B line (also served by tram Nos. 6, 9, 18, 21, 22 and 23). (See also 'Breweries and Brewpubs – Prague'.)
Daily 9–23.

U Petrské věže (21)

Petrská 12
Praha 1–Nové Město
T 222 329 856
www.upetrskeveze.cz
BEER: **Malý Rohozec**

This beautifully restored white-tablecloth fine-dining restaurant near New Town's Petrská věž ups the ante with Malý Rohozec, a little-seen Central Bohemian brew, to complement its fine wine list. With main

courses averaging 440 Kč, this is hardly a budget address by local standards, but it remains one of the only Rohozec taps in the capital. Near tram stop Bílá Labuť (tram Nos. 3, 8, 24 or 26).
Mon–Fri noon–midnight, *Sat & Sun* 18–midnight.

U Pinkasů (22)

Jungmannovo nám. 15
Praha 1–Nové Město
T 221 111 150
www.upinkasu.cz
BEER: **Unpasteurised Pilsner Urquell**

The first pub to serve Pilsner Urquell in Prague started up in 1843 before the drink was even called Urquell. For many years U Pinkasů was a run-down wreck before a total renovation just after the turn of the millennium brought it back to life. There are many levels, none of which have particularly friendly service – on the whole we prefer the dim, cool cellar; upstairs rooms are more restaurant-like and formal. Located at the bottom/northwestern end of Wenceslas Square, just a few steps from metro station Můstek.
Daily 11–23.

U Šumavy (23)

Štěpánská 3
Praha 2–Nové Město
T 224 920 051
BEER: **Budweiser Budvar**

This smoky New Town pub is a favourite for old-timers who long considered it to be the source for the city's best Budvar, at least until the opening of Dejvice's Budvarka. Good cheap goulash and other Central European favourites as well as weekday lunch specials, though most people come here for the beer alone. When there's no room inside, drinkers often spill out onto the pavement out front. We mean that figuratively. Near tram stop Štěpánská (tram Nos. 4, 6, 10, 16, 22 or 23).
Daily 11–23.

MALÁ STRANA (Lesser Town) & HRADČANY (Castle District)

Baráčnická Rychta (24)

Tržiště 23
Praha 1–Malá Strana
☎ 257 532 461
www.baracnickarychta.cz
BEER: **Svijany and Pilsner Urquell**

An excellent Malá Strana pub and restaurant whose name has various English translations, the closest sounding something like 'Small Homeowners' Association' and the weirdest being 'Patriot's Hall'. Located just up from the US, German and Irish embassies, Rychta is a lovely neighbourhood meeting place just below Prague Castle; an adjacent concert hall hosts concerts from surprisingly hip groups such as The Frames. Comfortable in the way pubs can feel only after 125 years of constant use. Near tram stop Malostranské náměstí (tram Nos. 12, 20, 22 or 23).
Mon–Sat 11–23, Sun 11–21.

Klášterní pivovar Strahov (25)

Strahovské nádvoří 10
Praha 1–Strahov
☎ 233 353 155
www.klasterni-pivovar.cz
BEER: **Sv. Norbert**

A newish brewpub in an old redoubt near Prague Castle with very good dark and amber lagers and very hearty Czech meals. Service can be a drag, but you're in the heart of the tourist zone just a few minutes from tram Nos. 22 and 23 at stop Pohořelec. (See also 'Breweries and Brewpubs – Prague'.)
Daily 10–22.

Malostranská Pivnice (26)

Cihelná 3
Praha 1–Malá Strana
☎ 257 530 032
www.malostranskapivnice.cz
BEER: **Unpasteurised Pilsner Urquell**

Despite the location in the heart of Malá Strana's tourist centre, this old-fashioned beer hall also sports old-fashioned menus, old-fashioned prices and traditionally surly service. That's probably why we love it. Just steps from the Malostranská metro and tram station, a short walk across Mánesův most (Mánes Bridge) from the Old Town.
Daily 11–23.

U Černého Vola (27)

Loretánské náměstí 1
Praha 1–Hradčany
☎ 220 513 481
BEER: **Velkopopovický Kozel**

Just across from the Loreta pilgrimage church at Prague Castle, the 'Black Bull' serves pilgrims of a different kind. The Strana přátel piva, or 'Party of the Friends of Beer', occupied this historic pub before it transformed into today's Sdružení přátel piva, or 'Union of Friends of Beer', the Czech equivalent of CAMRA. It is the kind of place where you might ask the man next to you to take your picture and then learn that your ersatz photographer has a day job as the Czech Ambassador to the United States and is only out for a beer here while home on holiday. You can walk all the way up from Malostranská metro, but both the Nos. 22 and 23 trams practically park by the pub doors at nearby tram stop Pohořelec. An excellent break spot while exploring Hradčany.
Daily 11–23.

184

U Hrocha (28)

Thunovská 10
Praha 1–Malá Strana
T 257 316 890
BEER: **Unpasteurised Pilsner Urquell**

Just below Prague Castle and not far at all
from the Malostranská metro station,
'At the Hippopotamus' is a nicely hidden
neighbourhood bar in the heart of the Malá
Strana tourist zone (if you pass the statue of
Winston Churchill, you've probably gone
too far). You might get stared at, but you
won't be unwelcome; at night empty tables
here can be extremely hard to come by.
Daily 11–23.

U Kocoura (29)

Nerudova 2
Praha 1–Malá Strana
T 257 530 107
BEER: **Bernard, Budvar** and **Pilsner Urquell**

Three great beers on draught with the rarely
seen Bernard *kvasnicové pivo* headlining over
Budvar and Pilsner Urquell. Despite the
tourist location at the bottom of Malá Strana's
Nerudova Street, the pub maintains its pre-
1989 cosy/dirty environs and 'people's prices'
– just 28 Kč per half litre as of January 2007.
A rare find in the now overpriced centre.
Daily noon–23.

BŘEVNOV

Klášterní šenk (30)

Břevnovský klášter
Markétská 1
Praha 6–Břevnov
T 220 406 294
www.intercatering.cz/en/index_brevnov.php
BEER: **Klášter**

Just past Prague Castle is Břevnovský
klášter (Břevnov monastery), founded in
993; one of the early battles of the Thirty
Years' War was fought less than a mile
from here at Bílá Hora (White Mountain)
in 1620. Today, the monastery pub has a
feel of similar historicity, though most of
the buildings, including the stately
Chapel of St. Margaret, only date from
the Baroque era. Klášter light and dark
11° have rarely tasted so heavenly,
possibly due to the atmosphere: there's
plenty of open space, lots of character
and a warming hearth in winter. Easy to
reach by taking tram Nos. 8 or 22 to stop
Břevnovský klášter.
Daily 11.30–23.

U klláštera (31)

Bělohorská 169
Praha 6–Břevnov
T 220 510 239
BEER: **Kláštér, Budvar, Pilsner Urquell, Primátor**

Right at the Břevnovský kláštér tram stop (tram Nos. 8 or 22), this old-style pub almost doesn't fit in with the rest of the city: instead of one brew, it stocks six draught beers (Kláštér light and dark lagers, Budvar premium, Pilsner Urquell, Primátor 16° special and Hoegaarden) and several special bottles from Primátor. Instead of charging high prices, its decent pub food is served at very moderate prices (e.g., goulash and dumplings for 70 Kč). Like almost everything else here, U klláštera is a smoke-friendly place, but a filter has been installed in the main room, keeping the air surprisingly fresh. Best of all, service is not actually surly. Are we still in Prague? *Daily* 10.30–23.30

DEJVICE, BUBENEČ AND HOLEŠOVICE

Bastard (32)

Kamenická 56
Praha 7–Holešovice
T 220 571 096
BEER: **Herold**

Take your nearest and dearest here as a means of letting them know what you really think of them. This neighbourhood pub stocks Herold's 10° golden lager and the brewery's spectacular 13° dark on tap, with the Bastard golden special (6.1%) available in bottles. Easy to reach in Prague 7's party zone, just three blocks over and two blocks up from tram stop Letenské náměstí (tram Nos. 1, 8, 15, 25 or 26).
Mon–Sat noon-21, *Sun* noon–20.

Budvarka (33)

Wuchterlova 22
Praha 6–Dejvice
T 222 960 820
www.budvarkadejvice.cz
BEER: **Budweiser Budvar**

Opened in mid-2006, this is the first Prague location of the Budvar pub mini-chain, serving two standard golden lagers, dark lager and Budvar's yeast beer, the so-called 'ring lager'. Room for 150, and often full. Two blocks south of metro station Dejvická or tram stop Vítězné náměstí (tram Nos. 2, 8, 20 or 26). *Daily* 11–midnight.

Dívčí skok (34)

Divoká Šárka 356
Praha 6–Dejvice
☎ 235 364 120
BEER: **Herold**

This pub in the Divoká Šárka or 'Wild Šárka' park to the north of Prague stocks two kinds of Herold beer on draught, including the stellar dark lager and the 10º Pilsner-style brew. The park, named after a mythical female warrior, is an excellent get-out-of-town destination for sunbathing, swimming, hiking, biking, golfing and rock-climbing as well as cross-country skiing in winter, in surprisingly rough terrain. (From metro station Dejvická, take tram Nos. 20, 26 or the airport bus No. 119 to the Divoká Šárka stop and follow the trails.) *Daily* 10–20.

Klášterní pivnice (35)

Ovenecká 15
Praha 7–Holešovice
☎ 233 376 150
BEER: **Klášter**

With few concessions to the modern age, this small taproom serves Klášter beer to a crowd of regulars just as Prague pubs have been doing for hundreds of years. Would that there were more like this one. Just one block south of tram stop Letenské náměstí (tram Nos. 1, 8, 15, 25 or 26) on the way to Letná park. *Daily* 9–21.

Letná (36)

Letenský sady 341
Praha 7–Holešovice
BEER: **Gambrinus**

The city's favourite beer garden has two taps pouring inexpensive Gambáč for poets, layabouts, skateboarders, young families and about 5 million dogs all seated under chestnut trees while enjoying wide-angle views across the river onto the rooftops of the Old Town. If Gambrinus in a plastic cup isn't your cup of tea, the nearby chateau (Letenský zámeček) goes way upscale with Pilsner Urquell in glasses. From the Old Town, walk across Štefánikův most (Štefánik Bridge) and climb the steps to the top, or take a tram (Nos. 1, 8, 15, 25 or 26) to stop Letenské náměstí and follow the crowds. *Daily* until late.

Na Mělníku (37)

Františka Křížka 28
Praha 7–Holešovice
☏ 233 378 731
www.namelniku.zde.cz
BEER: **Unpasteurised Pilsner Urquell**

Room for 170, give or take, with a few more crowding in at the end. This dank, bustling Prague 7 tank pub is just a block south of the Alfred v Dvoře theatre, where many of the performances are language-neutral (read 'silent'). For actors, directors and other layabouts, a separate room (Plzeňka) stays open until 2 a.m. nightly. Forget the tourist tax of city-centre destinations: meal prices here resemble those of remote villages... in bygone days. Two blocks up from the similar U Houbaře.
Mon–Thu 11.30–0.30, *Fri & Sat* 11.30–1, *Sun* 11.30–midnight.

Tanked Up

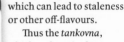

Most of the Pilsner Urquell served around the Czech Republic and around the world is the standard, pasteurised version. Around the Czech Republic, however, a limited number of pubs have been allowed to serve an unpasteurised version of Pilsner Urquell through the use of special kit. Instead of kegs, beer is pumped directly into replaceable, polyester-film sacks inside vast, sealed steel tanks. A pub which serves this style of beer is known as a tank pub, or *tankovna*. (You might see a sign that says *Plzeň z tanku*, or 'Pilsner from a tank'.)

Of course, pasteurisation itself is not a crime. After brewing, fermentation and lagering, beer is heated to around 63 °Celsius (145 °Fahrenheit) for at least 30 minutes, or longer for far-travelling exports. The result is a brew that is stable at the microbiological level, meaning that it is much more capable of withstanding the shocks it will receive during shipping and storage.

But that additional stability comes at a price. While pasteurisation does make beer more stable, heat also kills off much of the characteristic spicy flavours of Žatec hops. Additionally, pasteurisation can increase the beer's chance of oxidisation, which can lead to staleness or other off-flavours.

Thus the *tankovna*, which, at least in the case of Pilsner Urquell, only exists in the Czech lands. It is almost invariably a better pub, as only high-volume taprooms are allowed to serve tank beer: Pilsner Urquell requires that all unpasteurised brew it delivers must be consumed within two weeks. A further requirement is that pub owners must clean their lines – or have their lines sanitised by an outside service – much more frequently than with keg lager.

Consequently, the beer in a tank pub is often surprisingly fresh, with a much fuller, rounder malt body than the pasteurised version. An even greater difference lies in the unpasteurised beer's peppery hop aroma and bittersweet finish. The flavours are noticeably more dynamic and bright than those of the pasteurised version. Another benefit: due to the kit, the tank beer never comes into contact with oxygen, as the beer is 'pumped' out of the sack through the increased air pressure inside the sealed tank.

Pilsner Urquell was the very first to sell tank beer here. It was joined later by Krušovice, which now has two tank pubs in the capital. Could Budvar be far behind?

Plzeňský sklípek (38)

Eliášova 14
Praha 6–Bubeneč
☏ 224 316 808
BEER: **Unpasteurised Pilsner Urquell**

Not all of the Pilsner Urquell tank pubs lie on the Old Town's tourist trail: this Prague 6 favourite serves up the freshest, unpasteurised golden lager in Bubeneč.
Daily 11–midnight.

Pod Loubím (39)

Evropská 26
Praha 6–Dejvice
☏ 233 326 097
www.volny.cz/podloubim
BEER: **Pilsner Urquell**

Almost directly across from Hotel Diplomat and just a couple of blocks up from metro station Dejvická, Pod Loubím feels like something from an earlier era, with clean wood trim reminiscent of the International Modern and a surprisingly graceful pub cuisine: seared goose livers with toast, smoked duck with raspberry sauce, stuffed mushrooms with blue cheese. Excellent Pilsner Urquell for the neighbourhood and beyond.
Daily noon–midnight.

Pivní galerie (40)

U Průhonu 9
Praha 7–Holešovice
☏ 220 870 613
www.pivnigalerie.cz
BEER: **Various**

Petr Vaňek's 'Beer Gallery' is a Prague treasure, stocking 180 brands of rare bottles from regional producers throughout Bohemia and Moravia – if they don't have it here, you probably can't get it anywhere in town. In addition to the bottle store, a side room functions as a neighbourhood pub with two regional brews on tap. The gallery has been visited by the beer writer Michael Jackson and French crooner Charles Aznavour – presumably not at the same time. Essential. Tram Nos. 5, 12 or 15 to stop U Průhonu.
Mon–Fri 11–20.

Svijanský rytíř (41)

Jirečkova 13
Praha 7–Holešovice
☏ 233 378 342
www.restaurace-svijanskyrytir.wz.cz
BEER: **Svijany**

Just around the corner from the Klášterní pivnice, this pleasant restaurant-café serves five kinds of unpasteurised Svijany beer and full menus of Czech and international dishes. Volume drinkers or groups can purchase a table-top giraffe (4-litre/6¾ pints) portion, served with its own tap, for speedier consumption.
Mon–Fri 11–23, *Sat & Sun* private parties only.

U Houbaře (42)

Dukelských hrdinů 30
Praha 7–Holešovice
☏ 220 879 467
www.doma-houby-pivo.cz
BEER: **Unpasteurised Pilsner Urquell**

A great *tankovna* in the centre of industrial-cum-residential Prague 7, this bustling pub just across from the Czech National Gallery's Museum of Modern Art serves hearty Czech meals at very modest prices. Tram Nos. 1, 5, 8, 12, 14, 15, 17, 25 or 26 to Strossmayerovo náměstí.
Daily 11–midnight.

KARLÍN AND LIBEŇ

Pivovarský klub (43)

Křižíkova 17
Praha 8–Karlín
T 222 315 777
www.gastroinfo.cz/pivoklub
BEER: **Various**

A bottle-shop, brewpub and beer vendor, Pivovarský klub serves six draught beers from regional producers, including such rare birds as Hradec Králové's Rambousek, as well as meaty dishes like roast pork knuckle. Directly across from Karlín's newly refurbished *divadlo* (theatre), close to metro station Florenc. (See also 'Breweries and Brewpubs – Prague'.) *Daily* 11–23.30.

Richter Brewery (44)

Bulovka 17
Praha 8–Libeň
T 284 840 650
www.pivovarubulovky.cz
BEER: **Richter**

An extremely comfortable brewpub with live blues and jazz concerts, good food and some of the country's very best beers, including many great ales and other oddball styles. Essential. Tram Nos. 10, 15, 24 or 25 to stop Bulovka. (See also 'Breweries and Brewpubs – Prague'.) *Mon–Thu* 11–23, *Fri* 11–midnight, *Sat* noon–midnight.

U Českého Lva (45)

Sokolovská 7
Praha 8–Karlín
T 222 230 124
www.uceskeholva.cz
BEER: **Unpasteurised Pilsner Urquell**

In cold weather, this sprawling tank pub is limited to several atmospheric rooms with exposed stone walls and old wooden tables. Come May, the extensive outdoor area with seating for about 250 customers dwarfs the available interior space. Complete menus of Czech classics are available, and the location

right at busy metro station Florenc connects to two metro lines and numerous trams and buses. *Daily* 11–23.

U Jagušky (46)

Na Žertvách 28
Prague 8–Libeň
T 284 824 747
www.ujagusky.cz
BEER: **Unpasteurised Pilsner Urquell**

Just off the Palmovka metro, this spacious tank pub pours fresh Pilsner Urquell for the Prague 8 crowd with some of the lowest prices in the country. Excellent barbecued pork ribs and other hearty fare, with plenty of booths and tables for everyone. In the summer months, the backyard is a great spot for al fresco drinking. *Daily* 11–23.

ŽIŽKOV

Království (47)

Kubelíkova 36
Praha 3–Žižkov
T 222 716 288
www.kralovstvi.com
BEER: **Černá Hora**

This pleasant Žižkov pub offers breakfasts on weekdays with three kinds of hot cereal; lunch menus start with a 79 Kč special and include a free dessert, while dinner menus include Czech and Moravian specialities like

grundle (a popcorn-like fried river fish) and a Valašsko-style pork cutlet. Special events staged here include tastings of high-grade *slivovice* and concerts of Slovak folk music. Just a block and a half up from Palác Akropolis, the cultural centre of Prague 3, 'The Kingdom' is easy to find: it is just two blocks from tram stop Lipanská (tram Nos. 5, 9 or 26); the four kinds of Černá Hora beer on draught and two in bottles make it well worth the short hike. Menus are available in Czech, English and German, and though the posted closing hour is midnight, an evening here will probably go a bit later.
Mon–Fri 9–midnight, *Sat & Sun* 17–midnight.

Kuře v hodinkách (48)

Seifertova 26
Praha 3–Žižkov
T 222 734 212
www.kurevhodinkach.cz
BEER: **Bernard, Budvar, Pilsner Urquell**

Don't try to understand the name – the 'Chicken in the Watch' pub and restaurant is a shrine to the Czech bands of the 1960s and 1970s, and the name comes from a lyric by local rock legend Vladimír Mišík. Seeing Bernard, Budvar, Gambrinus and Pilsner Urquell in the same place is relatively rare; occasionally other beers have been served here as well.
Daily noon–1.

Parukářka (49)

Parukářka
Praha 3–Žižkov
T 603 423 140
www.parukarka.cz
BEER: **Gambrinus** and **Pilsner Urquell**

This hilltop beer garden is just a short walk up from tram and bus stop Olšanské náměstí (tram Nos. 5, 9 or 26; bus Nos. 133, 136 or 207), bordered by Olšanská, Lupáčová and Jeseniová streets. Lots of dogs, frisbees, occasional rock concerts, mellow people and plenty of cheap Gambrinus and Pilsner Urquell. Summer: *daily* 13–midnight; winter: *daily* 16–midnight.

Poja (50)

Seifertova 29
Praha 3–Žižkov
T 222 541 664
BEER: **Budweiser Bürgerbräu**

A modest pizzeria and bar overlooking the speeding trams of Seifertova. Decent pies and fresh Samson on draught.
Mon–Fri 11–2, *Sat & Sun* noon–22.

Šlechta (51)

Slavíkova 27
Praha 3–Žižkov
T 222 712 533
BEER: **Svijany**

Fair warning: this pleasant café currently hosts bi-weekly, English-language poetry readings on the second and fourth Sundays of each month at 18.30. Other times appear to be relatively safe.
Mon–Fri 13–22, *Sat & Sun* 14–22.

U Pižďucha (52)

Blahníkova 6
Praha 3–Žižkov
T 222 780 224
BEER: **Svijany, Regent** and **Staropramen**

Right off the Seifertova strip, this modest taproom serves bog-standard Staropramen as well as sought-after Svijany and Regent

brews at prices that rip the lid off the ubiquitous 35-Kč myth – by a factor of two at the time of writing the Guide.
Mon–Fri 11–1, Sat & Sat 14–1.

U Radnice (53)

Havlíčkovo náměstí 7
Praha 3–Žižkov
T 222 782 713
www.slevove-kupony.cz/u-radnice.html
Beer: **Podkováň**

This sprawling restaurant, pub, beer garden and sauna club (!) is one of the only addresses in Prague with Podkováň beer, serving light, dark and yeast varieties on tap in the colourful/gritty suburb of Žižkov. Live music Thursdays and Saturdays. Groups of five or more can book the sauna, though only true daredevils would combine sessions in the sweat-lodge with serious beer consumption.   *Daily 11–23.*

U sadu (54)

Škroupovo náměstí 6
Praha 3–Žižkov
T 222 727 072
www.usadu.cz
Beer: **Primátor** and **Pilsner Urquell**

The opening hours listed below are correct: serious pubs in Prague are open this early and this late, if not 24/7. Beyond serving great Pilsner Urquell, including bargain prices on take-away draughts if you bring your own *džbán*, U Sadu also has a constant supply of Primátor's excellent *Weizenbier* (wheat beer) on draught, as well as the brewery's seasonal specials. As if the good brewskis weren't enough, 'At the Orchards' also has very good Czech pub food and extremely gracious service for a real drinking joint, with pool tables in the cellar. The never-boring collection of eye-catching bric-a-brac includes several Communist flags and paintings of such reviled former ČSSR leaders as Klement Gottwald, as if to counterbalance the historic location: the busy tables outside face the square where Václav Havel made a historic speech on Human Rights on 10 December 1988. As an added bonus, the pub has great connections to the centre from nearby metro station Jiřího z Poděbrad.
Mon–Fri 8–4, Sat & Sun 9–4.

VINOHRADY AND VRŠOVICE

Cheers (55)

Belgická 42 (enter on Rumunská)
Praha 2–Vinohrady
T 222 513 108
www.cheers.cz
BEER: **Pilsner Urquell**, **Gambrinus**,
Staropramen and **Budvar**

Also known as 'Cheers: All Beer One', which
might sound strangely familiar. It's a good
premise, escaping the Big Three's 'exclusivity
contracts' which tie pubs to a single beer
supplier, but then Cheers somehow misses
the point: in this case, 'all' means 'all of the
Big Three'. Not a bad place considering,
especially if you want to compare draught
Pilsner Urquell, Gambrinus, Staropramen
and Budvar. Multiple TV screens show a
constant supply of sports and the food menu
includes hit-and-miss versions of Czech,
Thai, Mexican and American bar classics.
Daily 11–23.

Hrom do Police (56)

Moravská 40 (enter on Chodská)
Praha 2–Vinohrady
T 222 517 815
BEER: **Polička**
www.pivovar-policka.cz/hrom.htm

Serving traditional Bohemian fare, the
'Thunder into the Shelf' restaurant puns on
the name of the beer it serves, Polička – the
name might best translate as 'The Bull in the
China Shop'. In fact, Hrom do Police has a
complete array of excellent Polička beers on
tap, including two yeast beers, and bottles
are available for take-away.
Mon–Sat noon–midnight, *Sun* 18–23.

Pastička (57)

Blanická 25 (enter on Mánesova)
Praha 2–Vinohrady
T 222 253 228
www.pasticka.cz
BEER: **Bernard**

'The Mousetrap' is a cool pub on the ever-
appreciating Mánesova strip in the heart
of verdant Vinohrady. Two types of Bernard
are available on draught, as well as steaks,
chops, cutlets, salads and snacks.
Mon–Fri 11–1, *Sat & Sun* 17–1.

Riegrovy sady (58)

Riegrovy sady
Praha 2–Vinohrady
BEER: **Gambrinus**

Prague 2's favourite beer garden lies in this
verdant park, bordered by Polská, Italská,
Chopinova and Vozová Streets, contributing
much to the leafy feel of Prague's elegant
residential Vinohrady neighbourhood, a
particularly desirable address for the city's
expatriates. On summer nights, sometimes
it seems like half the conversations in this
bustling beer garden are taking place in
English, Spanish or at least some language
other than Czech. Easily reached by taking
tram No. 11 to stop Italská and walking
north, then following the buzz of the beer-
drinking throngs. No telephone, no
reservations, no problems.
Daily until late.

U Bizona (59)

Krymská 28
Praha 10–Vršovice
T 271 741 561
www.ubizona.info
BEER: **Platan**

Just a few minutes' walk from the
Bohemians' football stadium, the beer hall
'At the Bison' serves fresh Platan beer to a
crowd of Prague 10 neighbourhood locals.
It's small, dim, dingy and filled with smoke,
but U Bizona is also one of the few places
you can find Platan in Prague, including the
astonishing 14° Prácheňská perla on draught.
Daily 11–23.

SMÍCHOV

Anděl (60)

Nádražní 60
Praha 5–Smíchov
T 257 323 234
www.klubpp.cz/plzenskyrestaurantandel
BEER: **Unpasteurised Pilsner Urquell**

Located at metro station Anděl, this spacious
tank pub offers traditional Czech fare and
unpasteurised Pilsner Urquell, just a couple
of blocks north of arch-rival Staropramen.
Despite the space, the rough-hewn wooden
tables and booths are almost constantly full,
putting a loud buzz and lots of smoke in the
air. If you want to bowl, make reservations:
the lanes, located in the cellar, are extremely
limited.
Daily 11–23.

Jamajka (61)

Staropramenná 23
Praha 5–Smíchov
T 257 326 430
www.pivnicejamajka.cz
BEER: **Nymburk**

Across from metro station Anděl and down
the street from Staropramen, the gritty
Jamajka pub serves Postřižinské Pivo, aka
Nymburk beer, in smoky environs decorated
with (discarded? stolen?) women's handbags
and antique photographs. It has a series of
dark rooms where garrulous packs of
pensioners, English teachers and their
students and sprawling groups of teenagers
meet to slurp down inexpensive cold ones.
The non-liquid menu is limited to pickled
sausages and other beer snacks; the beer
menu at the time of writing the Guide includes
excellent draughts of Pepinova desítka,
Zlatovar and Francinův ležák. Fun, though
it definitely won't pass a white-glove test.
Mon–Fri 15.30–1, Sat & Sun 16–1.

Klamovka (62)

Podbělohorská 3
Praha 5–Smíchov
T 257 220 166
www.klubklamovka.cz
BEER: **Gambrinus**

One of the few beer gardens with an actual
street address, Klub Klamovka is a neighbourhood youth centre with concerts and
exhibitions, educational programme, a
theatre and an on-site youth hostel all
located in a Baroque building in a beloved
park once owned by the aristocratic Clam-
Gallas family. Easily reached (with a little
uphill walking) after taking tram Nos. 4, 7, 9
or 10 or bus Nos. 149 or 191 to stop
Klamovka.
Daily 18–23.

Na Verandách (63)

Nádražní 84
Praha 5–Smíchov
☎ 257 191 200
www.staropramen.cz
BEER: **Staropramen**

The house pub at InBev's Staropramen brewery has space for 130 or so of your closest friends, with another 50 or so stashed in the garden in warm weather and a separate-but-equal taproom on the other side of the hall. High-volume Staropramen is not the city's favourite beer, though Na Verandách ('On the Verandas') does a good job of serving up its own large volumes, and the pub food here is far better than average. In addition to Velvet, Kelt and Granát, all of which can be surprisingly good, Na Verandách serves Staropramen's only take on *kvasnicové pivo*. A quick walk or just one tram stop south of metro station Anděl (tram Nos. 12, 14 or 20 to stop Na Knížecí). *Mon–Thu* 11–midnight, *Fri & Sat* 11–1, *Sun* 11–23.

Olympia (64)

Vítězná 7
Praha 5–Smíchov
☎ 251 511 080
www.kolkovna.cz
BEER: **Unpasteurised Pilsner Urquell**

Housed in a former bank, this tank pub also from the Kolkovna group serves fresh Pilsner Urquell and very hearty traditional fare with funny names ('Moravian sparrow' is a pork recipe, 'Spanish bird' is beef). Seating for 160 plus 55 outdoor spaces and a small non-smoking area thrown in to boot. Just across most Legií (Legions Bridge) from the National Theatre at tram stop Újezd (tram Nos. 6, 9, 22 or 23). *Daily* 11–midnight.

U Mikuláše Dačického (65)

Victora Huga 2
Praha 5–Smíchov
☎ 257 322 334

www.umikulasedacickeho.cz
BEER: **Kutná Hora**

Upmarket Czech restaurant with white table-cloths, slightly higher prices and very good Central European cuisine. Though wine is probably more common with such fare, the restaurant is named after the aristocratic poet Mikuláš Dačický z Heslova (1555–1626), offering the beer from his home town of Kutná Hora on draught. Just north of metro station Anděl at tram stop Arbesovo náměstí (tram Nos. 6, 9, 12 or 20). *Daily* 11–midnight.

U Frgála (66)

Starokošířská 9
Praha 5–Košíře
☎ 775 374 259
www.volny.cz/kavarna_u_frgala
BEER: **Černá hora**

This pleasant café is dedicated to Moravia's remote Valašsko region, and especially that area's traditional *frgál*, a type of flat pie usually topped with peaches, cream cheese and poppy seeds. Not a pub, strictly speaking, but an interesting coffeehouse and bar with good beer, occasional live music and great desserts. Two stops west of metro station Anděl at tram stop U Zvonu (tram Nos. 4, 7, 9 or 10). CLOSED SATURDAY. *Mon–Fri* 12.30–21.30, *Sun* 14.30–18.30 or later.

NUSLE, CHODOV AND BEYOND

Megasportbar (67)

Roztylská 19 (Centrum Chodov)
Praha 4–Chodov
T 272 075 424
www.billiardcentrum.cz/chodov.htm
Beer: **Černá Hora**

Is that really one word? The Megasportbar is a spacious pool hall in the new Chodov shopping mall furnished with three snooker tables and 19 carom, pocket and Russian tables. Four kinds of Černá Hora beer on draught and herb-flavoured Black Hill in bottles. At metro station Chodov.
Daily 10–1.

Na Paloučku (68)

Žateckých 16
Praha 4–Nusle
T 241 401 426
www.vrpaloucek.cz
Beer: **Unpasteurised Pilsner Urquell**

At the Palouček tram stop (tram No. 18 or bus No. 193) and not far from metro station

Pankrác, this Pilsner Urquell *tankovna* has room for 112 spread out through several discrete chambers. Easy to combine with a trip to the U Klokočníka pub and První Pivní Tramway (see below), which is even further out, both geographically and metaphorically.
Daily 11–23.

První Pivní Tramway (69)

Na Chodovci 1a
Praha 4–Spořilov
T 272 765 683
Beer: **Primátor Hefeweizen, Gambrinus, Pilsner Urquell** and various

The winner of SPP's award for Pub of the Year 2006 is the truly bizarre 'First Beer Tramway', a tram-themed pub located way past the city's post-industrial sprawl, at the very last stop of the No. 11 line at Spořilov. The incoming tram pulls up not 3 m (10 ft) from the door; inside the pub are old tram seats, tram signs and a narrow, tram-like architecture, as well as three constant taps pouring Pilsner Urquell, Gambrinus and Primátor's terrific *Hefeweizen* with a fourth tap connected to an oddball keg, usually from one of the country's regional brewers. Smoky, dark and covered with semi-obscene

frescoes, První Pivní Tramway has a hard-partying atmosphere that the tourist-friendly pubs in the centre could never in a thousand years even hope to emulate. It's really quite lovely. The easiest way to get there is by metro to IP Pavlova, then transfer to the No. 11 and ride it to the end (approximately 15 minutes).
Daily 14–midnight.

U Klokočníka (70)

Na Veselí 48
Praha 4–Nusle
T 261 224 717
Beer: **Kácov**

This adorably dingy neighbourhood dive is one of the only taps in town with multiple variations of Kácov beer, including the 10° yeast beer, 10° and 12° light lagers and special draughts in season. It's modest as all get out and definitely a place for locals, as neighbourhood wags of all ages fill up the tables in the front yard in warm weather.

Located on the Pankrác-Nusle border, it's not the easiest to find, but the beer (and the prices) justify the trek. From metro station IP Pavlova, take tram No. 11 to stop Horky. Continue walking in the same direction one block down Nuselská to Na Jezerce. Turn right and walk up Na Jezerce to Pod Lázní; turn right and walk up to Na Veselí, turn right and U Klokočníka is up and on the right. Or take tram No. 18 to the end station at Vozovna Pankrác and walk down Soudní to Na Veselí and turn left.   *Daily* 11–23.

Brno Pubs

THE CZECH REPUBLIC's second city just might be the first choice for many beer lovers, especially those seeking variety. Far from the hegemony of Budvar, Pilsner Urquell and Staropramen, Brno rivals Prague in terms of beer diversity, though in a much smaller area, making it easy to try several great beers in a short space of time.

To start, hit one of the two fantastic brewpubs (Pegas or U Richarda) and perhaps take a tour or try the house pub and restaurant at Heineken-owned Starobrno, to put small-scale craft brewing into perspective. After that, you can choose from a number of independents (Černá Hora, Dalešice, Polička and Strakonice) which are rarely, if ever, seen in Prague.

The city is a lovely place to visit, especially for fans of Functionalist architecture (the domestic version of the International style); above all, Mies van der Rohe's Villa Tugendhat should not be missed. In case beer is not your only interest, the massive Janáčkovo divadlo is a font of world-class opera and ballet (the Covent Garden production of Bohuslav Martinů's *Greek Passion* played here, not in Prague). Best of all, Brno is an extremely walkable city, with many pedestrian zones and almost all of the pubs listed below within 15 minutes by foot from náměstí Svobody, the city's main square.

Černohorská pivnice (1)

Kapucínské náměstí 1
☏ 542 212 173
BEER: **Černá Hora**

An atmospheric cellar pub and restaurant with a special menu of fish and game dishes

and beer from local underdog Černá Hora, a brewery less than an hour to the north of Brno. Unfiltered 10° Sklepní golden lager, 10° golden lager Tas, golden 12° Ležák, dark 12° Granát and Kvasar 14° on draught. If you're walking from the train station towards the centre along Masarykova, this place is just off to the left on Kapucínské náměstí.
Daily 10–22

Černohorský sklep (2)

Náměstí Svobody 5 (at Rašínova)
☏ 542 210 987
BEER: **Černá Hora**

Right on the city's main square, this cellar splits into two rooms, a *pivnice* (beer hall) and a *restaurace* (restaurant). They are more or less the same, with the same rock radio, same smoky atmosphere and same great beers from Černá Hora: the standard 10° golden lager Tas, unfiltered 10° Sklepní golden lager, 12° golden Ležák, dark 12° Granát and Kvasar 14°, made with an addition of honey, apparently inspired by the delicious honey beers from Sentice's Kvasar brewery.
CLOSED SUNDAY. *Mon–Thu* 10.30–midnight, *Fri* 10.30–1, *Sat* 10.30–midnight.

Freeland (3)

Beethovenova 7
☏ 605 825 948
BEER: **Dalešice**

The hours listed below are for real: this downtown pub and restaurant is also a weekend dance club, attracting a very youthful clientele on weekend nights. That said,

Freeland's beers come from one of the country's best small brewers, Dalešice, with two or three varieties on draught (11° světlý, 12° řezané and 13° světlý speciál when last we checked). Various hearty meals, including a very good pork *koleno* (knuckle), round out the bill in this warm, neighbourly cellar furnished with rough-hewn booths. For fans of rare beers, this might be your first stop. And, considering the hours, perhaps your last. *Mon–Thu* 10–midnight, *Fri* 10–3, *Sat* 18–3, *Sun* 18–22.

Hluchá zmije (4)

Jugoslávská 34
T 776 385 935
BEER: **Strakonice** and others

A smoky den of iniquity on the south side of the Černá Pole neighbourhood, approximately 20 minutes by foot to the east of Janáčkovo divadlo, or take the tram (Nos. 3, 5, 9 or 11) to stop Jugoslávská. Normally pouring at least two types of Dudák beer from South Bohemia's Strakonice brewery, with a spare

tap running something special: Polička 10°, Svijany's 13° světlý speciál, or the like. Rock 'n' roll of the Jimi Hendrix/John Mayall variety is played here at high volumes, and two picnic tables out front provide al fresco boozing in fair weather. Noisy and fun. *Mon–Fri* 16–23, *Sat & Sun* 17–23.

Pegas (5)

Jakubská 4
T 542 210 104
www.hotelpegas.cz
BEER: **Pegas**

The Pegas hotel and micro-brewery offers some of the best beer in Brno, if not the country, with a standard line that includes a vanilla-like *světlý ležák* yeast beer, a yeasty *tmavý ležák*, a citrusy wheat beer and a luscious 16° golden *speciál*. Spacious and barnlike, but often crowded to capacity. Just steps from náměstí Svobody in the centre. (See also Breweries and Brewpubs: South Moravia.)
Daily 11–23

Starobrno (6)

Hlinky 12
661 47 Brno
T 543 420 131
www.starobrno.cz
BEER: **Starobrno** and **Heineken**

Starobrno is not the country's best-loved half-litre, nor is it the favourite even in its hometown, and Heineken's ownership doesn't seem to be doing much to help matters. However, the new overlords have chipped in serious money to clean up the on-site pub and restaurant just off the Augustinian Abbey of St Thomas at Mendlovo náměstí, leaving the upper level of the restaurant perversely dedicated to the Dutch import. The pub and restaurants serve Starobrno kvasnicové, the Tradiční 10° golden lager, 10° Černé (which seems to have changed its name to Karamelové), Řezák, Medium, Ležák and Baron Trenck, with Červený Drak and Black Drak available in bottles. (See also Breweries and Brewpubs: South Moravia.)
Mon–Sat 11–midnight, *Sun* 11–23.

Come again?

It's not quite a beer in the hand, but *pivo* fits into a number of Czech aphorisms and folk sayings. Almost every pub is decorated with the traditional brewer's greeting, *Dej Bůh štěstí*, or 'God give happiness', and many more are emblazoned with poetic lines such as:

Kde se pivo vaří, tam se dobře daří.
Where beer is brewed, things go well.

Kde se pivo pije, tam se dobře žije.
Where beer is drunk, life is good.

Lepší pivo v žaludku, nežli voda na plicích.
Better beer in the belly than water in the lungs.

Do půlnoci u pěny, od půlnoci u ženy.
On the suds until midnight; after twelve,
    on the wife.

Kdo pije mok pěnivý v posteli je lenivý.
Whoever drinks foamy liquid is lazy in bed.

Píme pivo s bobkem, jezme bedrník! Nebudeme stonat, nebudeme mřít!
Let's drink beer with bay, let's eat pimpernel! We won't get ill, nor will we die!

Pivo dělá hezká těla.
Beer makes a beautiful body.

Pivo hřeje, ale nepálí.
Beer warms, but it doesn't burn.

Pivo hřeje, ale nešatí.
Beer warms, but it doesn't clothe.

Vláda, která zdraží pivo, padne. (Jaroslav Hašek)
A government which raises the price of beer will fall.

Lepší teplé pivo než studená Němka! (Jára Cimrman)
Better a warm beer than a cold German girl!

Pivo mladé čep vyráží.
Young beer bursts from the tap.

Teprve pivo udělá žízeň krásnou.
Only with beer does thirst become beautiful.

Strakonický Dudák (7)

Vachova 8

T 542 213 001

BEER: **Strakonice** and **Polička**

Virtually unavailable on draught in Prague, South Bohemia's Strakonice has made a small beachhead in Brno. The brewery's advance party in Moravia is the Strakonický Dudák restaurant, which serves Strakonický Dudák 12° golden lager, the 12° kvasnicové (called Sklepák), and the 12° Záviš from the Polička brewery. Just around the corner from Freeland, and only a few minutes from náměstí Svobody.

Mon–Thu 11–midnight, *Fri* 11–1, *Sat* 17–1, *Sun* 17–midnight.

U Bláhovky (8)

Gorkého 54

T 543 233 310

BEER: **Unpasteurised Pilsner Urquell**

If you can get a seat here without a reservation, run out and buy a ticket for the Czech lottery: even at off-hours, Brno's best Pilsner Urquell tank pub is a very busy place indeed. Appearing much as it did 100 years ago, U Bláhovky (also known as Bláhovka) packs them in with fresh tank Pilsner, roast *koleno* (pork knuckle) and not much else. A treasure, well worth a trip to tram stop Úvoz (tram No. 4 or trolley-bus Nos. 26, 38 or 39), and it's only a 20-minute walk from náměstí Svobody.

Daily noon–midnight.

U Jošta (9)

Veselá 37

T 542 214 546

BEER: **Starobrno** and **Litovel**

This cellar pub and restaurant near náměstí

Svobody sits inside a typical Brno Functionalist building, yet it feels like a 200-year-old mountain cabin somewhere in the Orlické hory. Starobrno's golden lager and dark lager are available, as well as Litovel's Maestro and *kvasnicové pivo*. CLOSED SUNDAY. *Mon–Fri 11–23, Sat 11–midnight.*

U Richarda (10)

Ríšova 12, Brno-Žebětín
T 546 217 715
BEER: **U Richarda**

The Brno suburb of Žebětín is home to this cosy brewpub and restaurant with three craft lagers on draft. Special beers are occasionally brewed for the holidays, including a half-dark, 16° honey lager brewed with an adjunct of honey. Worth seeking out via taxi or public transport: from central Brno's Mendlovo náměstí, take bus Nos. 52 or 54 to the end station at Žebětín Ríšova, a 26-minute ride. (See also Breweries and Brewpubs: South Moravia.) *Sun–Thu 11–22, Fri & Sat 11–23.*

U Zlatého Meče (11)

Mečová 3
T 542 211 198
BEER: **Budweiser Budvar**

Though labelled a *vinárna*, or wine bar, 'At the Golden Sword' is a rustic restaurant and pub supplementing its wine list with three wonderful beers from the great brewer of Southern Bohemia: Budvar's 10° and 12° golden lagers and 12° dark. Between Zelný trh and Dominikánské náměstí in the centre. *Daily 9–midnight.*

Vegas Klub (12)

Milady Horákové 1a
(enter on třída Kapitána Jaroše)
T 545 571 435
BEER: **Xaver**, **Pilsner Urquell** and **Starobrno**

Not far from the Janáčkovo divadlo and about a 10-minute walk from náměstí Svobody, the hard-drinking Vegas Klub serves Pilsner Urquell and Starobrno, as well as an extremely rare bird: the **18° Oldřich** from Blučina's Xaver brewpub, a bitter and dark blend of three types of malt brightened with a blast of cardamom. CLOSED SATURDAY. *Mon–Fri 10.30–midnight, Sun 18.30–23.*

The use of the Džbán (beer jug)

As much as this book is about going out for beer, there's nothing quite like the occasional evening in. The only problem is, most of us don't have a keg in the kitchen. In the Czech Republic, the bottled beer is great, but it's never going to taste as good as the brews on tap. If you feel like drinking draught lager but don't want to spend the evening in the pub, what you need is a *džbán*.

The *džbán* is, literally, just a pitcher or jug, but it has a special connotation in Czech terms. Usually made of earthenware and sporting a bulbous, buxom bottom, the *džbán* is almost universally thought of as a device for transporting beer. With a typical diminutive, the most common expression using the word is *džbánek piva* (a little pitcher of beer).

The pitcher has a noble tradition dating back to the early days of brewing, before bottles were widely available. In the Middle Ages, usually just one person in every community was granted the right to brew beer by the feudal lord. Neighbours would come and purchase a fresh ration from the brewer for the evening, carrying it home in a *džbán* for consumption.

This custom survives today. Nowadays, locals still stop by their regular pub for fresh beer to take home for dinner or while watching a football game. In small villages, fathers send their young children off to the local pub with the family *džbán* before meal time. It's not quite legal, but in a country with such a strong beer-drinking tradition, it's widely accepted, especially in smaller communities.

In fact, anything will do: bartenders will pour your take-away beers into plastic water bottles, stainless-steel kettles or even terracotta flowerpots. But, historically, beer goes into earthenware – before the industrial revolution, glass (or Bohemian crystal) was reserved for the lords of the castle. A typical *džbán* is still made of earthenware today.

The form of the vessel makes for the best-possible beer-drinking experience. The insulating material helps to maintain the proper temperature, and the bulbous base holds the maximum volume. The narrow top reduces the brew's exposure to oxygen, which helps to keep it fresh. And the low centre of gravity makes the *džbán* easy to carry and prevents it from tipping over once set on the table.

The *džbán's* shape can even serve as a communication aide. This can be especially helpful if you're having trouble learning Czech. (The first time I walked into a pub with my *džbán*, the barmaid gave it a glance and immediately asked '*Dvě piva s sebou?*' – literally, 'Two beers to take away?' All I had to do was nod.)

The *džbán* is such a common part of Czech beer culture that one can be picked up almost anywhere here: most home stores, kitchen shops and ceramic stores offer them for sale. Make sure you get one that is not too big – the fresh beer in a *džbán* will only stay good for a few hours. On the other hand, it shouldn't be too small, as you probably won't want to make a second trip to the pub. On Štěpánská Street, one novelty goods store used to have a massive *džbán* prominently displayed in the shop window. Labelled *Král pivařů* (King of Beer Drinkers), it appeared to hold about eight pints.

Useful information

BEER SHOPS

At least by the bottle, rare Czech beers are pretty easy to find in the capital. While most shops stock only brews from the Big Three or their subsidiaries, the following shops carry a number of beers, including some very odd ones. If you're really stocking up, start at the supermarkets, where prices are lower than at the speciality stores, though the selection can be limited. Most have been shown to be fairly knowledgeable about beers, though the high bar in this regard is definitely set by Pivní galerie.

Galerie piva

Lázeňská 15, Praha 1–Malá Strana
T 257 532 687
www.czechbeershop.com

Not the best, but this small bottle shop just off the Malá Strana side of Charles Bridge (Karlův most) is one of the easiest to reach for tourists. The stock consists of a decent selection of products from smaller producers, especially strong beers, as well as mini-kegs, glasses and paraphernalia. On the first left off Mostecká Street after you cross Charles Bridge into Malá Strana. *Daily* 11–19.

Pivní galerie

U Průhonu 9, Praha 7–Holešovice
T 220 870 613
www.pivnigalerie.cz

The first regional beer store in the Czech Republic, the 'Beer Gallery' is a source of lore and wisdom about all things beery. In 2004, Pivní galerie formed the 'First European Beer Bridge', a beer-exchange programme

with the Beer Mania shop in Brussels. From seasonal brews to strong lagers and other rarities, if they don't have it here, you probably can't get it anywhere. Two unusual beers are usually also available on draught. (See also 'Prague Pubs'.) *Mo–Fr* 11–20.

Pivovarský klub

Křižíkova 17, Praha 8–Karlín
T 222 315 777
www.gastroinfo.cz/pivoklub

More of a pub and also one of the country's smallest breweries, 'Brewery Club' stocks about 200 bottles, mostly from the Czech Republic's smaller producers, though some Austrian, Swiss and German beers are also available. In addition, six brews are available on tap, including rarities never seen elsewhere in Prague. Bustling, as at sister brewpub Pivovarský dům, making reservations a necessity for pub visitors; those just picking up bottles should pick a quiet time in the mid-afternoon. And if you want to make your own, schedule about four weeks for lagering. (See also 'Prague Pubs'.) *Daily* 11–23.

CONSUMER GROUPS

Sdružení přátel piva

www.pratelepiva.cz
The Czech Republic's Sdružení přátel piva (Union of Friends of Beer) started life as a political party just after the Velvet Revolution. (At the time, other unusual platforms included the Society for a Merrier Present and the Independent Erotic Initiative, making Strana přátel piva – the Party of Friends of Beer – not such a strange sight by comparison.)

After competing in two parliamentary elections, the party changed into today's civic organisation in 1997, joining the European Beer Consumers' Union, or EBCU, on 15 April 2005. Today, the SPP is CAMRA's equivalent in the Czech lands, fighting for beer consumers' rights and giving out the most objective and well-deserved beer awards in the country.

Chrám chmele a piva

www.chrampiva.cz

The Temple of Hops and Beer is a small (but dedicated) beer lovers' group from Žatec, aka Saaz, which puts on the annual *Chmelfest* (Hopsfest), usually in May, and Chmelovín, at Halloween.

PUBLICATIONS

Kvasný průmysl

Published by the Výzkumný ústav pivovarský a sladařský (Research Institute of Brewing and Malting), the Czech brewing magazine began as *Kvas* in 1873 before changing to its present name in 1955. Contains summaries in English, German and Russian.

Pivař

This new, full-colour magazine launched in 2006 goes by the Czech word for a very serious beer drinker. Celebrating beer culture both Czech and international, *Pivař* appears every two months.

Pivovarský kalendář

The annual 'Beer Calendar', published by Prague's Výzkumný ústav pivovarský a sladařský, lists brewers, maltings, dates in Czech brewing history, as well as information about breweries in Poland and Slovakia.

Pivní kurýr

Available on most large newsstands, the 'Beer Courier' newspaper lists new breweries, pubs and beers and also hands out its own yearly beer awards, with many repeat winners, year after year, many of whom seem to advertise in *Pivní kurýr's* pages.

WEBSITES

The most up-to-date information about Czech brewing in any language is usually found online. The following websites have English pages.

www.beerresearch.cz

The other kind of beer research takes place at the Výzkumný ústav pivovarský a sladařský, the Research Institute of Brewing and Malting, whose laboratory sits above the Pivovarský dům brewpub in Prague. Founded in 1887, it has an extensive library of in many languages and publishes the annual *Pivovarský kalendář*, as well as the *Kvasný průmysl* journal.

www.cspas.cz

The Český svaz pivovarů a sladoven (Czech Beer and Malt Association) is the umbrella organisation for brewing in the Czech Republic.

www.csmnp.cz

The Český svaz malých nezávislých pivovarů are the Guys in the White Hats: the Czech Association of Small, Independent Breweries. English pages are perpetually under construction, but until they're finished, a click on '*členové svazu*' will get you to the list of members.

www.czhops.cz

The website of the Svaz pěstitelů chmele České Republiky (Hop Growers' Union of the Czech Republic) contains information about Czech hop strains, growers, history and culture.

www.europeanbeerguide.net

Ron Pattinson's European Beer Guide has dozens of pages on pubs and breweries around Europe. The Czech pages are well maintained and fairly accurate for a publication from outside the country.

www.pivni.info/mapa/index.htm

While the general pages of pivni.info are in Czech only at this point, the 'Czech beer map' is intelligible in any language.

www.pivovary.info
Czech breweries from the past as well as listings of current and upcoming breweries and the beers they make, with a consumer's eye on prices (listed year-by-year) per half-litre.

www.radio.cz/en/article/46095/breweries.html
Radio Prague's English-language stories about Czech beer and brewing. While some of the older stories are outdated, the history is extensive.

BREWERY HOTELS

By City

Brno, *Pegas Hotel and Microbrewery* 138
Chodová Planá, *Chodovar* 87
Dobrá, *Na Sýpce restaurant* 158
Dobřany, *Modrá Hvězda Hotel and Brewery* 50
Domažlice, *Pivovar Domažlice* 166
Dražíč, *Pivovarský dvůr Lipan* 81
Harrachov, *Novosad a syn* 108
Loket, *Svatý Florián* 98
Prague, *U Medvídků* 64
Průhonice, *U Bezoušků Pension and Brewery* 73
Štramberk, *Městský Pivovar Štramberk* 165
Trutnov, *Krakonoš* 119
Velké Meziříčí, *Jelínkova Vila* 135
Vrchlabí, *Krkonošský Medvěd Hotel s Minipivovarem* 121
Želiv, *Klášterní Pivovar Želiv* 135
Zvíkovské Podhradí, *Zlatá Labuť* 85

By Region

Central Bohemia, *U Bezoušků Pension and Brewery*, Průhonice 73
Hradec Králové Region, *Krkonošský Medvěd Hotel s Minipivovarem*, Vrchlabí 121
Karlovy Vary Region, *Svatý Florián*, Loket 98
Liberec Region, *Krakonoš*, Trutnov 119
Liberec Region, *Novosad a syn*, Harrachov 108
Moravian Silesia, *Městský Pivovar* Štramberk 165
Moravian Silesia, *Na Sýpce restaurant*, Dobrá 158
Pilsen Region, *Chodovar*, Chodová Planá 87
Pilsen Region, *Modrá Hvězda Hotel and Brewery*, Dobřany 50
Pilsen Region, *Pivovar Domažlice* 166
Prague, *U Medvídků* 64
South Bohemia, *Pivovarský dvůr Lipan*, Dražíč 81
South Bohemia, *Zlatá Labuť*, Zvíkovské Podhradí 85
South Moravia, *Pegas Hotel and Microbrewery*, Brno 138
Vysočina, *Jelínkova Vila*, Velké Meziříčí 135
Vysočina, *Klášterní Pivovar Želiv* 135

By Name

Chodovar, *Chodová Planá*, Pilsen Region 87
Jelínkova Vila, *Velké Meziříčí*, Vysočina 135
Klášterní Pivovar Želiv, *Želiv*, Vysočina 135
Krakonoš, *Trutnov*, Liberec Region 119
Krkonošský Medvěd Hotel s Minipivovarem, *Vrchlabí*, Hradec Králové Region 121
Městský Pivovar Štramberk, *Štramberk*, Moravian Silesia 165
Modrá Hvězda Hotel and Brewery, *Dobřany*, Pilsen Region 50
Na Sýpce restaurant, *Dobrá*, Moravian Silesia 158
Novosad a syn, *Harrachov*, Liberec Region 108
Pegas Hotel and Microbrewery, *Brno*, South Moravia 138
Pivovar Domažlice, *Domažlice*, Pilsen Region 166
Pivovarský dvůr Lipan, *Dražíč*, South Bohemia 81
Svatý Florián, *Loket*, Karlovy Vary Region 98
U Medvídků, *Prague* 64
U Bezoušků Pension and Brewery, *Průhonice*, Central Bohemia 73
Zlatá Labuť, *Zvíkovské Podhradí*, South Bohemia 85

Glossary of Czech Beer Terms

Czech words may change greatly according to how they are used in a sentence. Adjectives (marked "adj") may end with -ý, -é, -á and other endings. Nouns may also change according to case and number. The terms here are presented in their most common forms.

Balling a scale, akin to Plato, depicting the percentage of malt sugar present before fermentation (see page 54)
Bednář a cooper
Bednářství a cooperage
Čepovat to tap
Černý (adj.) black
Chmel hops
Chmelnice hop garden
Čtrnáctka a beer brewed at 14° Balling
Cukr sugar
Desítka a beer brewed at 10° Balling
Devítka a beer brewed at 9° Balling
Dia a special brew with lower carbohydrates for diabetics
Dvanáctka a beer brewed at 12° Balling
Džbán (or *džbánek*) pitcher
Granát garnet, a common name for a dark or half-dark beer
Hospoda pub
Jantar amber
Ječný (adj.) barley
Jedenáctka a beer brewed at 11° Balling
Kohoutek tap
Korbel a ceramic or porcelain beer vessel
Kvasnice yeast
Kvasnicové pivo (often *kvasničák*) yeast beer: a brew with a dose of young beer – fresh yeast and wort – added after lagering, thus reactivating fermentation
Láhev bottle
Lehké pivo a legal category for 'light beer'; brewed up to 7.99° Balling with less than 130 kJ per 100 ml
Ležák lager; a legal definition used for beers brewed between 11° and 12.99° on the Balling scale
Malé pivo a small beer, usually 0.3 litre
Mladina wort
Nealkoholické pivo non-alcoholic beer

Nefiltrované pivo unfiltered beer
Nepasterované pivo unpasteurised beer
Osmička a beer brewed at 8° Balling
Osmnáctka a beer brewed at 18° Balling
Pánev (mladinová pánev) brewing kettle
Patnáctka a beer brewed at 15° Balling
Pěna foam
Pitná (adj.) drinking (as in 'pitná voda', drinking water)
Pivnice beer hall
Pivo beer
Pito another term for non-alcoholic beer
Pivovar brewery.
Polotmavý (adj.) half-dark
Porter a dark beer in the Baltic style, usually bottom-fermented and brewed above 18° Balling
Pšeničný (adj.) wheat
Půllitr a half-litre beer glass
Řezané pivo cut beer: a 50:50 mix of světlé and tmavé
Sedmička a beer brewed at 7° Balling
Sedmnáctka a beer brewed at 17° Balling
Šestnáctka a beer brewed at 16° Balling
Slad malt
Sládek brewer
Sladař maltster
Sladovna maltings
Sladový šrot malt grist
Speciál a legal term for a beer brewed above 13° on the Balling scale
Spodní kvašení bottom fermentation
Sud barrel
Sváteční pivo holiday beer, usually a speciál
Světlý (adj.) light (in colour)
Svrchní kvašení top fermentation
Tankovna a pub serving beer (usually unpasteurised) from a tank
Tmavý (adj.) dark
Točený (adj.) draught
Třináctka a beer brewed at 13° Balling
Tuplák a 1-litre beer glass
Vaření (piva) brewing (beer)
Velké pivo a large beer, usually 0.5 litre
Višňové (adj.) sour cherry
Voda water
Výčepní pivo the legal category of 'tap beer', brewed between 8° and 10.99° on the Balling scale
Výčep taproom
Žitný (adj.) rye

Index of Beers and Breweries

CAMPAIGN
FOR
REAL ALE

Books for Beer lovers

CAMRA Books, the publishing arm of the Campaign for Real Ale, is the leading publisher of books on beer and pubs. Key titles include:

Good Beer Guide Belgium

TIM WEBB

Now in its 5th edition and in full colour, this book has developed a cult following among committed beer lovers and beer tourists. It is the definitive, totally independent guide to understanding and finding the best of Belgian beer and an essential companion for any beer drinker visiting Belgium or seeking out Belgian beer in Britain. Includes details of the 120 breweries and over 800 beers in regular production, as well as 500 of the best hand-picked cafes in Belgium.

£12.99   ISBN: 978 1 85249 210 6

Good Beer Guide Germany

STEVE THOMAS

The first ever comprehensive region-by-region guide to Germany's brewers, beer and outlets. Includes more than 1,200 breweries, 1,000 brewery taps and bars and more than 7,200 different beers. Complete with useful travel information on how to get there, informative essays on German beer and brewing plus beer festival listings.

£16.99   ISBN: 978 1 85248 219 9

Good Beer Guide

Editor: ROGER PROTZ

The Good Beer Guide is the only guide you will need to find the right pint, in the right place, every time. It's the original and the best independent guide to around 4,500 pubs throughout the UK; in 2002 it was named as one of the Guardian newspapers books of the year and the Sun newspaper rated the 2004 edition in the top 20 books of all time! This annual publication is a comprehensive and informative guide to the best real ale pubs in the UK, researched and written exclusively by CAMRA members and fully updated every year.

Beer Lover's Guide to Cricket

ROGER PROTZ

There are many books about cricket and many on beer, but this is the first book to bring the two subjects together. Leading beer writer and cricket enthusiast Roger Protz has visited the major grounds of all the First Class counties and gives in-depth profiles of them – their history, museums, and memorabilia, plus listings of the best real ale pubs to visit within easy reach of each ground and details of the cask ales available. This fully illustrated book also features individual sections on the birth of the modern game of cricket and the history of each featured ground, making it an essential purchase for any cricket fan.

£16.99   ISBN: 978 1 85249 227 4

Beer, Bed & Breakfast

SUSAN NOWAK AND JILL ADAM

A unique and comprehensive guide to more than 500 of the UK's real ale pubs that also offer great accommodation, from tiny inns with a couple of rooms upstairs to luxury gastro-pubs with country-house style bedrooms. All entries include contact details, type and extent of accommodation, beers served, meal types and times, and an easy-to-understand price guide to help plan your budget. This year, why not stay somewhere with a comfortable bed, a decent breakfast and a well-kept pint of beer, providing a home from home wherever you are in the country.

£14.99   ISBN: 978 1 85249 230 4

The Book of Beer Knowledge

JEFF EVANS

A unique collection of entertaining trivia and essential wisdom, this is the perfect gift for beer lovers everywhere. Fully revised and updated it includes more than 200 entries covering everything from the fictional 'celebrity landlords' of soap pubs to the harsh facts detailing the world's biggest brewers; from bizarre beer names to the serious subject of fermentation.

£9.99   ISBN: 978 1 85249 198 7

An Appetite For Ale

FIONA BECKETT / WILL BECKETT

A beer and food revolution is under way in Britain and award-winning food writer Fiona Beckett and her publican son, Will, have joined forces to write the first cookbook to explore this exciting new food phenomenon that celebrates beer as a culinary tour de force. This collection of more than 100 simple and approachable recipes has been specially created to show the versatility and fantastic flavour that ale has to offer. With sections on Snacks, Spreads and Dips, Soups, Pasta and Risotto, Seafood, Chicken and other Birds, Meat Feasts, Spicy Foods, Bread and Cheese and Sweet Treats it provides countless ideas for using beer from around the world. With an open mind, a bottle opener and a well-stocked larder, this exciting book will allow you to enjoy real food, real ale and real flavour.

£16.99   ISBN 978 1 85249 234 2   *Published September 2007*

Fuzzy Logic

TOM WAINE

A completely dispensable collection of intriguing nonsense devised or overheard in the pub, compiled and created by regular pub goer Tom Waine. Whether you experience a light-bulb moment while downing a swift half or think you have discovered the meaning of life while imbibing your favourite session beer, this book is packed full of smart ideas, fully-formed theories, unanswered questions – and sheer rubbish. Fuzzy Logic could well leave you entertained, amused and educated for longer than it takes to down a pint.

£9.99   ISBN: 978 1 85249 232 8   *Published October 2007*

Order these and other CAMRA books online at **www.camra.org.uk/books**, ask at your local bookstore, or contact: CAMRA, 230 Hatfield Road, St Albans, AL1 4LW. Telephone 01727 867201

It takes all sorts to Campaign for Real Ale

CAMRA, the Campaign for Real Ale, is an independent not-for-profit, volunteer-led consumer group. We actively campaign for full pints and more flexible licensing hours, as well as protecting the 'local' pub and lobbying government to champion pub-goers' rights.

CAMRA has 86,000 members from all ages and backgrounds, brought together by a common belief in the issues that CAMRA deals with and their love of good quality British beer. For just £20 a year, that's less than a pint a month, you can join CAMRA and enjoy the following benefits:

A monthly colour newspaper informing you about beer and pub news and detailing events and beer festivals around the country.

Free or reduced entry to over 140 national, regional and local beer festivals.

Money off many of our publications including the *Good Beer Guide* and the *Good Bottled Beer Guide*.

Access to a members-only section of our national website, **www.camra.org.uk** which gives up-to-the-minute news stories and includes a special offer section with regular features saving money on beer and trips away.

The opportunity to campaign to save pubs under threat of closure, for pubs to be open when people want to drink and a reduction in beer duty that will help Britain's brewing industry survive.

Log onto **www.camra.org.uk** for up-to-date CAMRA membership prices and information

CAMPAIGN
FOR
REAL ALE

Do you feel passionately about your pint? Then why not join CAMRA

Just fill in the application form (or a photocopy of it) and the Direct Debit form on the next page to receive three months' membership FREE!

If you wish to join but do not want to pay by Direct Debit, fill in the application form below and send a cheque, payable to CAMRA to: CAMRA, 230 Hatfield Road, St Albans, Hertfordshire, AL1 4LW. Please note that non Direct Debit payments will incur a £2 surcharge. Figures are given below.

Current rate		Direct Debit	Non DD
☐	Single Membership (UK & EU)	£20	£22
☐	Concessionary Membership (under 26 or 60 and over)	£11	£13
☐	Joint membership	£25	£27
☐	Concessionary Joint membership	£14	£16

Life membership information is available on request.

Title _____ Surname _____

Forename(s) _____

Address _____

_____ Post Code _____

Date of Birth _____ E-mail address _____

Signature _____

Partner's details if required

Title _____ Surname _____

Forename(s) _____

Date of Birth _____ E-mail address _____

Please tick here ☐ if you would like to receive occasional e-mails from CAMRA (at no point will your details be released to a third party).

Find out more about CAMRA at **www.camra.org.uk**

Instruction to your Bank or Building Society to pay by Direct Debit

Please fill in the form and send to: Campaign for Real Ale Ltd. 230 Hatfield Road, St. Albans, Herts. AL1 4LW

Name and full postal address of your Bank or Building Society

To The Manager

Bank or Building Society

Address

Postcode

Name (s) of Account Holder (s)

Bank or Building Society account number

Branch Sort Code

Reference Number

Banks and Building Societies may not accept Direct Debit Instructions for some types of account

Originator's Identification Number

9	2	6	1	2	9

FOR CAMRA OFFICIAL USE ONLY
This is not part of the instruction to your Bank or Building Society

Membership Number

Name

Postcode

Instruction to your Bank or Building Society

Please pay CAMRA Direct Debits from the account detailed on this Instruction subject to the safeguards assured by the Direct Debit Guarantee. I understand that this instruction may remain with CAMRA and, if so, will be passed electronically to my Bank/Building Society

Signature(s)

Date

✂ detached and retained this section

DIRECT Debit

This Guarantee should be detached and retained by the payer.

The Direct Debit Guarantee

■ This Guarantee is offered by all Banks and Building Societies that take part in the Direct Debit Scheme. The efficiency and security of the Scheme is monitored and protected by your own Bank or Building Society.

■ If the amounts to be paid or the payment dates change CAMRA will notify you 10 working days in advance of your account being debited or as otherwise agreed.

■ If an error is made by CAMRA or your Bank or Building Society, you are guaranteed a full and immediate refund from your branch of the amount paid.

■ You can cancel a Direct Debit at any time by writing to your Bank or Building Society. Please also send a copy of your letter to us.